The politics of   sector

The 1980s and early 1990s have been a period of radical change in the public sector; developments such as privatization, the creation of internal 'markets' and the increased use of competitive tendering remain at the heart of government policy. This volume examines one of the key features of this policy: the emphasis on 'quality improvement' and 'customer orientation'.

The contributors, leading experts from a range of academic disciplines, focus on a number of broad issues relating to the way the concept of quality has been used in the public sector. They discuss the macropolitical rationale behind quality-oriented projects, showing how they have served to add legitimacy to politically motivated changes. They also analyse how specific quality initiatives have actually been used within organizations: 'quality', they argue, may provide a convenient rhetoric to justify or force through changes in culture and working practices and a means of increasing control and discipline. A number of case studies illustrate such key issues as organizational change, shifts in occupational roles and the use of 'quality' by various interest groups. Throughout, the contributions highlight the contradictions and new sites of conflict that are emerging in the public sector around issues of quality and customer empowerment.

Bringing together a wide range of perspectives on quality-oriented management and change in the public sector, this collection will be required reading for students of public sector management and organizational behaviour, as well as for those interested in social policy and public administration.

Ian Kirkpatrick is Lecturer in Organizational Behaviour at Cardiff Business School, University of Wales, Cardiff. **Miguel Martinez Lucio** is Lecturer in Industrial Relations and Public Administration at Cardiff Business School, University of Wales, Cardiff.

The politics of quality in the public sector

The management of change

Edited by
Ian Kirkpatrick and Miguel
Martinez Lucio

London and New York

1148148 X

Learning Resources
Centre

First published 1995
by Routledge
11 New Fetter Lane, London EC4P 4EE

Simultaneously published in the USA and Canada
by Routledge
29 West 35th Street, New York, NY 10001

Selection and editorial matter
© 1995 Ian Kirkpatrick and Miguel Martinez Lucio
Individual chapters © 1995 the contributors

Typeset in Times by LaserScript, Mitcham, Surrey
Printed and bound in Great Britain by
Mackays of Chatham PLC, Chatham, Kent

British Library Cataloguing in Publication Data
A catalogue record for this book is available from the British Library

Library of Congress Cataloging in Publication Data
The politics of quality in the public sector: the management of
    change/edited by Ian Kirkpatrick and Miguel Martinez Lucio.
    p. cm.
    Includes bibliographical references and index.
    1. Administrative agencies – Great Britain – Quality control –
    Case studies. 2. Administrative agencies – Great Britain –
    Management – Case studies. 3. Total quality management – Great Britain.
    I. Kirkpatrick, Ian, 1965–. II. Martinez Lucio, Miguel, 1960–.
    JN425.P62   1995
    350'.000941–dc20   94–29560
                                                                CIP

ISBN 0–415–10665–6 (hbk)
ISBN 0–415–10666–4 (pbk)

Contents

Contributors

Annette Davies is Lecturer in Organizational Behaviour at the Cardiff Business School, University of Wales. While at Cardiff, Annette has been involved in a number of projects related to new technology and the management of change within organizations. Much of her recent research has centred on the strategic management of information technologies and on the cultural dynamics of corporate mergers. Key publications include *Industrial Relations and New Technology* (Croom Helm 1986) and 'Implementing Japanese manufacturing techniques: a tale of two factories' (with N. Oliver) in the *Journal of Management Studies*.

Alf Fitzgeorge-Butler is Lecturer in Strategic Management and Housing at the Centre for Housing Management and Development, University of Wales, Cardiff. He is also the managing director of his own company, Absolutely Essential Consultancy Ltd, which deals with organizational development issues in the housing sector. Prior to arriving in Cardiff, he was the main housing training adviser at the Local Government Training Board. His current research interests are in the fields of organizational culture, the allocation of council housing and organizational development. Recent publications include: *Strategic Planning* (Absolutely Essential Consultancy 1992) and *Strategic Management* (Absolutely Essential Consultancy 1992).

Robert Harris is Lecturer in Social Policy at the University of Wales, Bangor. He has just completed an extensive Welsh Office-funded study looking at the implementation of GP fundholding arrangements in Wales. His current interests are in neoliberal governmental rationality and the subjectivizing effects of market discourses in public services, with particular reference to health.

Mike Ironside read mechanical engineering at Aston University. He then worked as an environmental protection officer in local government and became a NALGO branch secretary. He completed his MA in industrial relations at Warwick University and then worked as the Head of Research for NASUWT. He is now Lecturer in Industrial Relations at Keele University involved in research in schools and local government.

Ian Kirkpatrick is Lecturer in Organizational Behaviour at Cardiff Business School, University of Wales. He is currently organizing (with Richard Whipp) the ESRC seminar series on 'Professionals in Late Modernity' and is also an active member of Cardiff's Employment Research Unit. At the moment he is involved in research looking at decentralization and management change in local government and comparative public sector developments in Britain and Germany.

Martin Kitchener gained a BSc (Econ) in law and politics and an MBA at the University College of Wales, Aberystwyth. After a period in retail management, he worked in the Management Services department of South Glamorgan Health Authority. During this time he also gained the Institute of Management Services Diploma. For the last four years Martin has been employed first as a management teaching fellow and more recently as a research associate at Cardiff Business School. Alongside his doctoral research, which investigates marketing change in the NHS, Martin is currently involved in two other major research projects. The first is an Economic and Social Research Council (ESRC)-funded study of the implementation of marketing into the NHS and R&D establishments. The second, funded by the Hans Bockler Foundation, is concerned with the management of local government change in the UK and Germany.

Miguel Martinez Lucio is Lecturer in Industrial Relations and Public Administration at the University of Wales, Cardiff. He has worked on the question of flexibility and work organization in both the public and private sectors. The changing identity of trade unions is another central concern of his work. He is also interested in the issue of trade union responses to new management practices and has written extensively on British and Spanish industrial relations issues.

Philip Morgan is Lecturer in Human Resource Management at Cardiff Business School, University of Wales. He is also a coordinator of the Modular MBA programme in health service management. His research interests include implementing total quality management (TQM) and organization development (OD) in hospital settings and problems associated with health service professionals becoming managers.

Andrew Pendleton is Lecturer in Industrial Relations at Bradford University Management Centre. He has written extensively on railway industrial relations and is the co-editor of *Public Enterprise in Transition: Industrial Relations in State and Privatized Corporations* (Routledge 1993). His other main research interest is employee ownership and participation.

Christopher Potter is Director of Christopher Potter Associates and part-time Senior Lecturer at University of Wales College of Medicine, Department of Epidemiology and Community Medicine. He has extensive experience teaching on both sides of the Atlantic and consults for a variety of health service organizations, including the Overseas Development Agency and the World Bank.

Michael Reed is a professor in the Department of Behaviour in Organisations, the Management School, Lancaster University. His major publications include *Redirections in Organisational Analysis* (Tavistock 1985), *The Sociology of Management* (Harvester 1989) and *The Sociology of Organisations* (Harvester 1992). He is currently researching the restructuring of expert work and organizational forms taking place within advanced industrial societies.

Roger Seifert read PPE at Oxford University. He then completed an MBA at the London Business School and a PhD at the London School of Economics. He worked for IDS before joining Keele University. He is now Professor of Industrial Relations and Director of the Centre for Industrial Relations at Keele University. His most recent book was *Industrial Relations in the NHS* (Chapman & Hall 1992), and his book with Mike Ironside, *Industrial Relations in Schools* (Routledge), will be available from early 1995.

Ian Shaw is the Director of Graduate Studies at the School of Social and Administrative Studies, University of Wales, Cardiff. He teaches social work students, and is active in the world of supported housing in England and Wales. The focal point of his recent writing and research work has been the relation between policies and programmes within the personal social services and in supported housing. He is presently developing computer-based learning materials for social work education and practice, and completing a text on practice evaluation skills for social workers.

Jackie Sinclair is Senior Lecturer at the University of the West of England (UWE). She has worked for a national trade union and has been a branch officer of a clerical workers' union. She later read politics and then completed an MA in industrial relations, both at Warwick University. She worked as a research associate on a study of minimum wages in the UK, at Warwick University. She then spent two years at Keele University researching industrial relations in the education sector. Since taking up a post at UWE, her research interests remain in this area.

Andrew Thompson is Lecturer in Quantitative Methods at the Cardiff Business School, University of Wales. Previously, he has worked as a researcher for Manchester University and has conducted numerous projects for local government social service departments and the Greater London Association of Community Health Councils. His publications are primarily within the field of health services, focusing on the measurement of patient satisfaction and quantitative modelling of appointment systems. He is currently an adviser to the World Health Organization and a member of the working group on citizen participation in health care.

Richard Whipp is Professor of Human Resource Management and Deputy Director of the Cardiff Business School, University of Wales. He has taught and researched at the Aston Management Centre, Warwick Business School and held a visiting professorship at the University of Uppsala, Sweden. He has published widely on the subjects of innovation, the management of strategic change and competition, and the institutional analysis of sectors. He has a specialist interest in the automobile, ceramics and book-publishing industries and in the NHS. His books include: *Innovation and the Auto Industry* (Frances Pinter 1986, with P. Clark), *Patterns of Labour* (Routledge 1990) and *Managing Change for Competitive Success* (Blackwell 1991, with A. Pettigrew).

Peter Williams is Visiting Professor at the Centre for Housing Management and Development, University of Wales, Cardiff. He is also currently Head of Research and External Affairs at the Building Society Association and Council of Mortgage Lenders. He is a board member of Housing for Wales and Chairman of the Housing Management Advisory Panel. Peter has conducted research on a wide range of housing policy and management issues. His most recent book publication was *Home Ownership: Differentiation and Fragmentation* (Unwin Hyman 1994, with Ray Forrest and Alan Murie).

Preface

Few who have studied recent developments in the British public sector can have failed to come across the issue of quality. The management of a whole range of public organizations, from Social Services departments to Royal Mail sorting offices, are now talking about how to implement or improve 'quality'. Some have tried to introduce total quality management (TQM), others quality assurance (QA) programmes, while yet others have sought ways of consulting their users. In recent years, these developments have provided a lucrative source of income both for quality consultants and the authors of 'how to do it' textbooks. Almost as numerous as the textbooks are the number of quality gurus and different theories of quality.

What has been lacking so far is a critical appraisal of what all these 'quality' projects have actually meant for the employees and users of public services. In this book the suggestion is made that the current interest in quality is the result of successive Conservative governments' policies reorganizing the public sector along 'market' lines. In this respect, efforts to improve quality are closely linked to a wider political project of radically changing the way in which public services are managed and organized. Quality itself, therefore, is something which is highly political. As such, we should try to discover how it has been *used*, what changes have been brought about as a result of it and what new tensions and contradictions have arisen.

This book draws together a range of case studies from different parts of the public sector, all critically analysing the impact of quality. These studies were carried out by leading academics in their respective fields. A substantial part of the book is drawn from the work of the Cardiff University Employment Research Unit. For some time now, this group has been looking critically at broad issues of change in the public sector. The work of other colleagues from Cardiff on new management practices, in particular Peter Turnbull, Paul Blyton and Paul Stewart, has fed into the work of this group. Other contributors from outside Cardiff are also well known for their critical engagement with the issue of new management practices and organizational change in the public sector.

Most of the contributors to this volume, both from inside and outside Cardiff, have worked together on numerous projects in the past. A workshop held in Cardiff, with the kind support of Routledge, also helped to bring together the different contributors in order to pool ideas and develop a degree of consensus around the core themes of the book.

Special thanks are due, first and foremost, to all the contributors without whose hard work and critical input this book would not have been possible. We would like to extend special thanks to Andrew Pendleton, Mike Reed, Richard Whipp and our ex-colleague, Peter Turnbull, for taking the time and effort to review the book and make invaluable remarks on how to improve it. Most of all, however, we would like to acknowledge the help of our colleague Andy Thompson whose excellent work in the field of consumer rights and health policy provided the initial inspiration for this book. Last but not least, we would like to thank Francesca Weaver and Laura Large of Routledge for listening to our crazy ideas, and Penny Smith and Karen Trigg for their hard work and support on the administrative side.

Introduction

The politics of quality in the public sector

Ian Kirkpatrick and Miguel Martinez Lucio

Over the last decade, public sector organizations in Britain have undergone radical changes. These changes were initiated by successive Conservative governments who asserted tight controls over public spending and, at the same time, pursued a neoliberal agenda of extending market forces into the public domain. Through markets, it was argued, public services would become more responsive to the choices and preferences of individual consumers. A market system was also seen as more efficient than bureaucratic forms of organization which tended to aggregate choice and waste public resources. To gradually introduce markets, a variety of policy mechanisms were used, including privatization and the creation of new institutional arrangements through which the planning and purchasing of services were separated from their delivery. In local government, this involved the widespread application of competitive tendering arrangements (Painter 1991), and in the National Health Service (NHS), an internal or quasi market (Le Grand 1991). Throughout the public sector, new trading relationships were created through which a variety of service providers (including those in the private sector) were forced to compete for service contracts (Stewart and Walsh 1992). Underlying this structural 'fragmentation' was also a desire to reduce the overall cost of public services.

In promoting these radical changes, the government has also argued that the 'quality' of public services would increase. Indeed, a rhetoric of quality improvement has been a key feature of government reforms since the early 1980s (Pfeffer and Coote 1991). By emphasizing quality, Conservative governments have tried to present change as legitimate and in the public interest. Much of the rhetoric is, however, highly problematic. Unlike previous debates about how to improve the standard of public services, during the 1980s Conservative governments engaged explicitly with concepts of 'quality' imported directly from the private sector. This reflected a more general belief in the superiority of the commercial enterprise and the values and assumptions of private sector management (Keat and Abercrombie 1991). The public sector, it was argued, could benefit not only from exposure to market forces, but from commercial models of management and of quality improvement. Such an approach was promoted despite the fact that it contrasted sharply with the views of many occupational groups working in the public sector. These groups held their own definitions of 'quality' and views about how *public* services should be managed in the public interest.

Prior to looking at how a variety of 'quality' initiatives were introduced into the public sector, it is necessary to explore briefly these commercial models of quality. Did they, for example, represent a coherent unified programme for transforming organizational performance, as some enthusiasts maintain, or were they a more diverse set of often competing ideas?

THE QUALITY REVOLUTION

Oakland, among others, has argued that western capitalism is now on the verge of a 'quality revolution'. This 'revolution' started in Japan and has since spread to the United States and Europe. The future competitive advantage of firms in rapidly changing markets, he argued, could best be achieved through strategies of quality improvement as well as a more traditional emphasis on price:

> In any competitive economy, continuous cost reduction and quality improvement are essential if an organization is to stay in operation. Competitiveness is measured by three things: quality, price and delivery. The theory behind the costs of quality shows that, as quality improves, costs fall through reduction in failure and appraisal costs. Satisfying the customer in terms of quality *and* price will clearly benefit market share.
>
> (Oakland 1991: x)

In this way, quality improvement strategies represent a most effective 'competitive weapon' for many firms. Through quality improvement, it is argued, firms will be able to increase their market share, reduce their costs and increase organizational flexibility, simultaneously.

Quality, in different formats, has been an important issue in the commercial world since the 1930s. Of particular importance were efforts made in the United States to improve the effectiveness of manufacturing operations. Well-known quality gurus such as William

Deming and J. M. Juran argued that by placing quality at the top of the agenda, production costs could be reduced and productivity increased (Deming 1986; Juran 1988). Management, they argued, could effectively control the quality of production systems and vastly reduce failure rates and general levels of waste. Another quality guru, Philip Crosby, also emphasized the importance of quality as conformance to standards and 'fitness for purpose'. He too talked about reducing waste through a quality control system based on prevention – 'getting it right first time' – as opposed to one based on retrospective monitoring and appraisal (Crosby 1979). To support these objectives, a variety of measurement devices for monitoring and assuring quality were promoted, such as statistical process control (SPC), quality function development (QFD) and failure, mode, effect and criticality analysis (FMECA). The aim of these, and other, monitoring techniques was to build quality assurance systems *into* the production process itself.

Although widely publicized in the United States, these ideas were first implemented on a wide scale in Japan in the 1950s. Their use, alongside other, home-grown quality assurance techniques such as just-in-time management, was seen to have played a key role in helping Japanese firms to achieve a strong competitive advantage in world markets during the 1970s. The challenge of Japanese competition and the perceived superiority of Japanese models of production also led to a growing interest in quality in the West and attempts to copy or transplant Japanese models (Oliver and Wilkinson 1988). These concerns have recently found their way into the debate surrounding 'lean production' (Womack *et al.* 1990; Anderson 1992).

In Britain, a range of approaches to 'quality' has been subsumed under the label of total quality management (TQM). The appeal of TQM travels beyond production systems to the management of human resources in a wider range of organizations. Aspects of this were also pioneered in Japan, for example, through the involvement of shop-floor project teams (or quality circles) in ongoing quality improvement exercises. TQM draws on this and other influences which emphasize the role of 'people' in quality improvement.

According to Hill, 'total quality management can be seen as a business discipline and philosophy of management which institutionalized planned and continuous improvement' (Hill 1991: 554). The emphasis is on finding ways to raise the standard of quality constantly by training staff and setting up project teams on the Japanese model. The idea is also to improve the quality and performance of a firm by paying attention to both 'external' and 'internal' customer requirements. As Hand puts it:

> Total quality embraces more than the external customer. It recognizes that everyone in a business provides a service. Some services happen to be provided to external customers, some to an internal customer. If the needs of an external customer are not met, he is likely to take his business elsewhere. If the needs of an internal customer are not met, he has to spend time putting things right. Either way, the business loses. In a total quality company, everyone strives to meet the needs of their customers (internal and external), and then to improve continuously the efficiency and effectiveness of the service provided.
>
> (Hand 1992: 27)

The quality of a service or product is therefore seen as arising from combining an emphasis on external customer needs with the continuous improvement of internal organizational processes.

Proponents of TQM often go to great lengths to stress the importance of involving everyone, from senior management down, in this process of 'customer-driven' continuous improvement. Nothing less than a complete cultural change, in which *all* employees undergo the same training and internalize the same values of 'customer orientation', will do if TQM is to succeed. According to Oakland:

> Total quality management is an approach to improving the effectiveness and flexibility of businesses as a whole. It is essentially a way of organizing and involving the whole organization; every department, every activity, every single person at every level. For an organization to be truly effective, each part of it must work properly together, recognizing that every person and every activity affects, and in turn is affected by, others.
>
> (Oakland 1991: 15)

Not only is cultural change necessary for TQM to succeed but, as the above quotation suggests, changes in organizational structures are required. To achieve this, many gurus have advocated setting up a variety of project teams and quality working groups. The objective of such groups is to improve communication between different functional departments, in order to coordinate efforts to improve quality. This, it is argued, would also make the organization more flexible and responsive to changing external (and internal) customer requirements.

A more radical aspect of TQM is the idea of increasing employee involvement and participation. Many TQM texts employ a rhetoric of delegating authority and power to staff lower down in an organizational hierarchy. Quality improvement, it is argued, can only be achieved if all staff are equally involved, committed, and given the space and responsibility to innovate and make decisions. According to Hill, 'An implication of this . . . is that responsibility should be decentralized downwards. Job enlargement and job enrichment leading to semi-autonomous work groups could create the conditions necessary for greater self-control among shop-floor employees' (Hill 1991: 555). In this way, TQM, as espoused by some, may require shifts in the balance of power within organizations between managers and the managed. As will become clear, however, this rhetoric of empowerment may also be interpreted as a more sophisticated means of surveillance and control (Sewell and Wilkinson 1992; Delbridge and Turnbull 1992).

Although TQM is primarily about affecting the management of human resources (HR), some have also insisted on the need for a battery of sophisticated measurement techniques for identifying problems and monitoring success or failure. In this respect, many have subsumed 'hard' as well as 'soft' HR developments under the definitional remit of TQM (Wilkinson et al. 1991; Garrahan and Stewart 1992).

Over the last decade, a number of organizations have attempted to implement TQM. Some of the most widely publicized examples have been firms such as Rank Xerox, Hewlett Packard and Texas Instruments. Others, however, including many banks, insurance companies and supermarket chains, have also tried to implement TQM or variants of it such as 'customer care' (Ogbonna 1992). What most have found is that change cannot be achieved overnight and may require years of committed management action to bring about (Wilkinson et al. 1991).

A less radical version of quality improvement than TQM is the worldwide movement towards quality accreditation. In Britain, the British Standards Institute (BSI) established its universal accreditation scheme, BS5750, as early as 1979. This was revised in 1987 to comply with the international, ISO9000, standard of quality assurance. By 1991, over 6,500 firms had achieved BS5750 quality accreditation (Incomes Data Services 1991). The BSI scheme, and others like it, emphasizes the need to establish formal systems of quality control in order to ensure that products and services conform to specified standards. Quality itself is understood as 'the totality of features and characteristics of a product or service that bear on its ability to satisfy stated and implied needs' (ISO 1990).

BS5750 and the many quality assurance programmes which are now commonplace in the public sector (for example, in higher education and health services) differ a great deal from TQM in their approach to 'quality' improvement. Whereas TQM talks about promoting a 'customer oriented' culture, BS5750 is mainly concerned with the written systematization of procedures for quality control. It could therefore be argued that 'the "paper bureaucracy" side of BSI may conflict with . . . TQM, which emphasises individual responsibility rather than rigid guide-lines' (Incomes Data Services 1990). When used in the same organization, these different versions of quality may then actually conflict with each other. While TQM adopts a rhetoric of flexibility and individual empowerment, BS5750 is more concerned with formal monitoring of quality and could imply even greater bureaucratic control. Furthermore, while TQM emphasizes ongoing continuous improvement and raising of standards, BS5750 – alongside many other similar quality assurance initiatives – involves specifying standards and ensuring that services conform to them. These are quite different approaches to quality, both in their scope and, to some extent, in their objectives.

A final dimension of this so-called quality revolution was the increased interest, especially in marketing circles, in defining the antecedents for and measuring levels of consumer satisfaction. A central concern has been to develop models for understanding how customers view the quality of intangible services. One of the most widely publicized of these frameworks was that developed by Parasuraman *et al.* (1985) who identified five 'universal' dimensions of service quality as perceived by 'external' customers: tangibles (the physical layout of buildings etc.), reliability, responsiveness, assurance (courtesy and knowledge of staff) and empathy. This framework has been used in a wide variety of service firms as a technique for measuring customer expectations and perceptions of quality. The logic behind it is that firms should become hyper-sensitive to consumer expectations and perceptions and should amend their own sales and marketing strategies accordingly (Gronroos 1984).

What is clear from this brief discussion is that a number of different approaches to defining and implementing 'quality' exist and that imple-mentation itself is by no means straightforward. While some advocates of quality concentrate on the management of production processes, others use a rhetoric of cultural change and empowerment, while yet others are developing sophisticated measurements of consumer satis-faction. Trying to reconcile or subsume these, for want of a better word, 'schools' of quality is unrealistic given their quite different aims and objectives. What is evident is not a clear, unified programme of quality improvement, but a wide variety of approaches which have in common only the most basic objective of somehow increasing the competitive advantage and profitability of a firm.

QUALITY IMPROVEMENT IN THE PUBLIC SECTOR

In the public sector, a similarly confusing diversity of approaches to quality has been advocated (Pfeffer and Coote 1991). This was due, in part, to the perceived 'benefits' of using private sector notions of quality to support a wider, government-inspired, project of reorganizing the public sector. Outside of the fact that the private sector and its managerial practices were seen as superior to the public sector's tradition of administration, these quality discourses had a range of features which were appealing to successive Conservative governments. Such features included the potential for cost saving and containment, the idea of introducing internal competitive relations, the dismantling of 'bureaucratic' cultures and the establishment of rational service specifications which were the responsibility of both employees and employers. Such perceived benefits led to a dynamic engagement with quality during the 1980s and 1990s.

It has been argued that underpinning many of the reforms of the last decade was an implicit project of remodelling the public sector along the lines of a commercial enterprise. A dominant image was one of an enterprise culture in which the needs and demands of sovereign consumers in the market-place were the key institutional imperatives (Abercrombie 1991). According to Du Gay and Salaman, this image was all-pervasive during the 1980s and has since led to a 'reimagination' of what public services are and what their purpose is:

> In the public sector . . . there can hardly be a school, hospital, social services department, university or college in the UK that has not in some way become permeated by the language of enterprise. Enterprise has remorselessly reconceptualized and remodelled everything in its path. Ostensibly different 'spheres of existence' have fallen prey to its 'totalizing' and 'individualizing' economic rationality – from the hospital to the railway station, from the classroom to the museum, the nation finds itself translated. 'Patients', 'parents', 'passengers' and pupils are all reimagined as 'customers'.
>
> (Du Gay and Salaman 1992: 622)

Within this wider process of 'reimagining' the public sector along commercial lines, the rhetoric of 'quality improvement' has been pivotal. *Improving quality was seen both as a justification for and an outcome of radical organizational change.* If private firms could increase their competitive advantage through improvements in quality then why, it was argued, should not public sector organizations? The fact that the public sector had traditionally been managed according to starkly different principles from those of the typical commercial enterprise was conveniently ignored.

At the heart of the government's critique of public services was the claim that state bureaucracies and the professional occupations working within them served their own producer interests before those of the consumer. This critique was motivated primarily by a desire to reduce the costs of public services and, in so doing, increase efficiency and remove so-called professional and trade union restrictive practices. At the same time, however, Conservative governments justified incursions into producer power by using a rhetoric of improving quality in the interests of the 'sovereign consumer'. What this implied was a fundamental challenge to the legitimacy and working practices of professionals and other occupational groups within the public sector. According to Wilding: 'Thatcherism has questioned and substantially damaged, the credibility of two basic instruments of collectivist welfare policy – bureaucracy and professionals. They are billed as self-interested, self-serving, inefficient and ineffective' (Wilding 1992: 202). In this sense, quality as it has been understood in the public sector during the 1980s was associated with a fundamental critique of established organizational structures, cultures and working practices.

The objective of this volume is to consider the impact of quality initiatives on public sector working practices and organizational structures. In so doing, we take quality not to be a neutral concept, but see it as essentially problematic and highly contested in its meaning (Laclau 1990). Not one but a variety of competing ways of defining and implementing quality have emerged in different parts of the public sector, just as in the private sector. As Pollitt reminds us, ' "quality" and "quality assurance" are terms which signpost a definitional battleground' (Pollitt 1990b: 436). For us, quality is not a politically neutral objective to which all parties are equally committed. On the contrary, it is intensely political and has been used to promote a range of new forms of management control and restructuring of traditional working practices, as well as genuine efforts to improve service delivery. For this reason, we concern ourselves less with what quality *is* and how it should be implemented, and concentrate more on the 'politics' of how quality has been socially constructed and *used* by different interest groups. In particular, the book will focus on the way the notion of quality formed part of a wider Conservative government-led project of change in the public sector.

The objectives of this volume are therefore to consider the micro-political uses of quality and investigate the problems and contradictions which arise from this. There are, we suggest, two key dimensions to the way 'quality' has been used for political purposes.

The first dimension looks at how 'quality' is used generally to legitimate intervention and change in public organizations; in particular, change in employment practices. It will be shown in chapter 1 how the rhetoric of improving quality at the macro level was associated with government plans to restructure whole parts of the welfare state around quasi markets. We also describe how quality was used as a justification for decentralization and the introduction of cultural changes to make service providers more responsive to user 'needs' and 'demands'. We argue that external representations of 'consumer interests' have been used to justify internal organizational changes (see also chapter 11 by Martinez Lucio). Such changes include the introduction of new working practices and the transformation of bargaining relations, and also changing terms and conditions through the use of techniques such as performance related pay and teamworking. Approaches to quality which emphasize 'value for money' have also been used as a legitimation device to make public managers more accountable for budgets and unit performance and, in some cases (for example, in the NHS), turning professionals into budget holders.

The second dimension relates to the way 'quality' has become associated with increased control over the public sector labour process. One can understand this in terms of: (a) how the rhetoric of quality was used as a legitimation device to justify increased managerial control, and (b) how actual mechanisms of quality improvement, such as decentralization, 'customer care' and performance measurement, acted in themselves as 'technologies' of control (Miller and Rose 1990). As a technology of control, quality may be associated with increased bureaucracy and methods of regulation which, in turn, have raised questions regarding the administrative 'costs' of quality (Wilson 1993). Alternatively, it could be associated with management exerting control over unions or over professionals in terms of reducing their workplace autonomy and undermining their 'restrictive practices'.

Although 'quality' may be understood as a 'governmental technology' – and as such may be associated with ever more intrusive systems of surveillance (Sewell and Wilkinson 1992) – the reality is that top–down efforts to introduce change and increase managerial control are mediated at the micro-organizational level. Public organizations, like any other, are 'negotiated orders' in which there exists ample scope for human agents to interpret top–down initiatives, transform them and use them for alternative purposes (Strauss 1978; Sturdy *et al.* 1992; Blackler *et al.* 1993). Most of the contributions in this volume therefore, illustrate how, at the organizational level, attempts to implement quality were manipulated, negotiated and in many respects altered beyond recognition. It is this essentially political process that the contributions to this book aim to illuminate.

OBJECTIVES AND STRUCTURE OF THE BOOK

All the contributions in this volume have adopted a critical stance towards the issue of 'quality improvement' in the British public sector. Most draw upon empirical research to illustrate different ways in which notions of 'quality' have been used to bring about change (successfully or otherwise) in organizational structures and working practices. The chapters focus on a variety of organizations within the British public sector including: the National Health Service, higher education, secondary education, local government housing, social services, Royal Mail and British Rail. Thematically, the chapters look at a range of issues including organizational change, the impact on professional roles and the transformation of collective bargaining. All the chapters address the core theme of this book which is the 'politics' of quality, its uses and the subsequent problems that emerge.

Our first chapter shows how the concern with 'quality' in the public sector was linked to a broader Conservative government-led project of change. We argue that this project concentrated on reforming the organization and management of the public sector and replacing what were perceived to be bureaucratic, inefficient and non-responsive forms of organization, with a public sector managed through contracts and structured around 'quasi markets'. This change was influenced by New Right thinking and by external pressures that emerged during the 1970s such as changing consumer expectations and a state fiscal crisis. We suggest that different concepts of quality, such as value for money and variants of consumerism (exit and voice), were used extensively to add legitimacy to Conservative government reform plans. This introductory chapter, therefore, considers the manifold political uses of 'quality' as part of a broad macro-project of change.

Chapter 2, by Mike Reed, shows how 'quality management practices' may be understood as a form of organizational control and surveillance. He suggests that the discourse of 'quality management' can be viewed as part of a larger ideological narrative and organizational strategy of the 'enterprise culture' which came into prominence in the 1980s. Within this, discourses of quality acted as 'intellectual technologies' which align central government programmes of change to local organizational practices. Such an alignment was (and is) both imperfect and contested. The operational capacity of quality to function as a 'relay device' effectively linking government 'mentalities' and policies with everyday organizational realities remains highly variable and uncertain. In this sense, the capacity of quality management projects to link the 'political', the 'cultural' and the 'technological' dimensions of governmental and organizational life is continually being 'distorted' or 'corrupted' by a socio-organizational environment that is heterogeneous, rivalrous and recalcitrant.

Chapter 3, by Andy Thompson, adopts a slightly different approach. Using the example of the NHS, Thompson considers how in New Right discourses of the sovereign consumer the user of public services has been redefined as a 'customer'. This, he suggests, is not only a highly problematic ideological project, but one which fails to deal effectively with more deep-rooted problems of user (or patient) passivity and professional expert power in service encounters. What is required, he argues, is a radical approach to 'quality' in which both patient involvement and the 'responsible autonomy' of the professional experts is emphasized. Quality would then be something which is negotiated by patients and professionals through new types of micro-political alliance, rather than an ideological project imposed top-down.

Chapter 4, by Annette Davies and Ian Kirkpatrick, moves away from the broader issues of change to the specific case of higher education. The authors look at how the emphasis there has been to define 'quality' in terms of greater efficiency and value for money. This has led to efforts both to measure and control what universities do through a range of local and national performance indicators. In the case of academic libraries, this use of performance indicators has facilitated greater bureaucratic control over professional librarians. As a result of this, much of their traditional workplace autonomy has been undermined. This chapter highlights a case where such changes appear to have been extreme and significant in their effect on the role of professionals.

In Chapter 5, Alf Fitzgeorge-Butler and Peter Williams look at the impact of quality in local government housing departments and draw similar conclusions. Government policy over the last decade has placed great emphasis on improving the 'quality' of housing services, while at the same time resources have been steadily reduced. To date, therefore, what has been achieved is a greater level of bureaucratic control and limited efficiency gains. Little progress has been made in terms of involving citizens in the process of housing policy decision making. Severe resource limitations have also undermined efforts to implement TQM in housing departments.

Chapter 6, by Ian Shaw, goes on to look at how attempts have been made to implement quality in social services. In contrast to the plight of professional academic librarians, Shaw suggests that professionals in the social services have been more successful in negotiating 'quality' and incorporating new managerial concerns into their own operating practices. Shaw also argues that the current emphasis on providing user choice will also be problematic in the social services context due to problems of defining 'customer needs'. In the light of this and other constraints, one should be highly sceptical about how far the recent quality fad will develop.

In the first of three chapters looking at the NHS, Robert Harris (Chapter 7) looks at the politics of negotiating 'quality' standards between general practitioners (GPs) and hospital trust managers. He describes how the new internal market in the NHS has turned GPs into budget holders with responsibility for purchasing the 'best-quality' services from a variety of provider agencies. Contrary to government rhetoric, however, the purchaser–provider set-up does not necessarily ensure the highest-quality outcomes. Because of the way contracts are structured, GPs are often unable to question or scrutinize the decisions of hospital consultants with regard to the quality or standard of service they provide.

Chapter 8, by Philip Morgan and Chris Potter, also looks at how quality has been used in the NHS. Their focus, however, is on how rival versions of 'quality' – TQM and quality assurance (QA) – are being pursued by the managements of trust hospitals. Whereas TQM involves continuous improvement and 'empowerment', a strategy which might be favoured by junior professionals and managers, QA is more concerned with conformance to standards which are set almost exclusively by powerful clinicians' groups. These differences in official approaches to quality can lead to wider conflicts of interest between various occupational groups competing for power and influence. A key issue discussed in this chapter is how professionals exercise power by taking over and determining the outcome of projects such as QA.

In Chapter 9, Martin Kitchener and Richard Whipp explore the introduction of 'market forces' in the professional service context of the NHS. They draw extensively on comparative studies of two hospital units in Wales set against the experience revealed by parallel case studies across the NHS in England. They show how concerted efforts have been made by NHS managers to sell the idea of marketing to professionals who are hostile to notions of commercialization. Such changes, however, have been skilfully presented by managers as leading to improvements in the quality of patient care. In this way, they suggest, NHS managers have been partially successful in using quality as a means of legitimating, internally, wider organizational changes associated with the creation of quasi markets in the NHS.

In Chapter 10, Andrew Pendleton moves the debate on from the subject of professionals and organizational change to the impact of quality initiatives on industrial relations in British Rail. He argues that quality has been both an objective and a tactic for bringing about change in British Rail, serving as a means of conceptualizing, justifying and legitimizing potentially contested innovations. He shows how a soft version of quality improvement has been associated with new management practices such as human resource management (HRM) and that this has had a major impact on industrial relations in British Rail.

In Chapter 11, Miguel Martinez Lucio continues the theme of quality and changing industrial relations practices, looking at management efforts to implement TQM in Royal Mail. An emphasis on quality formed part of a wider programme of commercialization in Royal Mail and has also been associated with changing shop-floor working practices such as the attempted introduction of teamworking and management references to the demands of the external customer. At the same time, however, Martinez Lucio shows how the discourse of quality itself is being rearticulated by Royal Mail trade unions at various levels in order to contest such changes. This kind of response, he suggests, may be part of a more general shift in the politics of British industrial relations which forces trade unions to consider certain broader issues of production.

Chapter 12, by Jackie Sinclair, Roger Seifert and Mike Ironside, also looks at the industrial relations implications of new quality initiatives, but in the context of secondary education. They show how discourses of quality and public choice have been used extensively to justify government reforms of secondary education, for example the creation of locally managed schools. These developments have also had an impact on teachers' unions and have raised the spectre of local bargaining arrangements. Unions, however, have been able to organize and respond to this change, especially by drawing attention to the inconsistencies in reward management and the financial constraints determining the character of these 'quality-related' developments.

The final, concluding chapter attempts to summarize the main problems and contradictions that are emerging in the public sector as a consequence of the politics of quality. It shows how new sites of struggle are emerging along with a whole range of issues in the management of the public sector. Such developments have in no small way been accentuated by the specific uses of quality-related controls. The authors argue that such contradictions and tensions are not leading to any decline in the public sector's interest in 'quality' (e.g. transparency, user empowerment, developing market relations through 'choice' mechanisms) but are further opening up the debate and interest in the issue. Alternative discourses and understandings of public service delivery and their quality are beginning to locate themselves in the political and institutional space unintentionally created by the government's restructuring of the public sector.

REFERENCES

Abercrombie, N. (1991) 'The privilege of the producer', in Keat, R. and Abercrombie, N. (eds), *Enterprise Culture*, London: Routledge.

Anderson Consulting (1992) *Bench Marking Project Report*, London: Anderson Consulting.

Blackler, F., Reed, M. and Whitaker, A. (1993) 'Editorial introduction: knowledge workers and contemporary organizations', *Journal of Management Studies* 30(6): 851–62.

Crosby, P. (1979) *Quality is Free*, New York: McGraw Hill.

Delbridge, R. and Turnbull, P. (1992) 'Human resource maximization: the management of labour in just-in-time manufacturing systems', in Blyton, P. and Turnbull, P. (eds), *Re-assessing Human Resource Management*, London: Sage.

Deming, W. (1986) *Quality is Free*, New York: McGraw Hill.

Du Gay, P. and Salaman, G. (1992) 'The cult(ure) of the customer', *Journal of Management Studies* 29(5): 615–34.

Garrahan, P. and Stewart, P. (1992) *The Nissan Enigma: Flexibility at Work in a Local Economy*, London: Mansell.

Gronroos, C. (1984) 'A service quality and its marketing implications', *European Journal of Marketing*, 18(4): 36–44.

Hand, M. (1992) 'Total quality management – one god but many prophets', in Hand, M. and Plowman, B. (eds), *Quality Management Handbook*, Oxford: Butterworth-Heinemann.

Hill, S. (1991) 'Why quality circles failed but total quality management might succeed', *British Journal of Industrial Relations* 29(4): 541–68.

Incomes Data Services (1991) *Total Quality Management*, study 457 (May), London: Incomes Data Services.

ISO (International Organization for Standardization) (1990) *Quality Management and Quality Systems Elements. Part 2: Guidelines for Services*, Geneva.

Juran, J. (1988) *Juran on Planning for Quality*, New York: Free Press.

Keat, R. and Abercrombie, N. (eds) (1991) *Enterprise Culture*, London: Routledge.

Laclau, E. (1990) *Reflections on the Revolutions of our Time*, London: Verso.
Le Grand, J. (1991) 'Quasi-markets and social policy', *The Economic Journal* 101: 1256–67.
Miller, P. and Rose, N. (1990) 'Governing economic life', *Economy and Society* 19(1): 1–31.
Oakland, J. (1991) *Total Quality Management*, London: Heinemann.
Painter, J. (1991) 'Compulsory competitive tendering in local government: the first round', *Public Administration* 69: 191–210.
Parasuraman, A., Zeithmal, V. and Berry, L. (1985) 'A conceptual model of service quality and its implications for future research', *Journal of Marketing* 49: 41–50.
Peters, T. and Waterman, R. (1982) *In Search of Excellence: Lessons from America's Best-run Companies*, New York: Harper and Row.
Pfeffer, N. and Coote, A. (1991) *Is Quality Good for You? A Critical Review of Quality Assurance in Welfare Services*, Social Policy Paper 5: London: Institute for Public Policy Research.
Pollitt, C. (1990a) *Managerialism and the Public Services: The Anglo-American Experience*, Oxford: Basil Blackwell
Pollitt, C. (1990b) 'Doing business in the temple? Managers and quality assurance in the public services', *Public Administration* 63: 435–52.
Ogbonna, E. (1992) 'Organizational culture and human resource management: dilemmas and contradictions', in Blyton, P. and Turnbull, P. (eds), *Reassessing Human Resource Management*, London: Sage.
Oliver, N. and Wilkinson, B. (1988) *The Japanization of British Industry*, Oxford: Basil Blackwell.
Sewell, G. and Wilkinson, B. (1992) 'Someone to watch over me: surveillance, discipline and the just-in-time labour process', *Sociology* 26(2): 271–89.
Stewart, J. and Walsh, K. (1992) 'Change in the management of public services', *Public Administration* 70: 499–518.
Strauss, A. (1978) *Negotiations: Varieties, Contexts, Processes and Social Order*, San Francisco: Jossey Bass.
Sturdy, A., Knights, A. and Wilmott, H. (eds) (1992) *Skill and Consent: Contemporary Studies in the Labour Process*, London: Routledge.
Wilding, P. (1992) 'The British Welfare State: Thatcherism's enduring legacy', *Policy and Politics* 20(2): 201–11.
Wilkinson, A., Allen, P. and Snape, E. (1991) 'TQM and the management of labour', *Employee Relations* 13(1): 24–31.
Wilson, D. (1993) 'Turning drama into a crisis: perspectives on contemporary local government', *Public Policy and Administration* 8(1): 30–45.
Womack, J., Jones, D. and Roos, D. (1990) *The Machine that Changed the World*, New York: Rawson Associates.

Chapter 1

The uses of 'quality' in the British government's reform of the public sector

Ian Kirkpatrick and Miguel Martinez Lucio

INTRODUCTION

The last decade saw an emerging interest in the question of quality. The need to review continuously production standards and refer to the changing demands of the consumer have become central to the language and practice of a range of organizations. The origins of such concerns are broad in both historical and political terms. A key issue in recent years, however, is that the state itself has been engaging with the question of 'quality'. The reasons for such an engagement are varied, but what is clear is that the contemporary restructuring of the public sector has been couched in terms of a language of new managerialism and informed by commercial paradigms. During the 1980s, 'quality' emerged as part of a political discourse pivotal to the aspirations of the New Right in the British government. These aspirations fed into an incremental government reform project aimed at transforming the management and organization of the public sector.

In this chapter we argue that 'quality' emerged as a key part of the Conservative governments' incremental strategy of reforming the management and organization of public services. A prime objective of this strategy was to reduce the state's role in the direct provision of public services, through a combination of privatization and the development of competitive tendering and quasi-market arrangements. These changes, it was argued, would result in increased organizational effectiveness and improved 'quality'. Underlying them, however, was a deeper objective of asserting greater managerial control over various recalcitrant interest groups, cutting the cost of public services and reducing the proportion of the nation's wealth directed towards state welfare provision.

An engagement with 'quality' and 'consumerism' along such lines was, in part, the result of the New Right's influence on successive

Conservative governments. By the New Right is meant an amalgam of different groups and intellectuals who have opposed the more moderate, centre-oriented developments in conservatism throughout the twentieth century, especially after the Second World War, and the move towards a broad 'social democratic consensus'. On the one hand, there is a range of political interests which have espoused the qualities of a minimalist state, and, on the other, a significant body of economists who, through their neoclassical and monetarist orientations, have sought to prove the superiority of free-market mechanisms. Paralleling these intellectual endeavours was a range of social groups and lobbies who, in the case of both Britain and the USA, organized themselves in the 1960s and 1970s around anti-taxation sentiments, traditional understandings of educational and social practices, and individual and market-oriented notions of liberty. Whilst never quite a harmonious project due to the recurrent tensions between the market libertarian and 'traditionalist' wings of the New Right, this broad movement did exhibit a major influence on British and American conservatism in terms of its re-encounter with the 'market' and with notions of the sovereign consumer.

Despite these New Right influences, 'quality' itself was (and is) an ambiguous and contested concept. Not one, but a variety of different approaches to quality improvement were espoused in Britain. In the first instance, emphasis was placed on achieving 'quality' in terms of the value for money and efficiency of public services. This provided a justification for the more extensive use of performance indicators throughout the public sector and new forms of managerial and (ultimately) bureaucratic control. A second, related approach to quality improvement employed a rhetoric of increasing the voice and choice of the consumers of public services. This too was used as a justification for change, although here it was more a case of 'decentralizing' public services in order to make them more responsive to user 'needs' and reorganizing whole sectors (such as health) into quasi markets supposedly to increase consumer choice.

The reform project of successive Conservative governments continues to be highly disjointed and uneven in its development. During the 1980s, one could argue that it developed from an exclusive input orientation, concerned with economy and efficiency, to embrace a wider emphasis on outputs and notions of 'consumer involvement'. Both themes, we argue, were incorporated and repackaged in the 1991 Citizen's Charter initiative. Despite this unevenness, however, a consistent theme running throughout was a desire to add legitimacy to change, not only in terms of the need for economy, but in terms of improvements in effectiveness and 'quality'. In this chapter we aim to show how an interest in quality improvement became associated with this reform project and how, given contradictions inherent within it, the future trajectory and development of the project now remain uncertain.

Prior to looking at the political uses of 'quality', we will try to illustrate why the issue of quality improvement became so central. We begin by discussing the origins of this reform project and link it to a wider crisis facing traditional approaches towards public administration. We show how a fiscal crisis and wider changes in the pattern of consumption in the 1970s undermined these traditional approaches. In particular, they posed a serious challenge to the 'Fordist' organizational structure of the public sector and to the professional interests which were retained within it.

In this chapter we take the view that the meaning of 'quality' is neither fixed nor politically neutral. Rather, the whole concept of 'quality' represents a contested terrain. That is to say, its meaning is being constantly rearticulated within different contexts by those who possess the power and institutional resources to do so. The objective of this chapter is *not* therefore to try and explain where concepts of quality come from (this issue is discussed in the introduction), or to produce our own definition. Our chief concern is to show how different approaches to quality have been *used* in the British government's project of reforming the organization and management of the public sector. In this respect, we concur fully with Du Gay and Salaman who argue that quality and notions of the 'sovereign consumer' have been used as a 'rationale for programmes of intervention in the public domain' (Du Gay and Salaman 1992: 623).

THE ORIGINS OF THE CRISIS OF PUBLIC ADMINISTRATION

What were the origins of this UK Conservative government reform project in which the issue of 'quality' became so central? In this section we argue that the impetus for change came about as a result of external pressures which, in different ways, were present in all western liberal democracies. The first of these pressures was a fiscal crisis in state resources brought about during the 1970s by rising oil prices and unemployment, along with broader problems in capital accumulation. This fiscal crisis imposed severe resource constraints on government spending just at the same time as a second set of pressures, relating to new and increasingly politicized consumer demands and expectations, was emerging. The relevance of this is that the output dimension of the state was becoming politicized in a similar manner to the input dimension. In combination, these pressures slowly undermined the effectiveness of traditional – 'Fordist' – approaches to public sector organization and management. In Britain, these developments were also articulated by the ideas of the New Right; their concerns fed into, and had great influence over, Conservative plans to reorganize incrementally public services in the 1980s.

Only by using a multidimensional approach will we be able to understand fully the origins of Conservative government attempts to bring about change. Each part of the crisis of the public sector can only be fully comprehended in relation to the others. Below, we explain this more fully by looking at two interrelated pressures which led to a crisis of public sector organization and management.

Fiscal crisis

During the 1970s, the British state began to suffer from an increasingly severe fiscal crisis. Transformations in capitalist structures, in terms of their increasing globalization and changing relation to the nation-state, undermined the traditional national 'loyalties' that had underpinned organized capitalism in Britain. This fact, combined with increasing competition – a consequence of globalization – the worldwide oil crisis and a decline in manufacturing capital, led to a general problem of capital accumulation and public resourcing. According to O'Connor:

> the capitalist state must try and fulfil two basic and often mutually contradictory functions – accumulation and legitimization . . . (i.e.) maintain or create the conditions in which profitable capital accumulation is possible . . . (and) try to maintain or create the conditions for social harmony . . . But a state that ignores the necessity of assisting the process of capital accumulation risks drying up the source of its own power.
>
> (O'Connor 1973: 6)

A fundamental problem for the British state during the 1970s was that the *external* environment became less supportive and conducive to its postwar expansionist social and welfare agenda. Accompanying this problem was a far greater degree of tax consciousness within civil society more generally (O'Connor 1973). This further exaggerated the financial pressures within the *input* dimension of the state.

Changes in welfare consumption

It would be impossible to comprehend the significance of this fiscal crisis of the state without reference to civil society and a range of broader social dynamics, especially those associated with the consumption of public services. Crucial here are what some authors have described as the fragmentation and differentiation of consumer demands and expectations (Sabel 1982; Hill 1991). These notions have often been used to describe changing market behaviour in the private sector, although we argue that they can also be used to understand similar transformations in public sector consumption. There are two basic elements to this transformation of public sector consumption.

First, at the same time as overall demand for public services was increasing during the 1970s (despite the fiscal crisis), new expectations relating to the content and 'quality' of services were also emerging. Educational and demographic developments, for example, were seen to be giving rise to a new set of fragmented demands within public services (Offe 1984). Increasingly, differentiated demands in the realm of health care were emerging, while in the case of social services, the recomposition of family structures was placing ever greater strains on traditional approaches to service delivery.

Second, the collective consumption of public services was being politicized by the advent of new interests and actors who challenged the traditional decision-making power of public managers and professionals. Broadly speaking, the administrators of public services traditionally functioned on the basis of a separation of 'production' from 'consumption'. At the level of collective consumption of public services, a range of contradictions began to emerge. Collective consumption in the areas of health provision, education and housing became the site of a range of new struggles. Collective consumption was steadily becoming politicized in a way that it had never been during the earlier stages of welfare state development (Castells 1979). A range of social movements was locating itself within the arena of collective consumption, calling not only for more welfare provision, but for democratic and transparent forms of decision making (Castells 1983). As the 1970s economic crisis deepened, many of these social movements began to articulate their opposition to further reductions in welfare state provision (Alonso 1992), regardless of their broad-based class character (Parkin 1968). The organizationally innovative and conflictual character of these movements, coupled with their questioning of traditional party and political processes, contributed to the high social expectations they were already articulating and the difficulty the state had in placating or diverting their demands. In this way, according to Offe: 'By expanding social services and infrastructure investment, the state not only exacerbates the symptoms of the fiscal crisis, it also makes itself the focus of conflict over the mode in which societal resources should be utilized' (Offe 1984: 143).

Crisis of public sector administration

The significance of these developments within the input and output function of the state becomes even more apparent when we focus our attention on the administrative apparatus of the state itself. This was being implicitly and explicitly challenged by these external developments which were leading to a crisis of what some have called 'Fordist' state organization. Prior to looking at the nature of this crisis, a brief note about what is meant by 'Fordism' in this context is necessary.

The Keynesian welfare state was, according to some, a Fordist state in terms of its organization:

> Like Fordist private capital, the Keynesian welfare state, including the local state, has developed by way of mass production of a limited range of standardised goods and services, economies of scale have been emphasised; and 'production' has in fact been organised on an assembly line 'principle' with professional and semi-professional 'people processors' replacing the material processing lines of mechanical factories.
>
> (Geddes 1988: 87)

Despite this, others have questioned the extent to which the state really was Fordist in its organization (Marquand 1988). Centralized administrative controls, they argue, were countered by professional interests with their restrictive practices and control over the labour process. In the National Health Service (NHS), for example, a careful balance of power has continued to be struck between government and professionals over financial and clinical controls respectively (Klein 1983). One could argue, therefore, that, although the welfare state resembled Fordism, it was never totally Fordist. According to Hoggett:

> The Keynesian welfare state . . . resembles Fordism without Ford. It resembles a kind of mongrel paradigm based on an uneasy marriage between a pre-Fordist craft (professional) productive system and a Taylorised (rational-bureaucratic) system.
>
> (Hoggett 1987: 223)

As will become clear, some recent developments within the government's state reform project, such as the promotion of 'rational executive management', look more like further extensions of Fordism than flexible (post-Fordist) modes of organization (Pollitt 1990a; Murray 1991).

Holding to one side the debate about Fordism, it could be argued that the postwar British welfare state was characterized by a planning ethos, 'mass consumption', bureaucratic techniques and professional power, which effectively neutralized any alternative consumer role. This internal bureaucratic culture was a key factor leading to crisis when public services were forced to contend with rapid changes (Hoggett 1987) in terms of shifts in external inputs and outputs outlined above. Whereas bureaucratic organization was once a successful feature of state development and intervention – organizing social provision – with these new pressures emerging, it gave rise to contradictions which were 'much broader than anything it can control in terms of its own logic' (Laclau 1990: 54).

In this way it can be seen how a range of external developments, both in the economy and within civil society, combined to undermine traditional approaches to public administration. Only by considering this multidimensional nature of this change can one fully understand the crisis of public sector organization.

ORIGINS OF THE PUBLIC SECTOR REFORM PROJECT

In this section we consider how, in Britain, this crisis of public administration was articulated by the New Right. Its ideas and policy prescriptions fed into Conservative government policies since 1979 of reforming the organization and management of the public sector. It was also partly as a result of New Right intervention that, as this reform project unfolded, a concern with quality became so central.

As outlined above, various social movements mobilized in the area of collective consumption, calling for more resources that would be delivered in a more democratic and participatory manner. Of greater relevance to this chapter, however, was the advent of the New Right and its reading of these developments. In Britain the New Right developed an anti-statist rhetoric that emphasized the role of privatization in restricting the scope of the public sector. On the one hand, the 'market' became the panacea for the ills of the public sector. Political systems 'aggregated decision making' and were thought to be largely ineffective as a way of bringing state bureaucracies to account. The solution to the complex crisis Britain faced in the late 1970s was therefore considered to be a gradual dismantling of the welfare state through cuts and privatization, deregulation, and a new emphasis on individual choice and consumption. All this, however, required quite fundamental and radical organizational changes in the public sector.

For many New Right thinkers and policy makers alike, 'public choice' exercised through markets represented a far more effective way of maximizing welfare benefits than did large, vertically integrated bureaucracies (Hayek 1944; Harris and Seldon 1971; Friedman 1980; Harris 1988; Robinson 1988). A consistent theme in New Right thinking was the idea that markets could simultaneously increase both efficiency and 'choice' in public services. For too long, it was argued, 'the emphasis had been on the production of standardized services, the control of resource inputs and professional definitions of need' (Wistow and Barnes 1993: 280). The traditional approach to public administration was considered to be inefficient, inward-looking and incapable of satisfying increasingly differentiated user needs and demands. Some thinkers also argued that state bureaucracies were inherently wasteful and inefficient, tending to oversupply services at the public expense (Niskanen 19971).

Not only were state bureaucracies criticized by the New Right for their inefficiency, but they were regarded as being non-responsive and detached from the needs and demands of individual consumers. Too much hierarchy, it was argued, had widened the distance of management decision makers and service providers from users. This distance was exaggerated, moreover, by professional groups who, according to New Right critics, acted as a 'narrow self-serving monopoly'. Professions, it was felt, also operated in a cost vacuum and remained unaccountable for their decisions both to managers and to the public more generally. They were also guilty of using their expert knowledge and skill to create an aura of indeterminacy between themselves and users, and to maintain 'restrictive practices, ineffective cartels and empire building' (Brooke 1989: 56). Over the years, these restrictive practices had become institutionalized within many large public sector bureaucracies, creating a strong power block resistant to top–down managerial control.

From this brief discussion one can see how a number of New Right critics directly addressed some of the core failings of traditional public sector organization and management. Their solutions required the extension of market forces in order to improve both the efficiency and responsiveness of public services. Such a change would, it was believed, also increase the quality of public services.

Adopting some of these assumptions, Conservative governments throughout the 1980s have 'insisted on the inevitable inefficiency and ineffectiveness of monopolistic provision of goods and services' (Wilding 1991: 201). As will become clear, they have also looked for ways of commercializing the public sector. A key question remains, however, of how far these ideas fully infiltrated the policy agenda of successive Conservative governments and to what extent they were responsible for the major reorganization of the public sector that began in the 1980s?

Authoritarian populism?

Of significance was how these New Right ideas fed into the British government's project for reforming the public sector and how far they shaped its *character*. Hall argues that one might understand this project in terms of 'authoritarian populism' (Hall 1988). Although criticized by a range of observers (Gamble 1988: Jessop *et al.*1988), this concept nevertheless illustrates the competing ways in which the New Right in Britain was politically responding to the complex crisis of public administration, addressing the kinds of feature we have outlined above. On the one hand, anti-statist and anti-collectivist popular sentiments that evolved during the crisis of the Keynesian welfare state were articulated within a project that emphasized the 'liberty' of market choice in the face of the bureaucratic monopoly of the state. On the other, these were tied into a project that was in effect authoritarian in that it mobilized popular sentiment against the public sector and its employees whilst also using a more coordinated state apparatus to police socially those most effected by anti-welfarist policies.

Critics of such an interpretation have been concerned with the way it reifies the role of Conservative government after 1979 and gives special prominence to its strategic and calculative abilities (Gamble 1988). Others drew attention to the way Conservative strategy appeared to be articulating a 'Two-Nation' discourse, incorporating into the 'market' certain social segments whilst, in effect, marginalizing and policing those who did not have the economic resources to find market-based solutions to their social needs (Jessop *et al.* 1988).

An important point to make is that the Conservative government project of change was disjointed and was never exclusively driven by New Right intellectual concerns. Yet, whilst it must be emphasized that the government's state reform project was diverse and uneven, constantly having to reproduce itself, it did nevertheless attempt to cope with varying aspects of the public sector's crisis. It did so through a strategy of both resource containment and economy on the input side, and by popularizing the 'market' and stigmatizing the public sector in terms of the quality and organization of service delivery. The dual aspects of such a strategy, in part a response to the complex nature of the crisis itself, would constitute a major theme for later developments in Conservative strategy both at the macro- and micro-level. Hence, the diverse nature of the project in social terms as expressed in the 'Two-Nation' approach, coupled with its strategic characteristic of combining authoritarian features with a market-based and individualistic populism, meant that the project was constantly developing, having to remake itself in the light of different external circumstances. It is this contingent aspect of state reform since the early 1980s which contributes to the complex development of quality-related discourses which we will now discuss.

PLANS TO REFORM THE PUBLIC SECTOR AND THE *USE* OF QUALITY

So far, we have seen how Conservative governments during the 1980s aligned themselves with New Right doctrines as a way of addressing the perceived deficiencies of traditional public administration. As a consequence of this, a rhetorical concern with improving the 'quality' of public services became a central part of plans to reform the organization and management of the public sector. More generally, the government's aim was to address what it perceived to be the deficiencies of a costly and bureaucratic public sector by subjecting it to radical change.

At the very heart of this project of change were competing objectives. To use Gunn's (1988) terms, not only did the government hope to improve the efficiency and effectiveness of public services, but it wished to achieve greater economy and resource containment. This meant that at the same time as the government used a language of quality improvement (efficiency and effectiveness), it was also trying to reduce (in real terms) the overall level of state resources directed towards the public sector. In this way, those aspects of the government's reform project ostensibly geared towards improving quality were contextualized by ongoing fiscal problems and demands to minimize inputs.

In this section we argue that the language of quality played a pivotal role in terms of legitimating government efforts to reorganize the public sector. Broadly speaking, notions of quality and quality improvement became associated with this change in two ways. First, linked to reforms aimed at raising efficiency – such as strengthening management and performance measurement – a notion of 'quality' as value for money and conformance to standards emerged. Second, and much later, concepts of quality that emphasized the role of consumers gained greater prominence (voice and exit). The latter were associated with reforms geared towards the actual restructuring of public services (around quasi markets and contracts) (Walsh 1994). These different concepts of quality were not mutually exclusive. During the 1980s they were invoked by policy makers, managers and professionals simultaneously in the context of change in such a way that they mediated each other's character.

Although different approaches to quality were (and are) present throughout the 1980s and into the 1990s, we suggest that they emerged and became prominent at different stages of the government's reform project. This project got under way first with an 'input' orientation in the early 1980s, stressing the importance of value for money and efficiency, and was only later complemented by an 'output' orientation which referred to the role of 'consumers'. In both cases, as mentioned above, the broad objective of economy and spending cuts mediated the character and trajectory of these developments.

VALUE FOR MONEY AND QUALITY CONFORMANCE

New Right criticisms of state bureaucracy manifested themselves during the early 1980s in government policies of top-down intervention to affect the efficiency of public services. This process, according to Geddes, involved a:

> tightening of surrogates for valorization criteria in the state, ranging from increased use of audit procedures stressing cost-effectiveness, and the development of cost centre based institutional reorganization to the imposition of harsh financial regimes on nationalized industries.
>
> (Geddes 1988: 92)

A key element of this process was the emergence of a narrowly defined concept of 'quality' (valorization criteria) as value for money and conformance to specified standards. In practice, this often meant trying to get more for less, or as Pollitt puts it, increasing 'the productivity of services, so that their quality can be maintained or even increased while the total resources devoted to them are held down' (Pollitt 1990a: 48).

Linked to a concern with efficiency and economy was a battery of techniques for implementing quality control and assurance. These approaches defined quality in terms of fixed standards representing 'fitness for purpose', and aimed to establish external modes of evaluation and accreditation such as quality audit or (much later) the British Standards Institute BS5750 programme. The latter defined quality as 'the totality of features or characteristics of a product or service that bear on its ability to satisfy a given need' (Ellis 1988). In the NHS, for example, numerous quality assurance (QA) programmes followed the publication of the Griffiths Report (Department of Health and Social Security 1983). These involved defining a service in terms of its 'fitness for purpose' and ability to satisfy a given need, and then monitoring the providers of the service to ensure they meet the specification. Under QA, public services, like manufactured goods, would have to conform to technical standards and specifications and, in the process, offer 'value for money' (Walsh 1991). The emphasis was on ensuring that clear standards were set and that limited resources were used as efficiently as possible to meet these standards.

To ensure that these quality objectives were achieved, elaborate systems of performance measurement and external audits were established throughout the public sector (Carter 1989, 1991). In 1983, for example, the Audit Commission was formed specifically to monitor the management and value for money of local government (and later health) services. Recently, it announced plans to collect extensive performance information from local authorities, scrutinizing every aspect of their services, from the efficiency of refuse collection and school meals to police response times. In the NHS, the Audit Commission has also required 'trust' hospitals to provide detailed measures of 'activity' such as waiting times, cancellation times and, by 1995, general practitioner (GP) referral times. In higher education, from 1986 onwards, performance indicators of university research (and later teaching), organized by the University Grants Committee (UGC) and, later, the UGC and Higher Education Funding Council (HEFC), were also implemented and, by the late 1980s, closely tied to resource allocations. Similarly, in secondary education there was extensive use of performance indicators and 'league tables' following the 1988 reforms which allowed schools to 'opt out' of local authority control and become grant maintained.

More recently, an interest in value for money has entered into initiatives more ostensibly geared towards increasing 'public choice' and competition, such as compulsory competitive tendering (CCT) (Painter 1991), 'Market Testing' and the *Working For Patients* reforms in the NHS (1989). The Citizen's Charter (HMSO 1991) also argued that as services were tendered out, their efficiency would simultaneously be increased. In this way, an emphasis on value for money and conformance has remained a key feature of government reform into the 1990s.

It could be argued that the concern with improving value for money also went hand in hand with the growth of a 'new public management' (Harrow and Wilcocks 1990; Hood 1991; Ferlie 1994). A key feature of this new management was the decentralization of responsibilities to staff lower down the hierarchy of state bureaucracies. Such 'decentralization' was, however, less about empowering managers and more geared towards budgetary control and enforced accountability (Geddes 1988) through a range of performance measures. The desire to increase efficiency provided a justification for a stronger management, capable of challenging professional power, transforming traditional working practices and asserting greater bureaucratic control (Hoggett 1991; Dunleavy and Hood 1994). Increasingly, responsibility for fiscal control and the achievement of 'value for money' fell into the hands of this more assertive new public management (Pollitt 1990a).

The first signs of this new public management emerged early on in the 1980s (Pollitt 1986). In the civil service, new managerial responsibilities for decentralized cost centre budgets were created following the Raynor scrutiny and Financial Management Initiative (1982) (Gray and Jenkins 1986). The trend towards decentralization continued with the Ibbs Report (1988) and programme for 'next step agencies'. Efforts to strengthen management through the creation of cost centres, internal trading accounts and new executive responsibilities were also present in local government during the 1980s (Brooke 1989), and in the NHS following the move towards general management after the Griffiths Report (DHSS 1983) (Harrison *et al.* 1992). There is not the space here to give a full appraisal of the growth of new public management, although it can be seen how, during the 1980s, efforts to strengthen management were closely associated with wider objectives of increasing the efficiency and value for money of public services.

So far, little has been said about the fact that much of the talk regarding improving 'value for money' actually meant, in practice, little more than attempts to contain, or even cut, public spending. The drive towards retrenchment and 'input minimization' which followed the fiscal crisis of the early 1980s was largely responsible for this more limited concern for economy. One might, as a consequence of this, question how far achieving value for money and efficiency really were genuine objectives, or whether they were merely convenient buzzwords used to justify successive government economy drives.

QUALITY AND CONSUMERISM

It has been argued that, in the late 1980s, the growth of an 'enterprise culture' led public and private organizations alike to become obsessed with meeting the demands of 'sovereign consumers' (Keat and Abercrombie 1991). In the context of the British government's state reform project, those discourses of quality linked to extending the role of 'consumers' became increasingly important. This occurred as the reform project unfolded and was transformed during the 1980s from one with an exclusively input orientation to one that was both input and output driven.

In the early 1980s, attempts to increase efficiency had been justified using a language of accountability to the taxpayer. In 1983, more explicit reference was beginning to be made to the consumption interests of citizens and to improving 'consumer satisfaction' (as noted in the Griffiths Report (DHSS 1983) on the NHS, for example). Only later in the 1980s, however, did references to the consumer become mainstream in the government's state reform project. They did so as part of a new emphasis on improving the 'outputs' of public services and on the role of users in determining and assessing them. As mentioned above, this did not undermine the earlier concern with inputs and efficiency, but developed from it and, as we will later argue, conflicted with it. An emphasis on outputs meant not just top–down state intervention and fiscal control, but a radical restructuring of public services and the widespread use of discourses of the 'sovereign consumer' to legitimate such changes. In the local government context, this was understood as a 'shift in the nature of Thatcher's challenge . . . from an emphasis on financial restraint in the early 1980s to a broad ranging concern with its role, organization, institutions and management which has emerged in the later part of the 1980s' (Stoker 1989: 157).

Consumerism might be described generally as 'attempts to redress the imbalance of power that exists between those who produce goods and services, and those for whom they are provided' (Potter 1988: 149). In this sense, consumerism is about removing barriers separating the consumption of services from their production. Following this, the providers of services – including professional experts – must adopt what Abercrombie terms 'want regarding' standpoints, whereby the needs and demands of consumers determine the content and organization of services. This contrasts with 'ideal' regarding standpoints in which the expert service providers themselves decide consumer needs (Abercrombie 1991). Consumerism, therefore, means increasing the power of consumers vis-à-vis the providers of services and, in so doing, affecting the quality of services.

In this section we suggest that discourses of consumerism, used as part of the government's reform project, have centred on increasing *individual* 'consumer power' through a mixture of what Hirschman referred to as user 'exit' and 'voice' (Hirschman 1971). These discourses have represented (and constructed) the user of public services not as a collective citizen with democratic rights and obligations, but as an individual 'customer' who makes choices in a market-place.

'Exit' and 'voice'

Hirschman suggests that when the performance of an organization deteriorates, so does the quality of its products and services. Management is made aware of this through the actions of consumers who may employ their 'exit' or 'voice' options. Not only do consumer exit and voice alert management to problems of deteriorating quality, but they supposedly act as a 'recuperation mechanism' for reversing decline and improving quality (Hirschman 1971).

By exit is meant the freedom of consumers (or employees) to choose alternative providers of a service in the open market. Such action represents the ultimate sanction against poor quality and is, according to many New Right theorists, also the most effective way of rectifying the problem. According to Hirschman, 'by inflicting revenue losses on delinquent management, exit is expected to induce that "wonderful concentration of the mind" ' (Hirschman 1971: 21).

By contrast, voice involves the consumer complaining, or in some way scrutinizing or placing pressure on the providers of a service so that improvements in quality are realized. New Right theorists have often rejected voice, assuming that 'political' channels for changing state bureaucracies will be largely ineffective. Consumer pressure from below is a lot 'messier' and more costly than exit, although such pressure can also vary a great deal in scope from a 'faint rumbling to violent protest' (Hirschman 1971).

Citizens or consumers?

Concepts of consumerism used in the British state reform project have embraced a mixture of exit and voice options. They have also defined the user of public services and the 'public' more generally in a very specific way. According to Gamble:

A central goal has been to discredit the social democratic concept of universal citizenship rights, guaranteed and enforced through public agencies, and to replace it with a concept of citizenship rights achieved through property ownership and participation in markets.

(Gamble 1988: 16)

The emphasis has been on promoting quality through the actions of individual consumers (or customers) and not through any extension of collective citizens' rights (Stewart and Walsh 1992).

This representation of the individual consumer largely contradicts alternative notions of consumerism developed on the political left around the concept of public service orientation (PSO) (Stewart and Clarke 1987). PSO, in contrast, combines individual consumer rights to high-quality services with those of citizens' rights to involvement and empowerment – through the democratic process – in the management and planning of public services. To date, these alternative notions of citizen-consumerism have not featured in the British government's agenda of reforming the public sector.

The New Right image of the individual consumer is one which would seem to place more emphasis on exit and individual choice. This, however, has not meant that voice options have been completely ignored. Recent government pronouncements have made extensive references to the idea of increasing consumer voice, especially in relation to local 'managerialist' initiatives geared towards changing the culture of service organizations and also in relation to the Citizen's Charter.

Throughout the 1980s, Conservative government references to 'quality' incorporated rival and even contradictory concepts of user exit and voice. Below, we describe the range of initiatives which have been pursued. First, we suggest, the language of public choice (exit) has been associated with moves to introduce 'competition' between the providers of public services through the creation of quasi markets. Second, we argue that there have also been numerous initiatives – some even independent of the top–down pressure from the government – to extend user voice. These initiatives centred on 'decentralization' and organizational change, supposedly to bring service providers 'closer to the customer' and make them more responsive to the needs of users. Finally, we consider the implications of the Citizen's Charter and its use of consumerist discourses combining exit, voice and an emphasis on 'value for money'.

Voice as 'responsiveness to consumers'

Some have described approaches to quality improvement which aim to extend user voice as 'managerialist consumerism' (Wistow and Barnes 1993). Various initiatives were launched during 1980s which aimed to make the structure and culture of public service organizations more responsive to the needs and demands of users. In this case, concepts of consumerism were associated with a similar critique of 'Fordist' modes of public sector organization to the one we described earlier. According to Stoker, 'the centralized hierarchical organization and the commitment to standard products, which followed Fordist principles, was criticized for its remoteness and lack of responsiveness' (Stoker 1989: 154). Only by changing the organization of public services, it was argued, could the voice of users be heard.

As mentioned, the notion of increasing responsiveness towards consumers involved changing both organizational structures and cultures. In particular, the ideas of Peters and Waterman's best-selling book, *In Search of Excellence*, were influential here (Hambleton and Hoggett 1987). This talked about creating less bureaucratic organizations with flatter structures, more integration between functions and departments, and greater decentralization to front-line staffs in order to bring service providers 'closer to the customer' (Peters and Waterman 1982). It also placed the management of public organizations in a proactive role of 'sensitizing service delivery to user needs and preferences' (Wistow and Barnes 1993: 286). During the 1980s, and increasingly in the 1990s, these and other similar ideas have been widely circulated among public sector managers through training programmes and appraisal schemes. It is less certain, however, how far they were successfully implemented or how willingly.

In some public sector organizations, notions of the 'internal customer' were articulated and promoted by management. In others, more emphasis was placed on decentralizing responsibility to front-line staffs while retaining overall control through systems of surveillance and 'loose tight' structures (Hoggett 1991). In the late 1980s, holistic change programmes such as total quality management (TQM) also became popular in the public sector. More than any other programme for increasing responsiveness to users, TQM required radical cultural change, or as Pfeffer and Coote cynically remark, the idea that 'the DNA of every atom of workers in an organization should be encoded to make them produce goods and services that satisfy customers' (Pfeffer and Coote 1991: 40). In theory, TQM meant greater integration of tasks and extensive use of teamwork to bring about continuous improvements in services.

Approaches to quality improvement as responsiveness to consumers became increasingly prominent as the government reform project developed in the mid- to late 1980s. Following the Griffiths Report on the NHS (DHSS 1983), there had been increased interest in surveying patient satisfaction and opinion (Thompson 1986). In local government there was also a growing concern, both on the left and right of the political spectrum, with extending the voice of users (Burns *et al.* 1994). In 1987, for example, the Local Government Training Board (LGTB) published *Getting Closer to the Public* which advocated greater decentralization to sub-units, the use of marketing techniques to discover consumer preferences and improved communication to improve access to local authority services.

It is, of course, less clear how far such rhetoric has been translated into reality. Some local authorities have clearly gone further than others in terms of decentralizing activities, producing A–Z user guides and improving information about local services. Generally, a concern with these issues has gathered pace in the 1990s. The Audit Commission's involvement became more pronounced, while independent bodies such as the LGTB (later called the Local Government Management Board, LGMB) have continued to promote changes in public service delivery: see the recent LGMB document, *Fitness for Purpose* (1993). More recently, these issues have been articulated in terms of a new form of 'entrepreneurial government' (Osborne and Gaebler 1992; Du Gay 1994).

Efforts to 'decentralize' other public services such as health and the civil service were also justified in terms of bringing providers 'closer to the customer'. By 1992, it was reported that more than half of all civil service employees had been transferred into executive agencies (*Financial Times* 2 June 1992). These initiatives were justified by the government as a means of increasing public accountability and as providing a counterweight to bureaucratic centralization, via 'a pull downwards and outwards – to the local provider, the user and the local community' (William Waldegrave, *Financial Times* 21 July 1992).

Exit and 'institutionalized consumerism'

The second aspect of the Conservative government's interest in consumerism relates to exit and choice. As discussed earlier, the exit option is favoured by many New Right public choice theorists who regard market structures as a more effective way of ensuring high-quality, efficient public services. The quality of services is increased under market conditions, they argue, not just because of the threat of consumer exit, but as a result of the competition it generates between service providers. These ideas were closely associated with policies of privatization, direct paying for services, contracting out and the restructuring of entire sectors of the welfare state to create quasi markets.

Notions of improving quality through consumer choice have also been linked to a general extension of contractual 'trading relationships' in local government that 'separate service policy-making and specification from delivery and production' (Stewart and Walsh 1992: 504). For the government this 'hands off', regulatory role for the local state is preferable to one which excludes competition and market forces. According to the senior Cabinet Minister, William Waldegrave, 'we have to restore the principle that the government's job is to govern, not to administer; to steer, not to row' (*Financial Times* 21 July 1992). As mentioned above, this could also imply a move towards a 'neo-Fordist' public sector in which:

> central government will contract with executive agencies, quasi-governmental organizations, the private sector, voluntary associations and local authorities to achieve its policy objectives. It will be able to choose to which organization to allocate resources and lay down performance targets and criteria . . . With only a little exaggeration, such a model turns the process of government into a dynamic paralleling that of a post-fordist Benetton!
>
> (Stoker 1989: 166)

In practice, the new government role has meant holding on to the purse strings while at the same time leaving the delivery of services and their quality in the hands of a mix of 'decentralized' public, private and voluntary agencies (Hoggett 1991, 1994).

In local government, restructuring has indeed led to fragmentation and the separation of planning from service delivery, 'stressing the importance of responsiveness to the public in the market' (Stewart 1989: 175). Initially, through compulsory competitive tendering (CCT) (1988), local authorities were forced to put out to tender a range of public services such as cleaning and catering. This principle, however, was extended to professional services following the Local Government Act in 1992, and later to social services. These moves, it was argued, would increase choice for non-standardized products and competition between providers which, in turn, would lead to greater efficiency (Painter 1991). They also heralded an era of 'welfare pluralism' in which so-called 'enabling' local authorities would concentrate on central planning while a mix of voluntary agencies, direct service organizations and private sector firms were held responsible for actual service delivery (Cochrane 1991). In interpreting these developments, local authorities may – depending on their political composition – adopt either a proactive focus on wider 'community' interests or a narrower 'market' focus in which 'local councils would only meet once a year – for lunch and to check all the contracts were in order' (Wilding 1993: 206).

A similar picture of restructuring around quasi markets can also be seen in the NHS where notions of extending consumer choice formed a core part of the *Working for Patients* reforms (1989). These reforms created internal markets which separated service providers ('trust' hospitals) from purchasers (GPs, regional and district health authorities). One result of these changes was that, in order to secure service contracts, individual providers were placed under increasingly 'intense' pressure to establish quality assurance systems and meet service specifications (Harrison *et al.* 1992; Harrison and Pollitt 1994).

Throughout the public sector, the language of extending consumer choice has been used to justify quite major plans to restructure and reorganize some public services around quasi markets. In a limited number of areas, such as secondary education and housing, the individual user *was* given a certain, albeit limited, amount of choice. In others, such as dental services, the government has extended the principle of 'user pays'. In the majority of cases, however, efforts to create quasi markets have not led to direct consumer choice (as in the private sector), but rather to an imperfect state of affairs which Pfeffer and Coote describe as 'institutional consumerism' (Pfeffer and Coote 1991). Here it is the contracting authority, or other institutional purchaser, rather than the individual user, who is the customer. The aim therefore is not necessarily to empower the individual user with choice but, in the short term at least, to break up the monopoly of services held by vertically integrated public sector providers. In this way, the only real choices in the new internal markets of health and local government services are those of contract managers and professional experts such as general practitioner fundholders.

The Citizen's Charter: mixing exit and voice

A variety of different approaches to quality improvement were formerly incorporated into the government's reform project through the *Citizens Charter* (HMSO 1991). The charter was a commitment on behalf of the government to guarantee standards of service, efficiency and value for money, as well as rights of complaint and redress if public services performed badly. More generally, it is debatable whether the charter represented a break from or a continuation of the politics of Thatcherism (Doern 1992). Side-stepping this issue, we argue that it represents an attempted formalization of the government's project at a time of growing political uncertainty, and a shift towards an output orientation, albeit one which was contextualized by strong financial controls. The key question for the government was how to get more outputs from public services in terms of quality and efficiency (involving consumers) without increasing inputs. According to Waldegrave: 'in reality people feel that they are already paying enough towards the provision of public services. They believe however they are entitled to more output from their input' (*Guardian* 17 February 1993).

The Citizen's Charter represented an attempted convergence of the various approaches to quality improvement described above (in part a response to the complexity of the projects related to the question of quality in the public sector). Furthermore, it could be argued that the charter was about deflecting the public's attention away from central government and broad resource issues of a political nature, towards service providers (Walsh 1994). The interface between individual and state was to be reduced to the interface between customer and service provider, depoliticizing expectations and forcing service providers to achieve high-quality standards with limited resources.

The core themes of the charter were listed as quality, choice, standards and value. In the preamble, emphasis is placed on value for money and extending user voice. The need to raise 'consumer satisfaction' and to 'increase choice, extend competition and thereby improve quality in all services' (HMSO 1991: 4) are also mentioned.

One could argue that the attempt of the Citizen's Charter to codify users' rights amounts to a tacit recognition by the government that the New Right obsession with exit consumerism was limited in the public sector. That is to say, there was a perceived need to make certain guarantees to users about standards and to regulate the activities of service providers (Pfeffer and Coote 1991). According to Willman, 'we are all charterists now', and, 'outside the ranks of a few die-hard libertarians, agreement is widespread that there are core public services which cannot be privatized and must be funded by the exchequer' (*Financial Times* 9 July 1992). This is not to say that the charter avoided all talk of extending public choice. It clearly argued for greater 'choice' and actually suggested ways of increasing it through internal markets and the restructuring of welfare state monopolies. Despite this, however, the key message was increased efficiency and extended 'voice' (talked about as choice) principally through limited rights of redress and complaint.

Most of the charter's mechanisms for achieving its objectives were simply continuations of existing policy, such as: more privatization, wider competition, further contracting out and the use of performance indicators. In the case of the latter, the charter was seen as a way of bringing together and repackaging various performance measurement initiatives across the public sector under a new label. More emphasis was placed on setting formal standards of service and on the production of what Sir Duncan Nichol termed 'accessible comparable information' or 'league tables' which would increase the public's 'ability to judge, influence and choose health services' (*Independent* 24 February 1993). In line with this, most public organizations were required to produce their own charters (thirty-three produced by late 1993) setting out clear standards and procedures for redress and complaint. These charters would be assessed independently by the National Audit Office, the Audit Commission and other inspectorates. Successful public organizations, meeting or exceeding their performance standards, would be awarded annual Chartermarks.

Other mechanisms specified by the Citizen's Charter for improving quality included new complaints procedures and rights of redress if services performed below standard. In 1992, for example, British Rail was forced to pay out £3 million to users for excessive delays, while the Benefits Agency paid out over £1 million in compensation for excess delays in benefit payments (both extremely low figures in relation to overall expenditure). Through a combination of often highly complex complaints procedures and rights of redress, the Citizen's Charter promoted a limited version of consumer voice in the management of public services. This threat of complaint was, in theory, supposed to make public organizations meet standards and deliver responsive, high-quality services.

A continuing characteristic of the Citizen's Charter was the Cabinet's ongoing attempt to rethink and reform it in response to the government's declining position in public opinion polls. A range of public meetings were held, for example, which were aimed at marketing and legitimating the role of the charter. This illustrated both the charter's centrality to the government's state reform project in the 1990s and its continued problems in the context of governmental crisis and re-evaluation.

In conclusion, the Citizen's Charter may be understood as an initiative which attempted to formalize, bring together and repackage a range of different quality discourses and practices. Consequently, the charter talked about often contradictory efforts to extend user voice and exit, while at the same time stressing value for money and efficiency of services. Continued efforts to privatize and restructure public services along the lines of both quasi markets and contracts were also subsumed under the Citizen's Charter initiative.

CONCLUSION

In this chapter we have outlined some of the key dimensions of a government-led, incremental strategy of reorganizing the public sector and the different ideas about 'quality improvement' which were associated with it. The government's interest in quality centred on notions of increasing 'value for money' and extending the role of the consumer (exit and voice). To some extent, the Citizen's Charter represented an attempt to consolidate and repackage these different objectives.

A rhetoric of improving the quality of public services was central to Conservative governments' plans to reform the management and the organization of the public sector. The objective of these reforms was to overcome the perceived deficiency of bureaucratic modes of organization, making public services more efficient, effective and responsive. This, in turn, was heavily influenced (although not completely dominated) by New Right doctrines.

'Quality' became associated with these changes first in terms of efforts to improve the value for money and efficiency of public services. Emphasis was placed here on setting standards and monitoring performance to ensure that levels of service were provided as efficiently as possible (often on budgets which were on the whole declining in real terms). In the late 1980s, as the government became increasingly concerned with outcomes and with the effectiveness of public services, a language of quality which emphasized consumer voice and exit emerged. This new emphasis on the role of the consumer in bringing about quality improvements went hand in hand with plans to restructure public services, first through 'decentralization' and later through the creation of quasi markets and new contractual relations between purchasers and providers.

In this chapter we have largely avoided the question of whether or not the quality of public services has improved as a result of these changes. Instead, we have focused on the political *uses* of quality. We have argued that the rhetoric of quality improvement provided a useful legitimation device to push forward a radical reorganization of the public sector. By arguing that such changes would enhance the 'quality' of public services, the government has, to a limited extent, been successful in representing its reform plans as being in the public interest.

What will be the future trajectory of this project of change and to what extent will an interest in quality improvement remain a central feature? To begin with, it looks increasingly likely that a larger proportion of what were once hierarchically controlled public services will become subject to what Hoggett (1991) and others describe as post-bureaucratic, contractual forms of control. This process has already gone quite far in the NHS and is moving at a rapid rate in both local and central government. Increasingly, it will be more difficult for central government to intervene in the way in which a complex variety of public service agencies (some increasingly in the private sector) are managed. Overall financial control will still, of course, be exercised by central government, as will some degree of policy control, albeit in a more strategic 'enabling' environment. The question remains how far the government will be able to control the detailed activity and service outputs of these increasingly decentralized agencies.

As mentioned, the Citizen's Charter was an attempt to achieve overall control over standards of service, while at the same time placing actual responsibility for quality improvement in the hands of service providers. It is too early to tell how successful the Citizen's Charter will be in providing a guarantee of standards and quality in this increasingly fragmented context of service providers and purchasers. All indications are that the charter will continue to face a range of diverse problems.

Given the problem of ensuring overall control over the outcomes of public services, it also remains uncertain how far, in future, emphasis on quality will be limited to the narrow concerns of the 1980s, i.e. of limited voice, institutional choice and emphasis on the user as an individual consumer, rather than an empowered citizen. In this chapter we have only mentioned in passing alternative ways of understanding quality and ways of implementing it, for example, around the notions of user empowerment and PSO. If structural changes continue to lead to greater fragmentation and decentralization then perhaps greater space may unintentionally have been created in which some of these alternative quality agendas can be constructed in the future. This has already happened to some extent in health and local government with numerous 'experiments' to increase user involvement in the planning and delivery of services being initiated (Burns et al. 1994). In this way, New Right concerns may increasingly be challenged and superseded as alternative conceptions of quality are promoted by local interests.

Also likely to characterize future developments are competing objectives within what we have so far described as a disjointed and highly uneven government project of change. These competing objectives rest at the very core of this project and relate to an espoused desire to improve quality and effectiveness while, at the same time, reducing – in real terms – the cost of public services. Rival messages of consumerism and value for money were often used as a 'smoke-screen to mask the effects of intensifying pressures on resources' (Pfeffer and Coote 1991: 2). This occurred, for example, in the case of early performance indicators which adopted the language of consumer interests, but focused almost exclusively on measuring inputs and processes, rather than service outputs or impact factors which might take into account users' views (Pollitt 1988a). Such contradictions have generated widespread 'demoralization' and cynicism amongst some public sector employees (Poole *et al.* 1994) who are told to increase quality while at the same time being expected to cut costs. If the government continues to promote long-term economy in public spending during the 1990s then there is no reason to expect this kind of contradiction to disappear.

These resource constraints not only lead to demoralization and uncertainty, they limit the space for alternative quality agendas to develop. Although we have argued that a more fragmented and 'decentralized' public sector may create opportunities for local interests to pursue their own agendas, this will take place within a context of severe resource constraints. What happens will depend on a variety of factors, in particular on how far local interests are capable of mobilizing and successfully negotiating change within this context of declining (real-term) resources.

REFERENCES

Abercrombie, N. (1991) 'The privilege of the producer', in Keat, R. and Abercrombie, N. (eds), *Enterprise Culture*, London: Routledge.

Alonso, L. (1992) 'Postfordismo, fragmentación social y la crisis de los nuevos movimientos sociales', *Sociologia de Trabajo* 16 (Autumn): 119–42.

Brooke, R. (1989) 'The enabling authority – practical consequences', *Local Government Studies* September/October: 55–63.

Burns, D., Hoggett, P. and Hambleton, R. (1994) *The Politics of Decentralization*, London: Macmillan.

Carter, N. (1989) 'Performance indicators: "backseat driving" or "hands off" control?', *Policy and Politics* 17(2): 131–8.

Carter, N. (1991) 'Learning to measure performance: the use of indicators in organizations', *Public Administration* 69: 85–101.

Castells, M. (1979) *City, Class and Power*, London: Macmillan.

Cochrane, A. (1991) 'The changing state of local government: restructuring for the 1990s', *Public Administration* 69: 281–302.

Department of Health and Social Security (1983) *NHS Management Enquiry* (Griffiths Report), London: HMSO.

Doern, G. (1992) 'The U.K. Citizen's Charter: origins and implementation in three agencies', *Policy and Politics* 24(4): 17–29.

Du Gay, P. (1994) '"Businessing" bureaucracy: entrepreneurial government and public management', paper presented at Employment Research Unit conference 'The Contract State', Cardiff.

Du Gay, P, and Salaman, G. (1992) 'The cult(ure) of the customer', *Journal of Management Studies* 29(5): 615–34.

Dunleavy, P. and Hood, C. (1994) 'From old public administration to new public management', *Public Money and Management* July–September: 9–16.

Ellis, R. (1988) 'Quality assurance: the professional's role', *Public Money and Management* Spring/Summer: 37–40.

Ferlie, E. (1994) 'Characterizing the "New Public Management"', paper presented at the British Academy of Management, Lancaster.

Friedman, M. (1980) *Free to Choose*, London: Pelican.

Gamble, A. (1988) *The Free Economy and the Strong State*, London: Macmillan.

Geddes, M. (1988) 'The capitalist state and the local economy: "restructruring for labour" and beyond', *Capital and Class* 35: 85–120.

Gray, A. and Jenkins, W. (1986) 'Accountable management in British central government: some reflections on the Financial Management Initiative', *Financial Accountability and Management* 2(3): 171–86.

Gunn, L. (1988) 'Public management: a third approach?', *Public Money and Management* 8(2): 21–5.

Hall, S. (1988) *The Hard Road to Renewal*, London: Verso.

Hambleton, R. (1988) 'Consumerism, decentralization and local democracy', *Public Administration* 66: 125–47.

Hambleton, R. and Hoggett, P. (1987) 'Beyond bureaucratic paternalism', in Hoggett, P. and Hambleton, R. (eds), *Decentralization and Democracy: Localizing Public Services*, Occasional Paper 28, Bristol: School for Advanced Urban Studies.

Hambleton, R. and Hoggett, P. (1993) 'Rethinking consumerism in public services', *Consumer Policy Review* 3(2): 103–11.

Harris, R. and Seldon, A. (1971) *Choice in Welfare 1970*, London: Institute of Economic Affairs.

Harris of High Cross, R., Baron (1988) *Beyond the Welfare State*, London: Institute of Economic Affairs.

Harrison, S. (1988) *Managing the National Health Service: Shifting the Frontier?*, London: Chapman Hall.

Harrison, S. and Pollitt, C. (1994) *Controlling Health Professionals: The Future of Work and Organization in the NHS*, Milton Keynes: Open University Press.

Harrison, S., Hunter, D., Marnoch, G. and Pollitt, C. (1992) *Just Managing: Power and Culture in the National Health Service*, London: Macmillan.

Harrow, J. and Wilcocks, L. (1990) 'Public services management: activities, initiatives and limits to learning', *Journal of Management Studies* 27(3): 281–304.

Hayek, F. (1944) *The Road to Serfdom*, London: Routledge and Kegan Paul.

Hill, S. (1991) 'How do you manage a flexible firm' *Work, Employment and Society* 5(3): 397–416.

Hirschman, A. (1971) *Exit, Voice and Loyalty: Responses to Decline of Firms, Organizations and States*, Massachusetts: Harvard University Press.

HMSO (1991) *The Citizen's Charter: Raising the Standard*, Cmnd. 1599, London: HMSO.

Hoggett, P. (1987) 'A farewell to mass production? Decentralization as an emergent private and public sector paradigm', in Hoggett, P. and Hambleton, R. (eds), *Decentralization and Democracy: Localized Public Services*, Occasional Paper 28, Bristol: School for Advanced Urban Studies.

Hoggett, P. (1991) 'A new managerialism in the public sector?' *Policy and Politics* 19(4): 243–56.

Hoggett, P. (1994) 'New modes of control in the public sector', paper presented at Employment Research Unit conference 'The Contract State', Cardiff.

Hood, C. (1991) 'A public management for all seasons?', *Public Administration* 69: 3–19.

Jessop, B., Bonnelt, K., Bromley, S. and Ling, T. (1988) *Thatcherism: A Tale of Two Nations*, Cambridge: Cambridge University Press.

Keat, R. and Abercrombie, N. (eds) (1991) *Enterprise Culture*, London: Routledge.

Klein, R. (1983) *The Politics of the National Health Service*, London: Longman.

Laclau, E. (1990) *Reflections on the Revolutions of Our Time*, London: Verso.

LGMB (1993) *Fitness for Purpose*, Luton: LGMB.

LGTB (1987) *Getting Closer to the Public*, Luton: LGTB.

Marquand, D. (1988) *The Unprincipled Society*, London: Cape.

Murray, R. (1991) 'The state after Henry', *Marxism Today* May: 22–7.

Niskannen, W. (1971) *Bureaucracy and Representative Government*, New York: Aldine.

O'Connor, J. (1973) *The Fiscal Crisis of the State*, New York: St. Martin's Press.

Offe, C. (1984) *Contradictions of the Welfare State*, London: Hutchinson.

Osborne, D. and Gaebler, T. (1992) *Reinventing Government: How the Entrepreneurial Spirit is Transforming the Public Sector*, Reading: Addison-Welsey.

Painter, J. (1991) 'Compulsory competitive tendering in local government: the first round', *Public Administration* 69: 191–210.

Parkin (1968) *Middle Class Radicalism*, Manchester: Manchester University Press.

Peters, T. and Waterman, R. (1982) *In Search of Excellence. Lessons from America's Best-run Companies*, New York: Harper and Row.

Pfeffer, N, and Coote, A. (1991) *Is Quality Good for You? A Critical Review of Quality Assurance in Welfare Services*, Social Policy Paper 5, London: Institute for Public Policy Research.

Pollitt, C. (1986) 'Beyond the managerial model: the case for broadening performance assessment in government and the public services', *Financial Accountability and Management* 2(3): 155–70.

Pollitt, C. (1988a) 'Bringing consumers into performance measurement: concepts, consequences and constraints', *Policy and Politics* 16(2): 77–87.

Pollitt, C. (1988b) 'Consumerism and beyond', *Public Administration* 66: 121–4.

Pollitt, C. (1990a) *Managerialism and the Public Services: The Anglo-American Experience*, Oxford: Basil Blackwell.

Pollitt, C. (1990b) 'Doing business in the temple? Managers and quality assurance in the public services', *Public Administration* 68: 435–52.

Potter, J. (1988) 'Consumerism and the public sector: how well does the coat fit?', *Public Administration* 66: 149–64.

Robinson, R. (1988) *Efficiency and the NHS: The Care for Internal Markets*, London: Institute of Economic Affairs.

Sabel, C. (1982) *Work and Politics*, Cambridge: Cambridge University Press.

Stewart, J. (1989) 'A future for local authorities' community government', in Stewart, J. and Stoker, G. (eds), *The Future of Local Government*, London: Macmillan.

Stewart, J. and Clarke, M. (1987) 'The public service orientation: issues and dilemmas', *Public Administration* 65(2): 161–77.

Stewart, J. and Walsh, K. (1992) 'Change in the management of public services', *Public Administration* 70: 499–518.

Stoker, G. (1989) 'Creating a local government for a post Fordist society: the Thatcherite project?', in Stewart, J. and Stoker, G. (eds), *The Future of Local Government*, London: Macmillan.

Thompson, A. (1988) 'The practical complications of patient satisfaction research', Health Services Management Research 1(2): 112–19.

Walsh, K. (1991) 'Quality and public services', *Public Administration* 69: 503–14.

Walsh, K. (1994) 'Quality through markets: the new public service management', in Wilmott, H. and Wilkinson, A. (eds), *Making Quality Critical*, London: Routledge.

Wilding, P. (1991) 'The British welfare state: Thatcherism's enduring legacy', *Policy and Politics* 20(2): 201–11.

Wilson, D. (1993) 'Turning drama into a crisis: perspectives on contemporary local government', *Public Policy and Administration* 8(1): 30–45.

Winkler, F. (1987) 'Consumerism in health care: beyond the supermarket model', *Policy and Politics* 15(1): 1–8.

Wistow, G. and Barnes, M. (1993) 'User involvement in community care: origins, purposes and applications', *Public Administration* 71: 279–99.

Chapter 2

Managing quality and organizational politics

TQM as a governmental technology

Mike Reed

INTRODUCTION

The objective of this chapter is to argue that the discourse and practice of 'quality management' should be understood as one critical component of a larger ideological narrative and organizational control strategy which came into political and institutional prominence in the 1980s. This narrative, and its related strategy of organizational restructuring, was geared to realizing a 'paradigm shift' in social values and managerial forms such that the principles and practices of bureaucratic rationality were to be replaced by those constitutive of market rationality. The latter also entailed, indeed demanded, a metamorphosis in prevailing organizational subjectivities or identities. The characteristic forms of motivation and action associated with 'organization man' or the 'bureaucratic personality' were to be replaced by those definitive of the 'enterprising or calculating self'. The 'culture of the customer' emerged as a 'total ideology' that was intended to sweep all remaining obstacles to cultural transformation and organizational re-engineering before it (Du Gay and Salaman 1992).

Relocated within this wider ideological and political context, total quality management (TQM) can be analysed as one crucial element within a broader 'intellectual or governmental technology', which is intended to align the broad objectives of governmental programmes – whether of the state, private sector corporations or public sector agencies – with the complexities and 'natural recalcitrance' of detailed organizational practice (Miller and Rose 1990). However, this process of alignment is highly partial and selective, given that the implementation and operationalization of governmental programmes at the 'organizational coalface' are likely to be characterized by an intense struggle between contradictory policy objectives and conflicting social interests.

The first section of this chapter will be concerned to develop this conceptualization of TQM as an integral component of an intellectual or governmental technology that attempts to link, if not integrate, governmental 'mentalities' and policies with everyday organizational realities. The chapter then moves on to a more specific and focused discussion of the organizational politics of quality management within public sector organizations undergoing the restructuring of surveillance mechanisms, and control practices associated with 'neo-Taylorism' (Pollitt 1990), the 'new managerialism' (Farnham and Horton 1993) or the 'new public sector management' (Hoggett 1991). Finally, the chapter will progress to examine the implications of these developments for the disciplinary regimes that are emerging in a wide range of public sector organizations, and the forms of control and resistance which are likely to crystallize around them. Recent developments within the health sector will be discusssed to provide further illustration of more general public sector restructuring and its implications for the emergence of new forms of governance within the latter.

TQM AS AN INTELLECTUAL/GOVERNMENTAL TECHNOLOGY

Hill (1991) has identified a number of principles normally associated with the concept and practice of quality management. These can be summarized in terms of customer-driven performance standards in both the market and within the organization; the implementation of these performance standards through the introduction of more advanced information control systems that pervade the work process; and a corporate culture which diffuses 'high-trust' work relations and a participative or collegiate decision-making ethos throughout all levels of the organizational hierarchy. These principles, he argues, 'can be seen to address the twin issues of how large corporations may increase the entrepreneurial propensity of their managers and debureaucratize their organizations' (Hill 1991: 401). This is so to the extent that TQM restructures organizational forms and practices to make them more open and responsive to customer needs, while simultaneously nurturing more flexible, decentralized and group-based forms of working. Both hierarchical control and bureaucratic closure are challenged by organizational and culture-change programmes that prioritize employee dedication to customer care above all other values.

Hill's characterization tends to conflate what Binns has called the 'procedurally based' and the 'culturally-based' approaches to TQM (Binns

1993). The former tends to emphasize a logic of standardized performance and control; the latter resonates much more strongly with long-term
attitudinal restructuring and cultural reconditioning aimed at instilling a
pervasive ethos of customer awareness and care throughout the whole
organization. In this respect, the concept of quality management
simultaneously carries a procedural imperative directed to effective
managerial control over product design and process performance, and a
cultural 'mission' geared to the manipulation of core organizational
values and beliefs that directly impact on work behaviour. The potential
contradiction, not to say conflict, between these two logics or rationalities of work design and organizational control – the former pressing
in the direction of enhanced external rationalization and the latter
towards extended internal autonomy – should not be underestimated
(Binns 1993; Delbridge and Turnbull 1992).

However, both of these conceptions of quality management can be
combined within an analytical framework that focuses on TQM as a
strategic component of an intellectual or governmental technology. The
latter is geared to the conceptual and practical retooling which needs to
be done to assemble the new disciplinary regimes within work organizations which the ideology of 'enterprise' or 'excellence' requires. An
intellectual or governmental technology, Rose and Miller argue,

> provides a mechanism for rendering reality amenable to certain kinds
> of action . . . it involves inscribing reality into the calculations of
> government through a range of material and rather mundane
> techniques . . . programmes of government have depended upon the
> construction of devices for the inscription of reality in a form where
> it can be debated and diagnosed.
>
> (Miller and Rose 1990: 7)

Thus, TQM can be analysed both as a symbolic form and as a technical
mechanism, which interweaves procedures for representing and inter-
vening in corporate life in such a way that thought is translated into the
domain of reality through languages and practices, which shape, normalize
and instrumentalize the conduct of organizational members.

On the surface, TQM may be seen as an apparently humble and
mundane procedural mechanism directed to the technical requirements
for operational efficiency and effectiveness within work organizations.
But this surface reality occludes an underlying logic and strategy of
control deployed in the service of values and interests held by those
occupying positions of governance within corporate hierarchies. The
sociopolitical and economic objectives of the latter frame the context

within which TQM renders a certain way of organizational living thinkable and practical; that is, amenable to techniques of calculation and forms of control which promise an attractive combination of individual autonomy, organizational effectiveness and economic success. Considered in this light, TQM can be interpreted as a potent mix of the 'sacred' and the 'profane', cultural transformation and procedural order. In its most conceptually pristine or ideal typical form, it offers an effective organizational integration of core values and control technologies through which ideological homogenization and behavioural conformity can be jointly secured (Hand and Plowman 1992). However, the actual implementation of TQM-type principles and methods is likely to be much more partial and contested than the ideal type would indicate. Indeed, judged as a practical control device, TQM has severe internal contradictions which will be reproduced in the form of highly selected and contested operationalization within the work organization.

As an intellectual or governmental technology, quality management can be viewed as one component of an overarching discourse and strategy of control that came to dominate political and academic debate over corporate restructuring in the 1980s (Reed 1993). This discourse focused on 'cultural re-engineering' as the primary means through which a new form of discipline was to be introduced throughout the private and public sectors. The underlying aim of this process of cultural transformation was to implant a mode of organizational governance in both private and public sector institutions which broke with the 'bureaucratic corporatism' characteristic of the post-Second World War settlement (Green 1987; Gamble 1988; Chapman 1991; Morris 1991). As an alternative to the inherent rigidities and inefficiencies of bureaucratic rationality and corporatist decision-making structures, this discourse of cultural transformation advocated a market-based rationality which was automatically assumed to guarantee 'enterprise', 'flexibility', 'commitment' and 'excellence'. Bureaucratic vicious circles were to be broken by programmes of attitudinal reframing and practices of organizational restructuring that swept away the collectivist constraints and sectional conflicts embedded in postwar culture and institutions.

In place of the restrictions and rigidities of corporatist compromise, the discourse of market-based enterprise and excellence anticipated, indeed demanded, the dismantling of failed institutional and organizational forms. The latter were to be superseded by organizational designs and managerial practices ideologically rooted in radical individualism and social Darwinism. As Silver has contended, the underlying project of this ideological critique is to legitimate a programme of cultural and technical change aimed at transforming 'workers attitudes – and thus to "unleash the forces of entrepreneurialism", "the psychological means of production" – without changing the nature of the job, without making tangible concessions to labour, and especially without increasing worker participation' (Silver 1987: 126). Thus, it is within this wider governmental discourse and its associated disciplinary technologies that the theory and practice of quality management must be set.

The specific representational, inscriptional and computational techniques associated with quality management need to be located within this broader ideological and political context. They provide the practical methods through which intellectual mastery and organizational control over a recalcitrant physical and social environment can be, at least partially, realized in order to secure the wider ideological and governmental objectives which that context specifies. As such, the practices associated with quality management facilitate a form of organizational governance based on an assumed technical and social expertise grounded in statistical and informational systems, and sociocultural management that permits 'control at a distance' (Cooper 1992) to be routinely achieved. Thus, Sewell and Wilkinson's study of 'total quality control' and 'just-in-time' regimes suggests that they:

> provide a whole paraphernalia of devices such as work flow simplification, set-up time reduction, cellular organisation, job rotation, stock reduction, Kanban controls, line balancing, statistical process control, etc., which can help take an organisation closer to the ideal (of 'total control') . . . where decentralization of tactical responsibility occurs at the same time as strategic control is centralized . . . Such surveillance and discipline is integral to TQC . . . management must erect a superstructure of surveillance and control which enhances visibility and facilitates the direct and immediate scrutiny of both individual and collective action.
>
> (Sewell and Wilkinson 1992: 278–82)

This analysis is entirely in keeping with Miller and Rose's argument that:

> domination involves the exercise of a form of intellectual mastery made possible by those at the centre having information about persons and events distant from them . . . Hence persons, organisations, entities and locales which remain differentiated by space, time and formal boundaries can be brought into a loose and approximate, and always mobile and indeterminate, alignment.
>
> (Miller and Rose 1990: 9–10)

The philosophy and practice of TQM thus provide a language and technique of governmental expertise which claims disinterested truth and specialized knowledge that will deliver desired results. The socio-technical infrastructure of the enterprise and its sociopsychological fabric are now subject to networks of control embedded in shared cultural vocabularies, theories and explanations. As Zeitz and Mittal's (1993) research on the institutionalization of TQM ideology and practice in the USA demonstrates, powerful institutional forces have supported the widespread diffusion of the values and techniques associated with that ideology in both the private and public sectors. The institutional forces which they identify range from state organizations and professional associations to major business corporations, such as Ford and Xerox, which endorsed and legitimized the adoption of TQM as a new philosophy of management which would completely transform the nature of organizational practice in both the private and public sectors in America.

Within the public sector in the UK, a series of structural and organizational innovations has been carried through in the name of 'quality', 'decentralization', 'deregulation' and 'contracting' . These combine a much more fragmented pattern of service delivery with political and informational control systems which much more closely, but unobtrusively, monitor and correct the decisions and activities of nominally autonomous agencies (Hoggett 1991; Pollitt 1993; Smith 1993). As Pollitt has argued:

A second problem with the coherence of public sector managerialism lies in its promises of, on the one hand, greater delegation to and autonomy for local units and, on the other, strengthened political and senior management control from the centre . . . In the public services, as in manufacturing, technological aids engendered visions of an 'information panopticon' in which top management could instantly access up-to-date information about whatever was going on anywhere within their fiefdoms . . . against the official Anglo-American rhetoric of decentralization must be set increasingly intensive top–down attempts to control information.

(Pollitt 1993: 115–18)

Hoggett's analysis of the changing control structures and relations within health, education and local government suggests that new forms of organizational surveillance and regulation are emerging which maximize operational decentralization and strategic centralization (Hoggett 1991).

These new control forms, Hoggett maintains, relate both to intra-organizational and inter-organizational restructuring in health, central and local government, education and social services. They simultaneously challenge bureaucratic and professional modes of organization by instigating much more devolved internal managerial control systems, and external contractual relationships that supersede the fragile balance between corporatism and syndicalism typical of public sector work organization (Hoggett 1991: 247–8). Under postbureaucratic forms of control, an underlying bifurcation between strategic and operational levels of decision making emerges, in which a process of 'decentralized centralization' dominates at all institutional levels of the public sector. This, Hoggett argues, entails a fundamental shift in the focus of control 'from a concern for internal methods and procedures to a concern for results' (Hoggett 1991: 250). Hierarchically based control systems, and their associated panoply of formal regulative control mechanisms, are replaced by contractual arrangements and practices that 'formalize informality'. This is realized by assembling a general framework of boundaries or limits within which a degree of operational autonomy, or at least discretion, can be exercised. Finally, Hoggett suggests, these developments lead to a much higher degree of administrative and spatial separation of strategic decision making and operational management – in which attempts are made to co-opt, if not incorporate, professionals into the management process. Control becomes both devolved and 'remote'; a framework of more extensive and intensive financial and informational control systems is put in place which closely monitors and regulates the actual exercise of delegated authority by 'front-line' staff.

Yet, like any other governmental technology, new forms of managerial control, based on decentralized operation and centralized monitoring, and directed at enhanced performance and service quality, are never implanted within the organization unscathed; they have to be adjusted and readjusted to the operational realities that they confront within everyday organizational life. As Miller and Rose put it, while the theory of 'governmentality'

> is eternally optimistic, the practice of 'government' is a congenitally failing operation. The world of programmes is heterogeneous and rivalrous, and the solutions for one programme tend to be the problems of another. Reality always escapes the theories that inform programmes and the ambitions that underpin them; it is too unruly to be captured by perfect knowledge . . . The 'will to govern' needs to

be understood less in terms of its success than in terms of the difficulties of operationalizing it.

(Miller and Rose 1990: 10–11)

Consequently, the micro-politics of quality management must be analysed before we can develop a more realistic appreciation of its organizational and governmental significance. Again, as Zeitz and Mittal's research shows, the theory and practice of TQM has been assembled, in a highly pragmatic and incremental fashion, out of a number of components such as sociotechnical systems theory, statistical process control and quality circles (Zeitz and Mittal 1993). The organizational impact of this 'bricolage' of concept and technique is mediated by inter- and intra-organizational politics which shape both the trajectory of its implementation and the substantive outcomes which this produces.

THE MICRO-POLITICS OF QUALITY MANAGEMENT

Empirical research on the implementation of quality management in work organizations suggests that the latter generates a centralization of indirect surveillance over individual and collective behaviour, and an intensification of direct supervisory control over task performance (Zuboff 1988; Wilkinson *et al.* 1991; Hill 1991; Sewell and Wilkinson 1992; Delbridge and Turnbull 1992). This conclusion sits rather uneasily with the ideology of 'individual empowerment' and 'high trust' work cultures (Fox 1974) aligned to TQM, in the sense that these concepts encourage an expectation of enhanced task autonomy and participative decision making which is rarely met in practice (Binns 1993). Nevertheless, the scale and intensity of the programme of cultural reconstruction and cognitive reconditioning, deemed necessary to establish the ideological infrastructure underpinning the development of the technical and administrative apparatus, through which total quality control and management become ubiquitous organizational realities, are real enough in themselves.

As Delbridge and Turnbull have argued, the underlying reality of TQM is 'management by blame'; that is, an ideologically mediated regime of product and process 'ownership', imposed through a system of 'employee peer surveillance', in which the rhetorical gloss of 'high trust' employment relations rapidly gives way to the practice of self-discipline and control:

The basis of quality control is, therefore, management through blame
. . . workers are encouraged to participate in the process of surveillance

which makes it possible to trace faults to individuals . . . a whole
system of self-subordination begins to develop . . . in which employees 'spy' on each other and report any deviant behaviour.

(Delbridge and Turnbull 1992: 65)

The pervasiveness of this culture of blame, and the internalization of
norms of self-discipline and control which it demands of workers and
managers, has also been documented in the work of Garrahan and
Stewart (1992) and Wilkinson *et al.* (1992). In particular, it requires a
fundamental reworking of organizational subjectivities and identities so
that the latter are redefined and reinscribed to form actively engaged and
highly motivated 'selves' – totally dedicated to the self-control and
subordination which must be achieved if continuous improvements in
customer responsiveness and care are to be realized (Du Gay and Salaman
1992). Thus, the individual workers and managers must subordinate
themselves to the structural imperatives and cultural dictates of TQM
without reservation. The mode of corporate governance and organizational design through which this can be realized involves a simultaneous
'autonomization and responsibilization of the self, the instilling of a
reflexive self-monitoring which will afford self-knowledge and therefore
self-mastery' (Du Gay and Salaman 1992: 627). This is to be achieved
through the culture and practice of 'total customer responsiveness',
which penetrates to the very 'soul' of individual employees, and requires
them to internalize full and complete responsibility for any organizational
failure to deliver perfect customer satisfaction. Thus, all organizational
members are required to submit themselves to a regime of control which
empowers them to take direct responsibility for organizational action,
while at the same time demanding that they exercise complete mastery
over their own behaviour in order to deliver the standards of performance which TQM systems expect.

However, we should be very wary of too easily accepting this imper-
ceptible merging of 'technologies of government' and 'technologies of
the self' that Du Gay and Salaman, and other researchers (Gordon 1991),
have identified and explained in terms of the 'totalizing reach' of the
governmental rationality constituted through the discourse of 'enterprise'. Indeed, as Miller and Rose's analysis indicates, the endemic
optimism and determinism of governmental rationalities is belied by
their highly partial and imperfect practical realization. The inherent
'recalcitrance of the tools of human action', so brilliantly exposed and
dissected in Selznick's study of the Tennessee Valley Authority (TVA)
(Selznick 1949), is echoed once more in the implementation of quality

management programmes – however sophisticated and advanced their theoretical designs may look. Selznick's work on the TVA pioneered a research tradition in organizational analysis (Perry 1979; Reed 1985) – continuing to be reflected, though in a somewhat modified form, in the research and writing of the 'new institutionalists' (Powell and Di Maggio 1992) – which focuses on the process of implementation and the moderating or qualifying effect that it inevitably has on the enactment of governmental programmes. Thus, Selznick's research demonstrates how the long-term policy objectives, and supporting control regimes contained within the latter, are always mediated by and through political processes which indelibly reshape the actual implementation of governmental technologies. This is particularly the case, he suggests, in public sector organizations, in which macro-level, as well as micro-level, political imperatives play a major role in determining the specific outcomes produced by reform programmes designed and legitimated within the somewhat rarified atmosphere inhaled by dominant elites occupying powerful positions within governmental structures.

Like intellectual/governmental technologies, systems of quality management require a relatively elaborate structure of surveillance and control practices to 'back up' ideological exhortation and cultural reprogramming, in the event that they prove less than effective in achieving the degree of self-discipline that the latter promise (Binns 1993). The 'self-steering and self-actualizing capacities' (Du Gay and Salaman 1992: 630) promised by TQM cannot be guaranteed by the range of cultural orders and technical practices through which TQM is instantiated as a regime of production management and control. Instead, these have to be buttressed by an apparatus of administrative, informational and organizational mechanisms that anticipates and copes with human frailty and resistance in all their multifarious forms and guises. This apparatus symbolizes and signifies, in a very concrete and practical way, that the design, implementation and evaluation of quality management systems, like all new technologies, have to be negotiated through highly complex micro-political processes, which substantially influence their long-term impact on prevailing governmental structures within work organizations (McLoughlin et al. 1988). The discourse of quality management anticipates and celebrates a radical process of attitudinal and behavioural restructuring, which will secure a deep-seated transformation in organizational identities and the work behaviour that flows from them. However, it has to confront the everyday realities of shop-floor and office politics that sculpt the 'contested terrains' on which control struggles are fought and decided. Self-subordination to the ideological and operational demands of quality management regimes is likely to be extremely imperfect, and to be mediated through the power struggles which actually shape organizational outcomes. Thus, in practice, the organizational reality of TQM will fall far short of the totalizing and universalizing ideals to which it aspires.

A number of studies illustrate the pervasive influence of micro-political processes – at all levels of the decision-making hierarchy within corporate structures and work organizations – on the practice of TQM. Hill's (1991) research demonstrates that quality management initiatives met with some degree of resistance – particularly from first-line and middle-level managers. Their task performance was exposed to much more intrusive and visible forms of external scrutiny, but they were prepared to sacrifice a degree of work discretion and autonomy in exchange for enhanced participation within higher levels of organizational decision making. Sewell and Wilkinson (1992) indicate that total quality control systems led to the introduction of more sophisticated and effective forms of surveillance over organizational behaviour, but this was moderated by avoidance tactics and strategies on the part of the workforce, which prevented management from completely appropriating the tacit knowledge and discretion of the latter. Smith's (1993) research on the actual use of performance indicators in public sector organizations reveals the extent to which the former are subject to a high degree of managerial and professional 'gamesmanship'. It also highlights the potentially dysfunctional impact of too rigid an application of performance indicators in which strategic control becomes overcentralized in 'command systems' that begin to resemble Soviet-style planning regimes. Delbridge and Turnbull (1992) suggest that the 'management by stress' control regime implicit in quality management theory and practice is being contested by shop-floor and trade union action, which challenges further restrictions on worker autonomy and discretion. Zuboff summarizes the general thrust of this research on the micro-politics of TQM when she argues that her own fieldwork demonstrates that:

> Unilateral techniques of control tend to evoke techniques of defence from subordinates who resent their own involuntary display . . . this battle of techniques of control versus techniques of defence signals the erosion of reciprocal relations as information becomes the field on which latent antagonisms are let loose. The electronic text can so insulate managers from the felt realities of their workplace that they will no longer have available the means with which to rekindle reciprocities if they should want to . . . Thus insulated, managers

often collude in ignoring the ever more slender relationship between their data and the organisational realities they are meant to reflect.

(Zuboff 1989: 316)

Zuboff's work shows us that the 'control and surveillance panopticon' promised to management by TQM and other governmental technologies is a chimera; these regimes have in-built constraints and limitations which cannot be overcome or erased by even further refinement of their design or functioning. In turn, the implementation failures of quality management systems will often drive organizations and their management to impose even more intrusive and ubiquitous control regimes, but the latter will usually be self-defeating (from a managerial perspective). This will be the case to the extent that they are likely to insulate managers from the political and moral realities of organizational life (Anthony 1990; 1994), and to open up new areas of conflict and struggle around the 'power/knowledge' discourses which innovative control strategies and practices generate. These new 'contested terrains' are also likely to destabilize, if not threaten, pre-existing forms of work organization based on relatively 'high-trust' organizational cultures and the moral foundations on which they rest – the very antithesis of what TQM ideology and philosophy promise. A 'vicious circle' (Crozier 1964) of partial control failures and reintensification of the very disciplinary regimes which have been successfully resisted by workers and managers sets in motion a downward sprial of social relationships that undermines the political and moral foundations on which organizational order was once negotiated.

Under the control regimes which TQM instantiates, specialized knowledge and information emerge as the most crucial of the critical power resources which different groups struggle over in their attempts to 'bend' those regimes to their advantage (Binns 1993). It also encourages management to become increasingly reliant, not to say dependent, on more technologically sophisticated informational and electronic control systems, which hold an extremely tenuous relationship with the social and political realities of everyday organizational life. Thus, managers become more and more skilled in the complexities of technical and informational control, while losing contact with the subtleties of political management. This encourages them to believe in the rhetoric of new ideologies and techniques of organizational governance which take them further and further away from the realities of negotiating and renegotiating order. They become entrapped in an ideological myth and technological apparatus of their own making which deliver the opposite of what they promise; that is, a technology of rule which can provide more effective 'control at a distance' and self-disciplining routines which reduce the need for external monitoring, but which simultaneously disable management from realistic engagement with the sociopolitical processes through which work organization is sustained. Managers become more insulated from the sociopolitical complexities and moral dilemmas which they would prefer, and are encouraged to avoid, while workers become more isolated from each other and the wider organizational communities with which they previously identified.

Recent developments in a wide range of public sector organizations attest to the new struggles for control crystallizing around 'restructuring' initiatives flowing from the imposition of the 'new managerialism'. They also provide further illustration of the vicious circles of internal managerial 'control at a distance' (Cooper 1992), and worker disengagement from the ethic of public sector service, that these control struggles often generate.

CONTESTED TERRAINS AND THE NEW MANAGERIALISM

A wide range of public sector organizations have experienced the full force of restructuring initiatives associated with TQM and other changes in control strategies during the second half the 1980s and early 1990s (Cousins 1987; Pollitt 1990; Chapman 1991; Farnham and Horton 1993; Pettigrew *et al.* 1992; Cox 1991, 1992; Reed and Anthony 1993; Smith 1993; Clarke and Pitelis 1993; Hoggett 1991). As Flynn has put it:

> neoliberal doctrines about inefficient and paternalistic state bureaucracies and professional monopolies converged with . . . public disquiet about the quality and effectiveness of welfare provision, and this convergence has provided a platform for the advocacy of market solutions and consumerism in the public sector.
>
> (Flynn 1992: 3)

These initiatives posed a serious threat to the 'professional syndicalism' and 'organizational corporatism' which had dominated the administration and management of the public sector since the post-1945 settlement. The ideology of market-led managerialism, and the control mechanisms which it legitimates, have challenged the hegemony of an institutional culture and organizational practice based on the morality of 'public service' and the politics of bureaucratic compromise. The latter are seen to buttress a form of governmental theory and practice which has prioritized the preservation of sociopolitical order and organizational consensus far above market efficiency, customer sovereignty and state impartiality. In turn, this is seen – by those who have been in positions of political, economic and social power during the 1980s and 1990s – to sanction an extreme form of administrative and managerial indulgence in relation to professional autonomy and power. The provider monopoly groups within the public sector are seen to be literally 'out of control' and free to determine the actual operation of public services, without any consideration of escalating financial costs and their implications for public spending. This has further embroiled the state in the morality and politics of public sector provision, from which it should ideally disengage so as to be in a position to act much more effectively as the arbiter of economic realism in a much more individualistic and competitive era (Green 1987).

Many of the cultural, structural and organizational reforms introduced in the public sector in the 1980s and 1990s can be interpreted as a general strategy of regaining managerial control over powerful provider groups (Loveridge and Starkey 1992). This was to be achieved through a programme of governmental restructuring aimed at introducing market discipline and related resource allocation mechanisms within public sector organizations which had been dominated by the monopoly power of provider interests (Ackroyd *et al.* 1989). This governmental programme, and the specific control regimes which its practical realization demanded, was underpinned by an ideology of 'cultural revolution' which legitimated the need for fundamental attitudinal and behavioural restructuring – particularly amongst powerful provider groups who were strong enough to resist the embrace of managerialism (Strong and Robinson 1990).

However, changing 'hearts and minds' proved to be somewhat more difficult than the direct imposition of a much harsher and authoritarian control regime indicative of the resurrection and revitalization of neo-Taylorism within public sector organizations (Pollitt 1993). Taylor and Lenin, rather than Mao, became the theoretical and ideological reference points for a programme of governmental restructuring, which would transform public sector organizations from bureaucratically protected provider guilds or professional fiefdoms into quasi-business enterprises. TQM became part, indeed a vital part, of this process of anticipated organizational change, insofar as it prioritized market discipline and customer sovereignty over administrative regulation and professional autonomy. The dominance of bureaucratic culture and provider power were to be directly challenged by quality management reforms which simultaneously centralized strategic control and deregulated supervisory control over operational performance. This was to be realized in such a way that the official image of triumphant public sector enterprise and entrepreneurialism could be, however tenuously, maintained in the face of growing evidence to the contrary. The 'velvet hand' of public sector quality initiatives, promising cultural re-engineering and behavioural restructuring, simply masks the 'iron fist' of intensified organizational control and the marketization of service standards and employment conditions.

There is also evidence to suggest that quality management reforms introduced into public sector organizations have led to a politicization of workplace and institutional conflicts; that is, they have increased the social visibility of, and political struggle over, decision-making processes concerned with resource allocation and deployment, which were previously hidden within the bureaucratic labyrinths of corporatist government and professional group bargaining (Martinez chapter 11). Such research also suggests that management is finding it increasingly difficult to cope with and contain these struggles within a mode of service governance and related organizational control which effectively emasculates the moral foundations of, and organizational preconditions for, the 'negotiation of order' between conflicting interests (Anthony and Reed 1990; Reed and Anthony 1993; Thompson 1987; Flynn 1992). As a result, the social and political pluralism which previously existed within the public sector as an institutional domain, and public sector organizations as 'mini-societies' within that domain, have been seriously threatened by control regimes based on unitary ideologies which delegitimate the need and opportunity for opposition between contending values and interests. A system of rule, based on an underlying belief in the dynamic quality and innovative potential of well-regulated social and political conflict, has given way to a new ideological orthodoxy extolling cultural conformity and organizational uniformity above all other values.

Nevertheless, the reality of operational practice within public sector organizations – which have supposedly been re-engineered by the transformational effects of quality management and other change programmes – suggests that the politics of 'negotiated order', in however attenuated a form, continues to define the limits of governmental reform. One of the most dramatic and insightful cases of the extent to which organizational politics continues to shape the processes through which institutional reform is actually managed within the public sector as a whole is provided by what has happened in the health service. The National

Health Service (NHS) was, and still remains, the institutional embodiment of an ethical and political doctrine based on universalism and pluralism; the governmental and organizational correlates of these core values were based on a compromise between centralized bureaucratic control and decentralized professional syndicalism (Klein 1990; Small 1989). The balance of power between these technologies of control changed and shifted over time, but a political trade-off between corporatist rule and professional autonomy continued to shape the institutional development and operational practice of the NHS until the early 1980s (Barnard 1989; Pollitt 1990; Reed and Anthony 1993).

However, political and organizational changes occurring from the early 1980s onwards signalled a decisive break with this compromise. This is true to the extent that they entailed an ideology of market sovereignty, and demanded a culture of consumer choice which was extremely difficult, if not impossible, to reconcile with corporatist bargaining and professional autonomy. As Flynn argues, managers emerged as the organizational carriers of this new ideology of market discipline and customer awareness. But they also had to contend with the much more open and intense political conflicts which crystallized around the new technologies of control that the implementation of this cultural revolution demanded (Flynn 1992). This was particularly the case when it became clear that the ideological abstractions of market logic and consumer choice would continue to be practically mediated by provider groups who were now much more sensitive to the wider political context in which they were operating. They were also much more aware of the substantial weakening, if not complete erosion, of the moral and cultural restraints which had previously moderated the intensity and impact of micro and macro power struggles between conflicting interests (Reed and Anthony 1993).

Indeed, recent empirical research suggests that public sector managers find themselves in a situation where they are caught in an 'organizational crossfire' between the financial and political imperatives driving centralized strategic control, and the operational realities of everyday work performance (Anthony and Reed 1990; Reed and Anthony 1993; Thompson 1987; Strong and Robinson 1990; Pettigrew *et al.* 1992; Flynn 1992). The latter requires negotiated compromises between conflicting interests and values, based on a relatively stable level of trust between competing organizational stakeholders (Burns 1992). The former rests on geographically, politically and socially remote systems of surveillance and control, which eat away at the moral and ethical foundations of high-trust work cultures (Anthony 1985). Inevitably, managers find themselves in a situation where their mediation of central policy directives and control mechanisms – so that they 'fit' the particular demands and constraints of organizational contexts – involves a substantial weakening of their authority as representatives of 'the service' and a corresponding strengthening of their new roles as subordinate agents of centralized control. As Pollitt argues:

> the managerialists conceive of management itself as the guardian of the overall purposes of the organization, and therefore it is wrong that another group of staff should be able to work to a different set of priorities and, when challenged, often successfully resist management's call for conformity. After all, in ICI or Dupont or McDonnell-Douglas there are plenty of professional experts, but they are 'on tap' for management, not 'on top'. What is unrealistic about the neo-Taylorian approach is that it assumes that these problems can be overcome and that meanwhile its prescriptions for rationalization (merit pay, appraisal, performance indicators, delegated budgeting systems, etc.) can go ahead. In practice, this assumption has contributed to the declining morale and led to a good deal of conflict . . . organizational realities proved stronger that an apparatus of managerialism founded too exclusively on economic logic.
>
> (Pollitt 1993: 131–2)

The imposition of a neo-Taylorist strategy of control, required to translate the ideology of market sovereignty and customer choice into some kind of organizational reality, has placed severe strains on the highly complex, and often fragile, political processes and moral understandings through which order was negotiated in health-service organizations. These strains and stresses are likely to result in further politicization of organizational decision making within the health sector, and to encourage enhanced fragmentation of institutional routines and operational services which previously defined health care as a 'national' service. They also provide additional support for the contention that the actual functioning of governmental technologies is mediated by micropolitical processes which cannot be completely marginalized through the more extensive and sophisticated control regimes which the former bring in their wake.

CONCLUSION

The overall thrust of this chapter has been to argue that TQM should be analysed as one vital component of an intellectual or governmental technology which attempts to align broad ideological mentalities and policy goals with the complex realities of organizational practice – but in a highly imperfect and contested manner (Miller and Rose 1990). By fabricating specialized informational technologies and expert routines, through which abstract concepts and propositions can be operationalized within a complex field of micro-political power processes and relations, the discourse and practice of TQM strive to build and maintain an effective ideological and technological bridge between the meta-narrative of 'enterprise culture' and the organizational reforms through which it is to be realized. However, the operational capacity of TQM to function as a relay device, effectively linking government mentalities and policies within everyday organizational realities, remains highly variable, uncertain and contested. Its ability to function as a translation or relay mechanism, through which general programmes of ideological reconditioning can be turned into practical institutional and organizational reforms, is dependent on the micro-political processes through which it has to 'pass'. In this sense, the capacity of TQM to link, much less integrate, the 'ideological', 'political' and 'technological' dimensions of institutional functioning and organizational life is continually distorted or corrupted by a socio-organizational environment which is heterogeneous, rivalrous and recalcitrant in the face of attempts to subject it to more effective forms of control. Yet, control regimes and technologies such as TQM, whatever their inherent contradictions and limitations, can, and do, enact very significant changes to our institutional landscapes and organizational settings. Webster and Robins' analysis of a 'social Taylorism' (Webster and Robins 1993), which empowers surveillance at the centre and controls the isolated individual at the periphery, may be rather more fatalistic and overdetermined than they intend. New information and control technologies, such as TQM, do provide much more flexible, portable and intrusive forms of government rule and managerial coordination. But their actual operation and results have to be set within the power struggles which are beginning to take shape around expert knowledge and the sociopolitical agendas that inform its application (Blackler et al. 1993). The analysis of new developments in control strategies and practices within public sector – or for that matter private sector – organizations must attempt to navigate a sensible theoretical and methodological course between the Charybdis of structural determinism and the Scylla of political voluntarism.

    This will be particularly relevant within public sector organizations in which the impact of these new control technologies is likely to be especially significant – given the inbuilt opportunities for resistance and modification which the former present. Accepting the inherent organizational complexity of public sector institutions, such as the NHS and the continuing moral and ideological appeal of its inherited traditions, the imposition of more intrusive and ubiquitous control regimes, which signify a radical discontinuity with the past, may not be so simple or straightforward. Indeed, it is likely to be fraught with a high degree of political and managerial risk which governing elites would do well to remember. It is also the case that new governmental technologies will have to pass through power struggles and control battles which will indelibly imprint themselves on the organizational forms that take shape in the 'public sector' in the closing decade of the twentieth century. The inevitable gap between 'governmentality' and 'government' will continue to cause serious control problems for those who would manage public sector organizations according to the logic and dictates of 'market rationality' and 'strategic command' – unfettered by the understandings and compromises made possible by quasi-corporatist modes of organizing and ruling.

REFERENCES

Ackroyd, S., Hughes, J. and Soothill, K. (1989) 'Public sector services and their management', *Journal of Management Studies* 26(6): 603–19.

Anthony, P. (1985) *The Foundation of Management*, London: Tavistock.

Anthony, P. (1990) 'The paradox of management culture or He who leads is lost', *Personnel Review* 19(4): 3–8.

Anthony, P. (1994) *Managing Culture*, Buckingham: Open University Press.

Anthony, P. and Reed, M. (1990) 'Managerial roles and relationships in a district health authority', *International Journal of Health Care and Quality Assurance* 3(3): 20–31.

Barnard, K. (1989) 'National Health Service management', in Taylor, I. and Popham, G. (eds), *An Introduction to Public Sector Management*, London: Unwin Hyman.

Binns, D. (1993) 'Total quality management: organization theory and the New Right: a contribution to the critique of bureaucratic totalitarianism', Labour Process Conference, Blackpool.

Blackler, F., Reed, M. and Whitaker, A. (1993) 'Knowledge workers and contemporary organisations, *Journal of Management Studies* November special issue 30(6): 851–1020.

Burns, T. (1982) *A comparative study of administrative structure and organizational processes in selected areas of the National Health Service*, Social Science Research Council Report, HRP 6725, London: Social Science Research Council.

Chapman, B. (1991) 'Concepts and issues in public sector reform: the experience of the UK in the 1980s', *Public Policy and Administration* 6(2): 1–19.

Cousins, C. (1987) *Controlling Social Welfare: A Sociology of State Welfare Work and Organization*, Brighton: Wheatsheaf.

Clarke, T. and Pitelis, C. (eds) (1993) *The Political Economy of Privatization*, London: Routledge.

Cooper, R. (1992) 'Formal organisations as representation', in Reed, M. and Hughes, M. (eds), *Rethinking Organisations: New Directions in Organisation Theory and Analysis*, London: Sage.

Cox, D. (1991) 'Health service management: a sociological view', in Gabe, J., Bury, M. and Calnan, M. (eds), *The Sociology of the Health Service*, London: Routledge.

Cox, D. (1992) 'Crisis and opportunity in health service management', in Loveridge, R. and Starkey, K. (eds), *Continuity and Crisis in the NHS*, Buckingham: Open University Press.

Crozier, M. (1964) *The Bureaucratic Phenomenon*, Chicago: University of Chicago Press.

Delbridge, R. and Turnbull, P. (1992) 'Human resource maximization: the management of labour in just-in-time manufacturing systems' in Blyton, P. and Turnbull, P. (eds), *Re-Assessing Human Resource Management*, London: Sage.

Du Gay, P. and Salaman, G. (1992) 'The culture of the customer', *Journal of Management Studies* 29(5): 615–34.

Farnham, D. and Horton, S. (eds) (1993) *Managing the new Public Services*, London: Macmillan.

Flynn, N. (1992) *Structures of control in health management*, London: Routledge.

Fox, A. (1974) *Beyond Contract: Work, Power and Trust Relations*, London: Faber and Faber.

Gamble, A. (1988) *The Free Economy and the Strong State: The Politics of Thatcherism*, London: Macmillan.

Garrahan, P. and Stewart, P. (1992) *The Nissan Enigma*, London: Mansell.

Gordon, C. (1991) 'Governmental rationality: an introduction', in Burchell, G., Gordon, C. and Miller, P. (eds), *The Foucault Effect*, Brighton: Wheatsheaf.

Green, D. (1987) *The New Right: The Counter-Revolution in Political, Economic and Social Thought*, Brighton: Wheatsheaf.

Hand, M. and Plowman, B. (1992) *Quality Management Handbook*, Oxford: Butterworth-Heinemann.

Hill, M. (1991) 'How do you manage a flexible firm: the total quality model', *Work Employment and Society* 5(3): 297–316.

Hoggett, P. (1991) 'A new management in the public sector?', *Policy and Politics* 19(4): 243–56.

Klein, R. (1990) *The Politics of the Health Service*, London: Longman.

Loveridge, R. and Starkey, K. (eds) (1992) *Continuity and Crisis in the NHS*, Buckingham: Open University Press.

McLoughlin, I. and Clark, J. (1988) *Technological Change at Work*, London: Macmillan.

Miller, P. and Rose, N. (1990) 'Governing economic life', *Economy and Society* 19(1): 1–31.

Morris, P. (1991) 'Freeing the spirit of enterprise: the genesis and development of the concept of enterprise culture' in Keat, R. and Abercrombie, N. (eds), *Enterprise Culture*, London: Routledge.

Perry, N. (1979) 'Recovery and retrieval in organisational analysis', *Sociology* 13(1): 38–50.

Pettigrew, A., Ferlie, E. and McKee, L. (1992) *Shaping Strategic Change*, London: Sage.

Pollitt, C. (1990) *Managerialism and the Public Services: The Anglo-American Experience* first edition, Oxford: Basil Blackwell.

Pollitt, C. (1993) *Managerialism and the Public Services: The Anglo-American Experience* second edition, Oxford: Basil Blackwell. .

Powell, W. and Di Maggio, P. (1992) *The New Institutionalism in Organizational Analysis*, Chicago: University of Chicago Press.

Reed, M. (1985) *Redirections in Organisational Analysis*, London: Tavistock.

Reed, M. (1993) 'Rediscovering Hegel: the new historicism in organisation and management studies', European Group for Organisation Studies Colloquium, Paris.

Reed, M. and Anthony, P. (1993) 'Between an ideological rock and an organisational hard place', in Clarke, T. and Pitelis, C. (eds), *The Political Economy of Privatization*, London: Routledge.

Selznick, R. (1949) *TVA and the Grass Roots*, Berkeley: University of California Press.

Sewell, G. and Wilkinson, B. (1992) 'Someone to watch over me: surveillance, discipline and the just-in-time labour process', *Sociology* 26(2): 271–90.

Silver, J. (1987) 'The ideology of excellence: management and neo-conservatism', *Studies in Political Economy* 24(8): 105–29.

Small, N. (1989) *Politics and Planning in the NHS*, Milton Keynes: Open University Press.

Smith, P. (1993) 'Outcome related performance indicators and organisational control in the public sector', *British Journal of Management* 4(3): 135–52.

Strong, P. and Robinson, J. (1990) *The NHS Under New Management*, Milton Keynes: Open University Press.

Thompson, D. (1987) 'Coalitions and conflicts in the NHS: some implications for general management', *Sociology of Health and Illness* 9(2): 127–53.

Webster, F. and Robins, K. (1993) 'I'll be watching you: comment on Sewell and Wilkinson', *Sociology* 27(2): 243–52.

Wilkinson, A., Marchington, M. and Goodman, J. (1992) 'Total quality management and employee involvement', *Human Resource Management Journal* 2(4): 24–31.

Zeitz, G. and Mittal, V. (1993) 'Total quality management: the Deming method as new management ideology, institutionalization patterns in the United States', European Group for Organisation Studies Colloquium, Paris.

Zuboff, S. (1988) *In the Age of the Smart Machine: The Future of Work and Power*, London: Heinemann.

Chapter 3

Customizing the public for health care

What's in a label?

Andrew Thompson

INTRODUCTION

Hardly anyone living in Britain today could have managed to escape the change in the terminology being used to describe them as they conduct their everyday activities of living in the public arena. Parents of pupils at state schools or students in higher education; passengers using British Rail; elderly clients in local authority residential accommodation or tenants of council housing; patients in hospitals or using GP services; they all have something in common. They are all users of public sector services and they are all now referred to as 'customers'. In other words, what used to be considered a distinct domain of human activity is now equated, linguistically at least, with the other daily activities of trade and commerce. Our position as users of public services is now essentially the same as that of a customer in a supermarket, a hotel or a car showroom. At least, this is what we are supposed to believe.

Is it, in fact, how we do view ourselves in relation to public services, or are we at least gradually opening our eyes to how we could become customers in this sector, hitherto shielded from the full glare of market dynamics? How do we want to be labelled and how should we be, given the nature of these social relations? Is the label important anyway, or does it simply provide a convenient hook for discussing one group of social actors in the service relationship?

It is to these questions that attention will be focused in this chapter, with specific reference to users of public health services. The importance of labelling is considered from the perspectives of sociology and critical discourse analysis (Fairclough 1989) within sociolinguistics to uncover meanings, implicit and explicit, of various discourses. The discussion proceeds with the theme of quality, and how the strategy is taking shape in the National Health Service (NHS), in order to understand the reasons for changes in discourse. This explores the broader contexts of ideology and economics, through the promulgation of an enterprise culture, to explain how quality has emerged as a dominant discourse in the management of change. The public, as users of the NHS, is seen as being co-opted into this discourse to effect as well as reflect the changes to the welfare state. The use of the term 'customer' is seen as reflecting the ideological shift from 'citizen-user' to 'market-consumer', as part of the process of commodifying health to take its place in the private market of goods and services. The related theme of choice is contrasted with evidence of an empirical nature drawn from recent studies of the private health sector to substantiate perceived, as opposed to intentional, manifestations of consumerism in health care. An alternative relationship between health-service users and professionals is proposed that recognizes the unequal access to information but promotes the interests of both. In summary, the evidence is appraised to determine to what extent and under what conditions 'the customer cap fits' and whether the public would benefit 'by wearing it'. In conclusion, I argue for the label 'patient' to be retained, but redefined to provide a more accurate and more liberating description from the public point of view.

LABELLING THE PUBLIC IN HEALTH CARE

Labelling is the social process by which people are classified as exhibiting certain social behaviours, and it indicates deviancy from a norm and certain valued attributes (Bond and Bond 1986). A state of illness is considered to be deviant and the status of patienthood is ascribed to those who are accepted as being 'diseased' by the medical profession or their substitutes. The process is essentially arbitrary and a social one. There has to be agreement between the individual, who feels ill, and the authorized practitioner, who diagnoses disease, before the patient role is confirmed. (There are a few instances where the state sanctions compulsory treatment, even if the individual does not acknowledge a need.) Evidence of strong professional influence on self-perceptions of ascribed roles is legion (Goffman 1968) and indicates the effect such labelling can have on a patient, an effect known sociologically as secondary deviance (Lemert 1964).

At this point we need to consider the nature of need itself, since this is the expression of health status for which health care is intended. At one and the same time we have to consider the duality of this concept, for we are concerned with both the positive promotion of health and prevention of illness on the one hand, and with the curing and caring during ill health, which may be episodic or chronic in nature, on the other. 'Illness is the night-side of life, a more onerous citizenship. Everyone who is born holds dual citizenship, in the kingdom of the well and the kingdom of the sick' (Sontag 1988). Patienthood is usually a temporary state concerned with illness, but needs are permanent when concerned with promotion and prevention and form a causal relationship with needs for treatment.

Related to this we need to explore the sociological conception of a patient in more depth, since it appears to offer, if not unique qualities, then at least qualities that are distinct and fundamentally unsuited to marketization. Certainly Titmuss (1969) long ago argued that medical care was qualitatively different since there is a demonstrable 'competence gap' between professional and patient. Despite the increasing evidence of an informed public, the advances in medical knowledge are clearly preventing a closure of that gap, particularly in certain specialties. Furthermore, the nature of human suffering, for which health services were developed as a response, gives these social relations a unique quality (Stacey with Homans 1978). It is this affective aspect, involving access to the private world of personal relationships, that marks out health care as a very different process from that conveyed in a customer relationship. Furthermore, as Light (1992) recognizes, there is a difficulty in defining a 'product' since what is produced and consumed is emergent and contingent during treatment. At all stages there is likely to be uncertainty and partial information at the points of delivery.

It appears, therefore, that a patient is someone who, in presenting a need and being accepted as worthy of that status through professional acknowledgement, enters the relationship with the professionals in a relatively weak position. Her interests may or may not be synergistic with those of the dominant professionals (Alford 1975). Where they are, this may be apparent, such as effective treatment, or inapparent, such as care during periods of unconsciousness. In cases of non-synergistic interests, these may be oppressed, such as in some issues relating to childbirth, or suppressed, where oppression exists but is not known about, such as in covert policies for age-limiting certain treatments (Williamson 1992). While many consumerist groups would place high value on the notion of autonomy, in apparent consonance with market ideology, it would appear that there is a need for professional guidance and support to make the most appropriate decisions.

Although rarely passive, in part the patient presents herself in the health-care system as a 'work-object', to have things done *to* rather than *for* her, which as Stacey (1976) has argued is an inappropriate concept for a consumer. In other words, the health service is a service that involves professionals and patients themselves working *on* patients who are ill or injured. However, as Williamson (1992) stresses, the traditional problem of professionals, in particular doctors, has been the way in which they objectify patients as parts of the body to be treated, rather than giving respect to the actual self of the patient. The need to be 'cared about' rather than 'cared for' is of vital importance to both clients and their informal carers (Wilson 1993).

Debate will undoubtedly continue over meanings and implications of various labels. For Brant, as a clinical audit adviser, approaches to patient empowerment would be discredited 'if the focus is allowed to wander far from the essential needs for clinical care which bring people to the health service's door. For that reason . . . the word "patient" will continue to be used' (Brant 1992: 5). For others, such as Ryan (1993), 'patient' denotes dependency or passivity, the object of treatment and diagnosis, whereas 'customer' creates for her a respected equal in the process. However, she gives the game away by going on to claim that customers can be any people along the path of a process, who receive something as the product of that process. This usage, therefore, does not distinguish patients from other participants in the process, nor does it recognize that patients are not simply on the receiving end of a commodity process. For Stacey the misconception of a patient as a consumer had many causes, but essentially she saw the importance of giving recognition to the health production function of patients, as well as their inevitably unequal relationship with professionals. For her the suggested, albeit rather cumbersome, terminology would be, 'the patient as partner but also work object' (Stacey 1976: 200).

As Williamson declares, 'the word "patient" is so rich in history and meaning that it deserves to be kept' (Williamson 1992: 13). However, in her case she goes on to use the term 'consumer' to include all recipients of health care (patients or users) as well as their close relatives or carers when they act on behalf of the patient. For her it provides a convenient generic term to relate with 'professionals', reserving 'patient' to relate with 'practitioner'.

In a study conducted to establish the perspectives of the various stakeholders to the implementation of quality changes in the outpatients department of a Welsh hospital, the reaction of staff themselves was also revealing of sensitivity to labelling (Thompson 1992). These included staff involved in direct care, technical support and system support services, for whom the newly introduced term of 'customer' was resented as being a way of depersonalizing patients. By and large they felt that they had a good rapport with the public, which they wished to preserve.

We can see, then, that while there are various opinions about which label is appropriate for a health-service user, there are a number of qualities which question the appropriateness of using a market term such as 'consumer'. To understand why such labelling has recently come to the fore, it is necessary to consider, albeit briefly, the broader changes taking place in the NHS and beyond in the economy as a whole.

THE QUALITY REVOLUTION

One of the global phenomena on which there is general agreement, at least in the post-industrialized nations of the world, is the emergence of 'quality' as a major rhetoric and strategy by which to manage goods and services in the economy. This is by no means a new concept, but it has grown to be arguably the dominant plank of competitive strategy in an otherwise converging world of technical advance. The services provided by British Airways, for example, are probably very little different from those offered by its principal competitors, but it cultivates its customers' perceptions of its quality to provide the competitive edge.

The emergence of quality as a key to strategy can be located historically in the manufacturing sector, and soon after in most sectors of private industry. The public sector adopted quality some time later, and in the case of the NHS could be seen to receive its catalytic boost through the Griffiths Report on management (Department of Health and Social Security 1983). This ushered in the private sector management model, replacing consensus management with general management. As part of its proposals, reference was made to the dearth of market research by which to focus service delivery to the views of its users. Prior to that significant document, quality had been assumed to be part and parcel of the professional services which made up health care.

Implementation of the Griffiths Report (DHSS 1983) began in 1984, followed by a number of efficiency measures, such as the Cost Improvement Programmes in 1984, concerned with non-clinical areas such as supplies and energy, and the Resource Management Initiative in 1986, which turned its attention to the clinical domain. A number of policy papers were also published on primary care, public health and community care, among others. While these reforms could be described as 'gradualist' (Griggs 1991), a much more radical shift occurred in 1989 with the publication of the White Paper *Working for Patients* (Department of Health 1989). This overall review of the NHS was in response to a perceived financial crisis, and yet its recommendations were concentrated on organizational and managerial reforms, rather than financial ones (Griggs 1991), of which quality was seen as a central part of the new 'contract culture'.

Over the last decade, the NHS has witnessed a plethora of gurus, systems and approaches to establishing quality as a key strategy. As Pfeffer and Coote (1991) outline, these encompass the range from traditional views of superior services that confer status on users or providers, through the scientific/expert approaches of 'fitness for purpose', to the more recent managerial/'excellence' approaches of responsiveness to customer demand, or alternative consumerist empowerment models of active citizenship. We need to recognize, therefore, that 'quality', although widely discussed and implemented in organizations, is not a concept with a single definition, but varies according to the perspective of the person who defines it. Quality, depending as it does on values and roles, is by definition contestable, as it is not simply concerned with a technical solution to problems (Wilding 1994). Different interest groups produce their own definitions of quality, and with them their own approaches and respective levers of power, 'in the struggle to determine which definitions, methods and measurements will be adopted' (Pollitt 1993: 161). Total Quality Management (TQM) has been brought in explicitly to make patients the centrepiece of service strategy. However, despite much local enthusiasm, it has not yet produced the wholesale cultural change promised, although it is being used 'to promote and accelerate piecemeal and incremental change, both in attitudes and practices' (Pollitt 1993: 168).

Much of the current organizational restructuring, in the private and public sectors, is concerned with replacing bureaucratic regulation with market regulation, centred on an emphasis on relations with customers, as a model for effective forms of organizational relations. As Keat and Abercrombie attest, 'meeting the demands of the "sovereign" consumer becomes the new and overriding institutional imperative' (Keat and Abercrombie 1991: 3). In the case of the NHS, the sovereignty has been forced through central government legislation over issues such as competitive tendering, service level agreements and patients' charters. As Du Gay and Salaman remark, 'Paradoxically, we . . . find that the adaptation of market relations and structures in organizations is frequently a result of formal, centralized and bureaucratic compulsion' (Du Gay and Salaman 1992: 620).

Consumerism is part of the general decentralization of decisions 'to increase responsiveness and efficiency at the local level' (Light 1992: 466).

This decentralization to self-managing trust hospitals and fundholding GPs, who may refer patients where they wish (subject to their budgetary constraints), is, however, according to Walsh (1994), likely to be matched by an increasing centralization of power as government steps in to resolve conflicts which were previously resolved at a lower level of the control hierarchy, at regional or district level.

The political project is clearly one of creating the conditions for an enterprise culture, where employees and clients of organizations are all locked into relationships aimed at competitive advantage, for personal as well as organizational gain; so-called 'freedom' through choice in the market, rather than civil rights. To understand the new framework it is necessary to consider the discourse of enterprise, with which the state and managements are attempting to 'reimage' social relations. Attempted control of citizens can be carried out by governments by organizing their realities for them, through censorship, fragmentation of information and rumour. In a society where 'public relations' competes with dissemination of information, image admits to fabrication and the claim for '[t]ruth gives way to appearance, substance to style' (Bolinger 1980: 151). Of course, discourse has a dialectical relationship with society, in that it shapes and is shaped by it, helping to constitute and change knowledge and its objects, social relations and social identities (Fairclough 1992a). The process of shaping discourse is a stake in power struggles for control of the meaning of terms and labels used to describe and define quality, which tend to 'conform to the prevailing contours of power, authority and autonomy' (Pollitt 1993: 162). It would be interesting, therefore, to know to what extent 'sovereign consumers' affect or are affected by the discourse of service.

Quality has been recognized as providing the competitive edge to organizations in the quest for efficiency. This concept is new to the NHS, which has long remained a popular public institution. The change from a welfare state to an enterprise culture requires the public to reframe its understanding of what the NHS provides in terms of a market relationship, and the notion of health as a commodity to be traded within that market.

COMMODIFICATION OF HEALTH

The change from 'consumer' to 'customer' has been a much more recent development and reflects the ideological project of the state, in the Althusserian (1970) sense of interpellation, to transform citizens from apparently 'passive recipients' into 'active individuals' making choices in the market. 'As market concepts gain credence in society, more and more types of human activity come to be treated as commodities to be made available through the market' (Sax 1990: 12). For the capitalist state, the ideal conditions occur when every owner of a unit of value can exchange it as a commodity (Offe 1984). This provides the link between the economic and political substructures of society, whose stability depends on commodity universalization. Although Offe (*ibid.*) believed that the state would require organizations, such as those related to health, to remain 'uncommodified', for reasons of creating use value rather than exchange value, the focus on active customers requires individuals to seek 'competitive advantage' through the exchange process. Health, therefore, is prey to 'customerization' as the logic of enterprise.

Linguistically, the perspective generated by a society that sees itself as fundamentally an economy allows 'economic beliefs and practices [to] guide the metaphoric structuring of reality' (Bolinger 1980: 151). The main function of entities in the metaphor of reality is to support the attached verbal illusions in a way that persuades the public that things are as they seem to be. While there is evidence of a continuing strong public support for the NHS and the values it traditionally embodies (Calnan *et al.* 1993), the new realities of ideology and praxis are increasingly likely to fragment and confuse such allegiance.

Commodification, then, can be defined as the 'process whereby social domains and institutions . . . come . . . to be organised and conceptualized in terms of commodity production, distribution and consumption' (Fairclough 1992b: 207). While advertising has been identified as the most visible practice and discourse of consumerism (Fairclough 1989), there is a case to be made for a parallel 'technology' of public relations and public charters displacing traditional communities with new 'consumption communities'. These act in a way to provide citizens with subject positions, within a constrained relationship of limited content: of procedural rights, but not substantive ones relating to outcomes (Walsh 1994; Wilding 1994). In other words, rather than allowing the public to participate in decision making at the macro level, they are confined to a role at the micro level of choosing what to consume from the limited range on offer, in competition with other members of their 'ersatz community'. This clearly labels them as market-consumers, rather than citizen-users (Wilding 1994).

In order to 'sell' the notion of health as a commodity, I argue, the public is offered choice as a means to become empowered, with the apparent support of local management, by wresting some control from the prevailing power of health professionals.

THE CHIMERA OF CHOICE

We need to consider the nature of consumption itself and how this has been changing within the new culture of enterprise. There appears to be widespread acknowledgement of the importance of the increasing differentiation of demand in advanced capitalist societies (Hill 1991). Offe (1984) claimed that consumption only has meaning in societies having undergone differentiation, for example between work and non-work. However, postmodernist analyses would suggest that the distinction between production and consumption is increasingly blurred or 'dedifferentiated': 'As the language of "the market" becomes the only valid vocabulary of moral and social calculation, "civic culture" gradually becomes "consumer culture", with citizens reconceptualized as enterprising "sovereign consumers" (Du Gay and Salaman 1992: 622). Hence we are witnessing the colonization of the public sector discourses by a new enterprise culture of meaning, which is designed to impose consumer relations within a centrally managed market, and in turn exert more control over people's lives (Habermas 1984).

One of the key policies contained in the *Working for Patients* document (DH 1989) was the adoption of the ideas of Enthoven (1985) on 'internal markets'. This effectively separates the purchasing of care from the providing of care, which previously had been under the same authority in the NHS. The effect is to create competition between provider units to secure the cash which flows with patients, either on the basis of contracts with 'purchaser' health authorities or 'fundholding' GPs. This latter category of GP is distinguished from other GPs who are obliged to follow their health authority contracts. This represents a change with respect to patients' referrals to care outside the GP surgery, since prior to this the primary care budget was theoretically unlimited. Choice of specialist or unit was made by the GP, irrespective of price (which was unknown). The government's avowed intention is now to provide patients with choice, although it would appear that this is confined to deciding whether to have a GP with or without a budget.

The British version of the market, therefore, provides incentives for changes in the supply side of health services, with public control over the consumption of care and an empowerment of management, unlike, for example, new Swedish forms of public competition, which provide incentives for change in demand, with public control over the production of services and an empowerment of patients (Saltman and von Otter 1992).

The current consumer is seen as being active and enterprising, rather than passive and easily pleased as under Fordist production

(Abercrombie 1991). From the 'active citizen' standpoint is there evidence of an increasing demand to be customers of public service? Has the public seized the chance to increase its power through sovereignty in the market-place? This needs to be considered from the perspective of the characteristics of such power, namely choice and autonomy, as exemplars of neoliberal values of freedom and individuality. The 1989 White Paper on the reform of the NHS heralded greater user choice in its title (*Working for Patients*) and through the internal market strategy discussed above (DH 1989). However, as many health 'consumerist' commentators noted 'patients can only go where a contract has been placed; we have less choice than before' (Pratten 1992: 1). Furthermore, '[w]e have moved from a situation where doctor knows best, to the general manager knows best' (*ibid.*). However, current uncertainty surrounds the commissioning function of districts vis-à-vis the growing strength of fundholding GPs to determine where contracts will be placed. It may, in fact, reverse the situation once again to one where doctor knows best, albeit now within financial constraints. Even if not, better informed management does not equate with greater autonomy for users. Nor does greater choice for patients equate with stronger representation in the management of services. The 'supermarket model' of health care denies the right to decisions about investment or, in other words, what should be 'on the shelves'.

What evidence is there that the public subscribes to one or other of these labels and under what conditions? For this it is instructive to consider the varying positions in relation to private health care. This sector has been growing since the beginning of the NHS, as evidenced by the increase in the number of subscribers to private health insurance and the increased number of private hospitals and private beds (including those in NHS hospitals). Given how well it fits in with the government's market model of health care, it is worth reflecting on why it has not been fully implemented to date. One of the reasons put forward by Calnan *et al.* (1993) is political in that there has been a lack of popular or professional support for a private system. There appears to be an ambivalence among the public between supporting the NHS and wanting more to be spent on it and yet for some the existence of private medicine is also valued. Various explanations have been put forward for this. Taylor-Gooby (1987) suggests the NHS is supported due to its beneficence, but capitalist ideology provides a means of recognizing value through exchange relations which are seen to pertain in the private sector. Saunders and Harris (1989) see people as 'trapped consumers' having to pay tax, but ideally wanting the private sector to express their need for autonomy and control. Busfield (1990) sees support for both as material self-interest, since both offer something which can give benefit. For Calnan *et al.* (1993) their empirical study suggested strong support for the NHS in principle, but for some the private sector offered other benefits. For many insurance holders it was given as a perk of employment, which implies that nothing is lost by having it.

As far as the increased demand for private health care is concerned, it appears that although there is dissatisfaction with the NHS, this is not a reason for subscription to private insurance by those who personally choose it. The evidence is that only about half of them actually use their insurance, the main reason being related to concerns over waiting time for treatment and consequential loss of income. Private insurance was recognized as giving status but was viewed negatively by many (subscribers and non-subscribers) and it was only seen as a necessity, rather than a luxury, by those who individually subscribed and valued their time greatly (Calnan *et al.* 1993). It is very interesting that in this study there was little evidence of 'shopping around', with choice of hospital or consultant being largely left to the GP. In a survey of over 3,000 readers of the Consumers' Association magazine, *Which?*, only 7 per cent gave choice of consultant as the most important reason for taking out private health insurance, and only 1 per cent gave choice of hospital, with avoidance of long waits being the main reason (Consumers' Association 1992). In another study, by Wiles and Higgins (1992), reasons for using the private sector (from a sample of over 700, of whom 89 per cent had private insurance) were primarily to avoid waiting, and for 38 per cent because they wanted to use their insurance. The consumption communities alluded to earlier do not seem to have taken root as yet, but rather private health care may be a symbol of the producer communities of social class. In other words, even in private health care, patients do not appear to act as customers, in terms of making positive choices between providers, but rather to avoid perceived (and often unsubstantiated) problems in the main supplier, or to use something they would otherwise waste.

The notion of choice is ultimately problematic when considered in relation to health care, since the aim, as mentioned earlier, is not to satisfy demand but rather to meet needs. First, as Offe (1984) recognizes, choices made by economic subjects in the consumer goods market do not accurately express real needs, which is necessary for an adequate theory of consumer welfare. Nor can it be assumed that people are in a position to recognize their needs. Historically, this identification of needs has been characterized by the unequal struggle between professionals and users with their 'consumerist champions'. However, as Williamson (1992) argues, it may be more liberating in a non-commercial context to consider people's interests, which can be met without knowledge or power residing in their hands. In other words, where need is problematized in this way, it may be as important to consider it from an existential perspective as simply from the political one. At least, the political may lag behind more immediate requirements for service.

The prevailing dominant position of professionals, and in particular the medical profession, has been widely documented from several perspectives (Navarro 1976; Illich 1977; Allsop 1984). A number of challenges have been levelled against such power, including: cultural critiques of medical ineffectiveness, iatrogenesis and patriarchy; neo-liberal challenges to their monopolistic position as inhibiting consumer choice (Green 1988); and challenges from dissatisfied patients through increased complaints and litigation (Elston 1991). Recent debates in the USA have centred on the notion of proletarianization of doctors, through increased corporatism and managerial control (McKinlay and Arches 1985), and deprofessionalization, through increasing patient knowledge and power (Haug 1988). However, academic support for either of these theses is far from evident either in the USA or UK (Elston 1991). Certainly, the second of the theses would seem from the discussion earlier to have little substance. It is instructive to consider the first proposition in the context of the quality strategy for the NHS.

The large degree of 'territorial sensitivity' over quality has led to a tribal approach involving three types: medical quality (or clinical audit as it is now termed), which concerns professional technical matters; service quality, which includes all services except the medical input; and the experienced quality of users (Pollitt 1993). The mobilization of external pressure from patients and governments to force the professionals to take quality assurance more seriously was identified as a possible tactic by the World Health Organization (WHO) (1983), although they feared the risks of moving from the professional to the political arena due to the potential loss of professional autonomy.

Where clinical audit, as a mono-professional, provider-focused tool fits into corporate, consumer-oriented TQM is not clear. However, it does appear that, unlike other professionals and NHS employees, the medical elite is being protected to encourage them to carry out the micro-level rationing decisions which would otherwise prove politically embarrassing to the management or politicians. The other telling developments which reveal medical power, yet within a changing context of co-option, have been the setting up of clinical directorates within hospitals, where doctors are responsible for the activities and budgets of several specialties, thus combining medical and specific management responsibilities, and, in primary care, the new fundholding general practices. The evidence thus far would seem to suggest that medical power is still a major force within the NHS (Hunter 1992), although it remains to be seen whether it becomes subordinated to general management and the discipline of TQM.

The interdependent roles of NHS management and government would seem inescapable, despite the increasing emphasis on local decision making rather than centrally driven directives. The removal of all locally elected members of health authorities and the imposition of government-selected chairpersons would seem designed to ensure that the will of the centre is carried out at local level. The ideological thrust behind the cultural revolution of enterprise is not likely to be challenged by general management and, where it is, will quickly lead to removal under the new short-term contract arrangements and individual performance review techniques of control. In this sense, they can be seen as the instruments of central government, or 'corporate rationalizers' in Alford's (1975) terminology.

Choice, therefore, is offered on a very limited basis and continues to be under the control of the GP as gatekeeper. Where private insurance is taken up it does not seem to place the policy-holder in the role of informed decision maker positively choosing between alternative suppliers. There seems to be little substance to a changed role for medical professionals, especially given the way clinical auditing has remained entirely divorced from other measures of quality. The need remains for a model of care that empowers individuals in need and harnesses the skills of professionals to work with them towards a common aim, without their being juxtaposed in an adversarial relationship.

AN ALTERNATIVE TO THE MARKET

Foucault (1973) traces the history of the conceptualization of the patient in relation to the social practices of the time. The notion of a discrete, passive and objectified body emerged in the late eighteenth century, in parallel with the development of scientific techniques for surgery. Nightingale's recognition (1859) of the importance of the physical environmental context led to patients being objectified in terms of their physical and physiological realities. It was not until the 1950s that personality was included in the make-up of the patient as having a subjective state (Bond and Bond 1986). However, an analysis of medical advertising suggests that 'patient as cyborg' is increasingly seen as the ideal, requiring only servicing, maintenance and parts replacement, with no messy entrails, emotions or need for human contact (Lupton 1993). (Cynically, one may be tempted to view this as the model for which the commodity market has been designed.)

The relationship with professionals is also symptomatic of changes in theory and practice of patient care. For example, Gadow (1992) discusses the evolving comprehensiveness of the 'clinical gaze' from uninterpreted subjectivism, through abstraction, objectification, holism and finally to an interpreted subjectivism. The recent emphasis on the nursing process has redefined the patient from a biological object to a subjective being. In tandem with this, the nurse has been redefined from a part of the machinery of surveillance to being responsible for monitoring and evaluating the patient's personal identity, constructing and sustaining it. Social relations are seen to be the site for work for professionals, with discourse offering possibilities for subjectification, although not necessarily democratization of the relationship (May 1992). Armstrong even asserted that, '[u]ntil recently the relationship between the patient and nurse was similar in its mechanistic passivity to that between customer and cashier' (Armstrong 1983: 458). In other words, each participant in the process had very limited social relations, which is a key feature of the commercial exchange relationship connoted by the term 'customer'.

As the seminal work by Stacey (1976) emphatically recognizes, patients may be as much producers as they are consumers of health. In fact, it is obvious that the vast majority of health-related activity occurs in the private personal domain and with the support of informal carers, as has belatedly been recognized by government. The term 'consumer', deriving as it does from economics, has been engineered into a social actor's term, replacing patient or client, to legitimate changes in the power structure. It appeared as early as the 1974 NHS reorganization (DHSS 1972), when the public was removed from the executive arm of the NHS and sidelined into the Community Health Councils, which, while statutory, have no executive power. It has encouraged the keeping of patients as quiet, docile and compliant, due to failing to recognize the decision-making role of patients, an accusation which the state shares with health professionals.

The need to treat patients as people, rather than objects to be processed, requires professionals working for and with patients as 'person-subjects', as well as patients maintaining their own subjective state (Gadow 1980). In this way, recovery, as a goal of health services, can be understood not simply in terms of cure or return to health, but possibly in terms of the person-self transcending the work-object, which may have more relevance in cases of chronic or terminal illness. From this we can recast the social relationship between patients and professionals as one of a collaborative autonomy (Williamson 1992), where unequal knowledge and power is acknowledged to exist, but accepted when the interests are synergistic and information is shared in the decision-making process. The demand for a partnership which this implies is contradicted by a market relation where adversarial stances are counterposed between sellers and buyers (Wilding 1994). As Light claims, '[t]he seller is the buyer's agent, and the buyer wants it that way!' (Light 1992: 467).

CONCLUSIONS

In considering the theoretical context for the management of change in the public sector, we have recognized the importance of strategies for quality as the dynamo of enterprise, of which TQM can be seen to epitomize cultural change based on the notion of the 'sovereign consumer'. However, through the process of deconstructing the health service user, we can begin to understand how inappropriate the notion of consumer and, even more so, the notion of customer are in the present context.

Nevertheless, discourse does not merely function to describe social relations but can have a strategic intent (Habermas 1984) of instrumentally orienting them to reach certain goals. In this instance, the neoliberal project is identified as using the discourse of the market in an ideological sense to reimage the social relations (Laclau 1977) between patients and professionals, and between patients and health service organizations, as well as intra-organizationally among health service workers. Through commodifying health, the optimal conditions for market relations are put into place.

Language and the labelling of social actors is crucially important but can only be understood in the context of specific historical situations (Silverman 1985). Critical discourse analysis, as with economics, is not concerned with essential meanings, but with value. Meanings arise in the use of language. The empirical evidence would seem to point to the inappropriateness of market discourse at the current time, but it would be difficult to predict how this may change given the alteration in the material reality of the NHS. The greater the distance between the traditional normative aims of equity and comprehensiveness and current reality, the more the public may feel subordinated to the requirement to

compete for an adequate slice of the cake. This may not reflect a turning
away from former values so much as a turning to material opportunities
to meet existential needs.

The apparition of choice that has been promised by the health service
reforms may not necessarily accord with public desires, let alone needs.
It may be illusory in the sense that 'rational' managerial protocols may
not offer what patients want, the tension between consumer choice and
efficiency being clear in the *Working for Patients* document. Also,
patients may not want to absolve professionals from responsibility and
to have to carry total personal responsibility for decisions about health
care (Elston 1991). Rather, it is likely that joint decision making would
be preferred during the process of health care, as argued through the
concept of collaborative autonomy.

What alternative is there to the paradigm of enterprise that currently
dominates the health policy arena in many post-industrialized countries?
How can the public be empowered if not through a TQM model of
quality? The model itself does not have intrinsic value, but reflects the
current dominant forces through the method of its implementation.
TQM can represent a learning model for cultural change based on values
of a different order. Pfeffer and Coote (1991) propose a quality strategy
based on the democratic components of equity, responsiveness at all
levels to people's needs, and empowerment through public participation, established rights and an open system of public accountability.

How can it be possible that such an alternative be achieved? The
culture of enterprise has managed to colonize the public sector domain
through the specific conditions of the failure of the welfare state and the
crisis of Keynesianism. This contingent reality points to the possibility
of further transformation through changes in the environmental conditions.
Although forms of social struggle seem to be giving way to more
individualistic reactions (the 'voice' versus 'exit' concept of Hirschman
1970), people have to accept responsibility for accepting or rejecting the
adoption of language that reproduces social relations. As Janks and
Ivanic state, '[h]egemony depends on the consent of the masses' (Janks
and Ivanic 1992: 330), which breaks down when there is a refusal to
conform.

The future of health care in Britain depends, therefore, on public
participation, not only in the management of services, but in the public
giving voice to how they wish to be labelled. My only suggestion would
be to develop Stacey's formulation of 'the patient as partner but also
work object' (Stacey 1976: 200) by adding 'and person subject as an
individual and equal member of the social collectivity'. In this way, we

can include concepts of subjectivity, equity and participation. Perhaps the most useful abbreviation that distinguishes this person from other stakeholders is to keep the word 'patient', but defined in this more liberating way. At least this would offer a more honest and relevant label for someone in a relatively dependent state than an illusion of empowerment which shrouds the subordination of people within the culture of the market.

REFERENCES

Abercrombie, N. (1991) 'The privilege of the producer', in Keat, R. and Abercrombie, N. (eds), *Enterprise Culture*, London: Routledge.

Alford, R. (1975) *Health Care Politics*, Chicago: University of Chicago Press.

Allsop, J. (1984) *Health Policy and the National Health Service*, London: Longman.

Althusser, L. (1970) 'Ideology and ideological state apparatuses', in *Essays on Ideology*, London: Verso.

Armstrong, D. (1983) 'The fabrication of nurse–patient relationships', *Social Science and Medicine* 17: 457–60.

Bolinger, D. (1980) *Language – the Loaded Weapon*, London: Longman.

Bond, J. and Bond, S. (1986) *Sociology and Health Care*, Edinburgh: Churchill Livingstone.

Brant, S. (1992) 'Hearing the patient's story', *International Journal of Health Care Quality Assurance* 5(6): 5–7.

Busfield, J. (1990) 'Sectoral divisions in consumption: the case of medical care', *Sociology* 24: 77–98.

Calnan, M., Cant, S. and Gabe, J. (1993) *Going Private*, Buckingham: Open University Press.

Consumers' Association (1992) 'Is it worth going private?', *Which?* August: 426–9.

Department of Health (1989) *Working for Patients*, Cmnd. 555, London: HMSO.

Department of Health and Social Security (1972) *Management Arrangements for the Reorganised National Health Service, London: HMSO.*

Department of Health and Social Security (1983) *National Health Service Management Enquiry*, (Griffiths Report), London: HMSO.

Du Gay, P. and Salaman, G. (1992) 'The cult(ure) of the customer', *Journal of Management Studies* 29: 615–33.

Elston, M. (1991) 'The politics of professional power: medicine in a changing health service', in Gabe, J., Calnan, M. and Bury, M. (eds), *The Sociology of the Health Service*, London: Routledge.

Enthoven, A. (1985) *Reflections on the Management of the National Health Service*, London: Nuffield Provincial Hospitals Trust.

Fairclough, N. (1989) *Language and Power*, London: Longman.

Fairclough, N. (1992a) 'Introduction', in Fairclough, N. (ed.), *Critical Language Awareness*, London: Longman.

Fairclough, N. (1992b) *Discourse and Social Change*, Cambridge: Polity Press.
Foucault, M. (1973) *Birth of the Clinic: An Archaeology of Medical Perception*, London: Tavistock.
Gadow, S. (1980) 'Body and self: a dialectic', *Journal of Medicine and Philosophy* 5: 172–85.
Gadow, S. (1992) 'Existential ecology: the human/natural world', *Social Science and Medicine* 35(4): 597–602.
Goffman, E. (1968) *Stigma: Notes on the Management of Spoiled Identity*, Harmondsworth: Penguin.
Green, D. (1988) *Everyone a Private Patient*, London: Institute of Economic Affairs Health Unit.
Griggs, E. (1991) 'The politics of health care reform in Britain', *The Political Quarterly* 62(4): 419–30.
Habermas, J. (1984) *The Theory of Communicative Action* vol. 1, London: Heinemann.
Haug, M. (1988) 'A re-examination of the hypothesis of deprofessionalization', *The Millbank Quarterly* 66 (Supp. 2): 48–56.
Hill, S. (1991) 'How do you manage a flexible firm?', *Work, Employment and Society* 5(3): 397–416.
Hirschman, A. (1970) *Exit, Voice, and Loyalty*, Cambridge, MA: Harvard University Press.
Hunter, D. (1992) 'Doctors as managers: poachers turned gamekeepers?', *Social Science and Medicine* 35(4): 557–66.
Illich, I. (1977) *The Limits to Medicine*, London: Penguin.
Janks, H. and Ivanic, R. (1992) 'CLA and emancipatory discourse', in Fairclough, N. (ed.), *Critical Language Awareness*, London: Longman.
Keat, R. and Abercrombie, N. (1991) 'Introduction', in Keat, R. and Abercrombie, N. (eds), *Enterprise Culture*, London: Routledge.
Laclau, E. (1977) *Politics and Ideology in Marxist Theory*, London: New Left Books.
Lemert, E. (1964) 'Social structure, social control, and deviation', in Clinard, M. (ed.), *Anomie and Deviant Behaviour. A Discussion and Critique*, New York: Free Press.
Light, D. (1992) 'Equity and efficiency in health care', *Social Science and Medicine* 35(4): 465–69.
Lupton, D. (1993) 'The construction of patienthood in medical advertising', *International Journal of Health Services* 23(4): 805–19.
McKinlay, J. and Arches, J. (1985) 'Towards the proletarianization of physicians', *International Journal of Health Services* 15: 161–95.
May, C. (1992) 'Nursing work, nurses' knowledge, and the subjectification of the patient', *Sociology of Health and Illness* 14(4): 472–87.
Navarro, V. (1976) *Medicine under Capitalism*, London: Croom Helm.
Nightingale, F. (1859) *Notes on Nursing*, London: Blackie.
Offe, C. (1984) *Contradictions of the Welfare State* (ed. Keane, J.), London: Hutchinson.
Pfeffer, N. and Coote, A. (1991) *Is Quality Good for You?*, Social Policy Paper 5, London: Institute for Public Policy Research.
Pollitt, C. (1993) 'The struggle for quality: the case of the National Health Service', *Policy and Politics* 21(3): 161–70.

Pratten, B. (1992) 'Health off the shelf', in *Health Rights Report: Consumerism in the NHS*, London: Health Rights.

Ryan, M. (1993) 'The future is continuous quality improvement', *Quality Management in Health Care* 1(3): 42–8.

Saltman, R. and von Otter, C. (1992) *Planned Markets and Public Competition*, Buckingham: Open University Press.

Saunders, P. and Harris, C. (1989) *Popular Attitudes to State Welfare Services*, London: The Social Affairs Unit.

Sax, S. (1990) *Health Care Choices and the Public Purse*, Sydney: Allen and Unwin.

Silverman, D. (1985) *Qualitative Methodology and Sociology*, Aldershot: Gower.

Sontag, S. (1988) *Illness as Metaphor*, New York: Anchor Books.

Stacey, M. (1976) 'The health service consumer: a sociological misconception', in Stacey, M. (ed.), *The Sociology of the National Health Service*, Sociological Review Monograph 22, Keele: University of Keele.

Stacey, M. with Homans, H. (1978) 'The sociology of health and illness: its present state, future prospects and potential for health research', *Sociology* 12(2): 281–307.

Taylor-Gooby, P. (1987) 'Welfare attitudes: cleavage, consensus and citizenship', *Journal of Social Affairs* 3(3): 199–221.

Thompson, A. (1992) 'Better patient services at East Glamorgan General Hospital', Report 3, unpublished report to the Welsh Office, Cardiff Business School, UWCC, Cardiff.

Titmuss, R. (1969) *Commitment to Welfare*, London: George Allen and Unwin.

Walsh, K. (1994) 'Citizens, charters and contracts', in Keat, R., Whiteley, N. and Abercrombie, N. (eds), *The Authority of the Consumer*, London: Routledge.

World Health Organization (WHO) Regional Office for Europe (1983) 'The principles of quality assurance', report on a WHO meeting, Barcelona 17–19 May 1983, EURO Reports and Studies 94, Copenhagen.

Wilding, P. (1994) 'Maintaining quality in human services', *Social Policy and Administration* 28(1): 57–72.

Wiles, R. and Higgins, J. (1992) *Why Do Patients Go Private? A Study of Consumerism and Healthcare*, Southampton: Institute for Health Policy Studies, University of Southampton.

Williamson, C. (1992) *Whose Standards?*, Buckingham: Open University Press.

Wilson, G. (1993) 'Users and providers: different perspectives on community care services', *Journal of Social Policy* 22(4): 307–26.

Chapter 4

Performance indicators, bureaucratic control and the decline of professional autonomy

The case of academic librarians

Annette Davies and Ian Kirkpatrick

INTRODUCTION

During the 1980s, questions of university quality and performance formed part of a wider debate concerning the 'modernization' of higher education (Kerr 1987). Policy makers argued that universities had for too long been 'showered with money' from the public purse and had, in effect, become playgrounds for self-indulgent and inward-looking cliques rather than engine rooms for a post-industrial economy. These assumptions were translated into more direct state intervention in the activities of universities which, up to then, had enjoyed considerable institutional autonomy and 'academic freedom'. According to Pollitt (1990), this intervention was motivated by three factors. First, by a desire to cut public expenditure across the board and at the same time improve overall levels of cost-effectiveness and accountability. Second, by the government's objective of increasing access and consumer 'choice', forcing universities to plan more for the training needs of an 'enterprise economy'. Finally, by the government's ideological distaste for higher education and, in particular, for certain disciplines in the arts and social sciences. The issue of 'quality' in higher education can only be understood in relation to these political imperatives, aimed at bringing about radical change in the management and goals of universities.

In this chapter we argue that attempts to implement 'quality' in British higher education have been concerned mainly with the use of performance indicators, and the measurement of efficiency and value for money. These practices were often justified using a language of accountability to external 'consumer' interests. In the 'old' universities, performance indicators were also associated with new forms of 'neo-Taylorist' management intervention and bureaucratic control (Smith 1993). Such intervention posed a direct challenge to the workplace autonomy of certain professional groups, including academics. Nowhere, however, was this more the case than with weaker, quasi-professional occupations such as academic librarians. These groups have suffered a marked reduction in their traditional workplace autonomy over the last decade. This process, we argue, was driven by the desire of an increasingly assertive management to measure performance and, as an unintended consequence of this, exert greater bureaucratic controls.

To illustrate these points, this chapter draws on case-study data collected in summer 1993 from six 'old' university libraries. The cases were representative of a wide spectrum of approaches to library management and included: one well-resourced research library; two large research and teaching libraries; two smaller teaching-led libraries; and one technical university library. In each case, interviews were conducted with senior management and (with one exception) with groups of junior professional staff. The interviews focused on new quality initiatives, management practices and recent changes in professional work roles. Prior to discussing this data and the question of professional change in academic libraries, however, it is necessary to describe the main historical developments in British higher education. We also attempt to trace the origins of current performance indicators in academic libraries and the political imperatives which affect their use.

CHANGES IN THE MANAGEMENT OF BRITISH HIGHER EDUCATION

The advent of a Conservative administration in 1979 marked a sharp change in government policy towards higher education. Long-established commitments to preserving institutional autonomy and academic freedom were largely abandoned. A new relationship between the state and higher education was established, in which the former slowly transformed its role from being an allocater of grants to a more discerning and selective purchaser of teaching and research services. New criteria of cost-effectiveness and value for money were used to appraise the success or failure of academic institutions. Universities were, in short, to be made more accountable.

For some time prior to 1979, policy makers were questioning the high cost of the post-Robbins 'social demand' approach to higher education funding whereby rights of access were virtually guaranteed (Pearson 1990). In 1977, the University Grants Committee (UGC) abandoned its quinquennial system of five-year block grants to universities in favour of an annual allocation (Rodger 1988). In 1981, this trend towards declining resources was accelerated by the UGC's sharp cut in recurrent grant allocations, forcing many universities to make drastic reductions in staff and student numbers (Sizer 1988). After 1981, the real decline in recurrent grants was combined with pressure from the Department of Education and Science (DES) to improve the 'management' of universities. This culminated in 1985 with the publication of the Committee of Vice Chancellors and Principals' (CVCP) Jarratt Report (CVCP 1985) on efficiency. This report not only called for improved strategic and financial planning, but urged university councils to adopt a less consensual, 'executive' approach towards the management of their institutions (Lee and Piper 1988). As the CVCP saw it, university managers needed to become more accountable for existing resources and, in the process, improve the effectiveness and the value for money of their institutions more generally. To achieve this, universities were urged to develop 'reliable and consistent performance indicators, greater awareness of costs and more full cost charging' (CVCP 1985: 36).

In 1986, following the recommendations of the Jarratt Report, the UGC, in collaboration with CVCP, published its first statement of university performance indicators. At the time, both parties were under considerable pressure from the government to quickly develop some form of measurement (Cave *et al.* 1989). Most of the early performance indicators, developed in 1986 (and in 1987), were primarily measures of university costs and expenditure. All were expressed in the form of ratios, 'expressing some aspect of the internal balance of institutional processes' (Pollitt 1990a: 70), for example computer services expenditure per FTE staff, or per FTE student. These early attempts at developing performance indicators were followed in 1989 and 1992 by the University Funding Council's (UFC) more comprehensive research selectivity exercises. These included assessments of the research output of *all* universities in the new unitary system established after 1991. More recent Higher Education Funding Council (HEFC: the UFC's successor) assessments of university teaching 'quality' took longer to set up, and did not get under way until early 1994.

In the 1991 White Paper, *Higher Education: A New Framework*, the government made performance assessments linked to resourcing a key element of its plans to create a new 'unitary' system out of the old binary system of polytechnics and universities (HMSO 1991). At the same time, there was mention of an increasing divide between 'comprehensive research universities' and 'teaching only' universities. The 1991 White Paper also outlined plans to double student numbers in higher education over the next twenty-five years. This expansion was to be achieved, however, without any increase in financial support for universities and with a steady fall in unit costs (Trow 1992). Additional costs would be borne by the 'consumers' of academic services and through the increased efficiency of the universities themselves. This fact added to the already considerable government and CVCP pressure on universities to achieve greater control over the 'performance' of their institutions (Pearson 1990; Trow 1992).

In response to this government pressure, the university sector launched its own quality assurance initiative and established the Academic Audit Unit (of the CVCP). Major changes also took place at the institutional level as individual university departments pursued their own quality assurance plans and, in a few cases, Total Quality Management (TQM) programmes (Becher 1992; Tannock and Burge 1992; Middlehurst 1992).

Following the recommendations of the Jarratt Report, some universities departed from older traditions of 'consensus' or administrative management and moved towards an assertive, 'executive' approach to management (Lee and Piper 1988). Many also reorganized their academic and support departments as internal cost centres with their own decentralized budgets. These departments were given greater independence in academic and financial planning; all departments were also assessed separately as part of the HEFC's research selectivity exercise. Gradually, in response to external pressures, the management of British universities became more concerned with internal planning, objective setting and cost-effectiveness. All departments, including libraries and other support services, faced greater internal scrutiny of their activities by university managers who were themselves responding to external pressures to improve value for money. In those institutions where the cost-centre logic was taken furthest, the need to demonstrate effectiveness at departmental level also became essential if they were to compete for a finite pool of internal resources.

ACADEMIC LIBRARIES: BACKGROUND

During the 1980s, this external pressure on university managers to demonstrate value for money led them, in turn, to raise questions about the cost-effectiveness of internal support services such as the library. Below, we describe how academic librarians, like the rest of the higher education sector, were forced as a result of these pressures to address the issue of performance measurement.

Traditionally, academic libraries were viewed by the UGC and others as an integral part of academic life, at 'the heart of the university' (Enright 1990). In the post-Robbins era many libraries were well resourced and given considerable scope to build up large, self-sufficient research collections. By the late 1970s, however, the rising costs of these activities came under close scrutiny. Following a sharp fall in 1981, library funding declined steadily during the 1980s. Recent CVCP figures show that, while library expenditure has risen by 27 per cent in 'cash terms' since 1984/5, this still represents a 23 per cent cut in 'real' terms when measured against factors such as rising book prices and inflation (CVCP 1993). In real terms therefore, library expenditure failed to reach the levels at which it could adequately meet rising user (especially under-graduate) demand, or the costs of books/journals, staff and information technology (Mann 1990). Today, academic libraries are being forced to meet rising demand for their teaching and research services through ever greater efficiency gains.

THE 'POLITICS' OF QUALITY IN ACADEMIC LIBRARIES

Traditionally, many university administrators have viewed the library as a 'bottom-less pit' into which almost unlimited funds could be poured without any discernible result (Munn 1968). In the harsh economic environment of the 1980s, however, this assumption led to increased scrutiny of library costs. Also, in the wake of the Jarratt Report, many universities reorganized their library service as separate cost centres, accountable for their own one-line budgets (Burrows 1987). Even those universities which did not adopt this approach found themselves under external pressure to scrutinize the costs and value for money of their libraries. In this way:

> As a group, university libraries face pressures at the national level to demonstrate that they are using resources effectively and efficiently . . . Individually, libraries face pressures within their own institutions to justify their use of scarce resources, when they have been allocated in competition with other activities, not least the teaching departments.
> (SCONUL 1992: 1.7)

To survive in this competitive environment, library managers were forced to play a political game of demonstrating value for money by collecting their own performance indicators and showing, whenever possible, that the needs and demands of their 'consumers' were being met. Only by actively demonstrating the value for money and 'quality' of their service could most academic libraries hope to make 'reasonable' claims for additional resources (Enright 1990). Prior to looking at how this process led to greater bureaucratic controls in academic libraries, it is necessary to consider how 'quality' and 'performance' were defined.

WHAT IS MEANT BY 'QUALITY' IN ACADEMIC LIBRARIES?

Most observers recognize that 'quality' in higher education is a contested terrain. Different interest groups and stakeholders hold sometimes diametrically opposing views of what quality *is* and on how it should be implemented. According to Barnett: 'There is less a genuine debate about quality . . . than a babel of voices, their different messages reflecting alternative starting points and claims on higher education itself' (Barnett 1992a: 4). One could argue that in higher education, interpretations of 'quality' differ greatly among 'consumers', providers and payers (the government and university administrators).

Despite these differences, we argue that the most powerful force defining 'quality' in recent years has been that of the payer (the government). Their main concern has been with how 'quality', defined in terms of efficiency and value for money, could be measured and controlled using performance indicators. This, according to Barnett, reflects the fact that:

> the state is less in the business of improving the system and more in the business of controlling the system . . . the costs have to be kept in check. In turn, performance indicators are favoured which reflect an institution's efficiency: student:staff ratios and student output.
>
> (Barnett 1992a: 9)

Current performance indicators are therefore an expression mainly of the payers' (the government) objective of ensuring value for money and the strict control over the costs of higher education.

'Consumerist' approaches to 'quality' have also featured in some universities' plans to introduce teaching assessments, as well as in the rhetoric surrounding performance indicators more generally. A language of responsiveness to consumers may be used, for example, to justify performance indicators, i.e. as providing 'objective' market information – via league tables – on the comparative performance of universities. Such information, some argue, increases the choice of higher education consumers and allows them to differentiate between high- and low-'quality' providers. Generally speaking, however, talk of responding to consumer needs has been largely subsumed by a more instrumental desire to measure performance and achieve control over the activities and goals of universities. This fits well with the government's key objective of increasing the value for money of universities, while at the same time paying lip-service to a more general ideology of market forces and the 'sovereign consumer'.

Historically, the UGC has always collected statistical information on libraries as part of its *Universities Statistical Record*. Library information was also included on the UGC's 1986 and 1987 performance indicators, albeit in the very crude form of ratios of library expenditure to full time equivalence (FTE) students, staff and total expenditure (Henty 1989). The academic libraries' own representative body, the Standing Conference of National and University Libraries (SCONUL), also began collecting statistics on expenditure during the 1980s. These were more comprehensive than the UGC's indicators, covering a variety of activity measures such as the number of loans, enquiries and seat hours per FTE (SCONUL 1992: 5).

In many academic libraries, quality assurance and management information systems were set up to cope with the increased demand for performance information (Line 1990). The practice of setting objectives at strategic, departmental and individual levels is, for many, now commonplace. These objectives form the basis upon which standards are set and performance regularly assessed. Often, the easiest things to measure are those aspects of library work which can be quantified, such as the effectiveness of inputs or efficiency of processes. One might, for example, compare inputs such as staff time or book/journal budget allocations with outputs such as stock utilization. Some libraries have also pioneered more sophisticated output measurements which look, for example, at the effectiveness of book acquisitions, inter-library loans (Lines 1989; Abbott 1990), stock availability, accessibility and delay (Ford 1989).

As mentioned, performance indicators were used by academic librarians to demonstrate their accountability to external 'consumers'. Some have taken this argument further and argued that libraries not only need to demonstrate their value for money and efficient use of resources, but need to become 'customer led'. This would involve adopting certain principles of TQM and of 'customer care' which would, in turn, require fairly substantial changes in the organizational structure and culture of libraries (Abbott 1990; Davies and Kirkpatrick 1995). In the majority of cases, however, talk of responding to consumer needs has had more to do with collecting performance indicators and demonstrating cost-effectiveness than with real cultural or structural changes.

PERFORMANCE INDICATORS: INTERNAL AND EXTERNAL CONTROL

Most performance indicators which have been used in university libraries aimed to measure a range of organizational processes and outputs. Their focus was primarily on evaluating efficiency, value for money and the effectiveness with which limited resources were used to maintain (or increase) standards of service. Many claimed that these performance indicators were politically neutral and that they provided 'objective' measures of organizational effectiveness. In this chapter such claims are disputed. Far from being 'neutral', we argue that performance indicators were a clear expression of the payers' (the government and university managers) desire to control not only the costs and the performance of higher education institutions, but also the detailed activities of professional staffs. According to Pollitt (1988), most 'have been "top down" affairs, propelled by the interests of politicians and senior officials in controlling both the expenditure and the range and types of activities engaged in by lower level officials, particularly the "street level" service deliverers' (Pollitt 1988a: 77). In the case of academic librarians, a key outcome of this use of performance indicators was the extension of bureaucratic controls and a subsequent decline in professional autonomy.

The question remains, exactly how do performance indicators lead to greater bureaucratic control? In this and the following sections we will try to explain this process.

According to Smith (1993), current performance indicators in the public sector are associated with two modes of control: external and internal. In both cases their function is to provide quantifiable, so-called 'neutral' information about different activities. First and foremost, performance indicators are associated with control exercised by external agencies, payers or user interest groups, over the organization. Many public sector organizations are increasingly being 'decentralized' and made accountable for the cost-effective use of resources and for meeting standards (Carter 1989). External interest groups may regard performance indicators, especially those which measure outputs, as 'objective' information which they can use to evaluate the effectiveness of different public services (i.e. through league tables). In this way, output-related performance indicators may also be linked to discourses of extending consumer voice and choice, being used, for example, to 'furnish external users with information about the outcome of the organization's activities so that they can make informed judgements about the organization's performance, and informed choices about future activity' (Smith 1993: 136). In the context of higher education, there are clearly numerous external pressures forcing universities to provide performance information. This pressure, as we have seen, was relayed downwards to internal support services (including the library), which were managed, 'hands off', as accountable cost centres.

Closely linked to the external control function of performance indicators is an internal control function. The main objective of internal control is to ensure maximum efficiency of organizational processes and the cost-effective use of (limited) resources. Pressure to achieve this has increased in higher education following cuts (especially in academic libraries) and the increased external scrutiny mentioned above. What internal control implies is measuring the costs (both time and resources) of every activity or process in the organization to ensure that it is fully effective. Such information about relative costs and benefits can then be used to make decisions about service priorities, an exercise which, it might be argued, is especially relevant in the context of limited (or declining) resources.

In this way, performance indicators are associated with two dimensions of control: the external and internal. Both dimensions overlap in practice. It would, for example, be impossible to measure process efficiency without also looking at outputs. Likewise, one could not properly measure outputs without first looking at internal organizational processes. Management may therefore use performance indicators both as a means of exerting its own internal control over organizational processes and as a way of complying with external demands.

PROFESSIONAL VERSUS BUREAUCRATIC CONTROL

British higher education has traditionally been characterized by a mixture of bureaucratic and professional controls. The key elements of the latter are: self-regulation, collegiality, credentialism and semi-autonomy (Hoggett 1991). Professional control depends in part on the ability of occupational groups to use their expert knowledge base to mystify or to create an 'aura of indeterminacy' which, depending on the context, precludes managerial or user involvement (Boreham 1983; Murphy 1990). Many aspects of the professional work process may therefore remain highly indeterminate and difficult for 'outsiders' to evaluate. This indeterminacy, combined with other institutional resources (such as certified expertise), may also help professionals obtain a considerable degree of workplace autonomy. Historically, this has meant that some professional occupations were able to maintain 'restrictive practices' and determine, sometimes independently of management, the priorities and objectives of the organizations in which they worked.

The current use of performance indicators in academic libraries has, we argue, greatly facilitated the erosion of professional autonomy. Performance indicators provided management both with a technology and a 'rational' *justification* for exerting increased bureaucratic control. According to Hoggett (1991), the key aspects of this bureaucratic control are: greater formalization of tasks and routines; specialization of roles and increased hierarchy; more standardization and simplification (where possible) of tasks; and clearer objective and target setting. All this implies greater managerial power to define the content and the operational goals of professional work.

Through performance indicators, managers have at their disposal an effective information system which allows them to identify inefficient working practices and poor individual or group performance. Using this information, managers can make convincing and 'rational' claims for removing inefficient or 'restrictive' professional working practices. They can also justify increased bureaucratic control on the grounds that it will help to ensure value for money and, in the long term, better serve the interests of the external consumer (or payer).

As mentioned above, performance indicators can be used to measure the efficiency and cost-effectiveness of different work processes, and in so doing identify areas which are inefficient or perform badly. One consequence of this is that performance indicators may make previously indeterminate professional activities more explicit. This, in turn, increases the transparency of professional knowledge/expertise, demystifies it, and allows management to monitor, assess and control the professional work process more easily. In theory, then, performance indicators allow management to scrutinize the costs of previously indeterminate working practices. If these practices are found to be wasteful, inefficient and non-cost-effective, then management might be able to justify increasingly bureaucratic forms of monitoring and control.

This process, if successful, will have a number of consequences. In the first place, it might lead to the formalization of professional work by subjecting it to bureaucratic timetables and routines which aim to prevent wastage. Second, it might call for greater specialization of professional work and the formal separation of roles and responsibilities to avoid expensive duplication. Another aspect of this might be the establishment of more formal hierarchies which differentiate between junior professional and managerial roles and, more importantly, those of professional and clerical staffs. All this may require greater standard-ization and, in some cases, simplification of professional work tasks. The setting of formal targets and objectives for individual professionals may also be an important aspect of this bureaucratic control. Such objectives would be decided by management and monitored through regular performance appraisals and feedback meetings. Finally, it might also be the case that professionals themselves are incorporated and given new managerial responsibilities such as supervisory control over junior staff or the management of their own unit budgets.

During the 1980s, the desire of university managers to use perform-ance indicators as a means of achieving greater internal control was in direct conflict with that of professionals to defend their workplace autonomy and 'restrictive' practices. According to Middlehurst:

> in institutions with traditions of autonomy, self governance and a professional ethic, such external incursions into their territory . . . may engender fear amongst staff about the consequences of change in terms of a loss of power, status and financial security.
>
> (Middlehurst 1992: 35)

Despite this potential conflict, it was argued that only by subjecting professionals to greater 'bureaucratic controls' could greater efficiency and value for money be achieved.

PERFORMANCE INDICATORS AND BUREAUCRATIC CONTROL IN ACADEMIC LIBRARIES

As we have seen, during the 1980s, academic libraries came under intense 'political' pressure from university managers to demonstrate value for money and responsiveness to 'consumers'. This led in some cases to new library funding arrangements and the establishment of service contracts with individual departments. It also forced many library managers to scrutinize the costs of their own professional services. In so doing, they have developed performance indicators and management information systems which measure the efficiency and effectiveness of professional work.

Like many other professional occupations, academic librarians traditionally enjoyed a high degree of autonomy. This was autonomy primarily to carry out 'core' professional tasks such as book classifi-cation, cataloguing, reference work and dealing with user enquiries. These activities, more often than not, were carried out by professionals without direct reference to managerial or cost concerns. The semi-collegiate structure of many academic libraries also helped ensure that core professional activities remained largely indeterminate and not subject to managerial scrutiny or evaluation. In a small number of resource-rich institutions, the professional librarian was given considerable freedom to develop as a subject specialist and engage in scholarly work of his/her own, largely independent of bureaucratic rules, routines and timetables (although this was less the case in teaching-led institutions). Most librarians also saw their workplace autonomy as being in the client's interest and essential for providing high-quality professional services.

Some have already noted how an emphasis on performance indicators may threaten professional autonomy. According to Lines, for example:

> In university libraries it was not unusual for subject specialists to operate with a high degree of autonomy in the use of their time, giving them considerable freedom to react to users' demands . . . The process of performance measurement, with an emphasis on balance between economy, efficiency and effectiveness can easily be seen as politically threatening.
>
> (Lines 1989: 114)

These efforts to measure performance also seem 'politically threatening' because they coincide with a deeper crisis facing the librarian profession (Davies and Kirkpatrick 1995). This crisis relates to the fact that many core professional skills – for example, in cataloguing and classification – have now been largely displaced by new information technologies (Gunson 1990). This development has also increased the potential for user 'self-service' (Cronin and Davenport 1988), and has threatened to blur the divide between professional and clerical spheres of work (Prince and Burton 1989).

During the 1980s, the number of 'academic related' professional staff fell by 7 per cent (Mann 1990), a trend which some argue was synonymous with the gradual deprofessionalization of librarians. As Roberts argues:

> Reductions in professional staffing ratios now owe more than is openly admitted to managerial assumptions that professional status, and hence salaries, cannot be justified in practice. In other words, claims to professionality have been challenged and found wanting.
>
> (Roberts 1991: 452)

The use of performance indicators may have accelerated this process by encouraging managers to search for ways of making professional work more efficient in order to cut costs. The increased transparency which this has created may also have furnished managers with information they can use to undermine librarians' 'claims to professionality'. The net result, we argue, was a decline in the traditional autonomy of professional librarians and a steady increase in bureaucratic control. As the case data (discussed below) suggests, this was a general trend in most academic libraries, albeit one which was subject to local negotiation and uneven development.

PERFORMANCE INDICATORS, BUREAUCRATIC CONTROL AND PROFESSIONAL AUTONOMY: CASE DATA

In this section the case study data from the six 'old' university libraries is considered. Our findings reveal a general trend towards greater bureaucratic control in academic libraries. This, in turn, we argue, has led to a decline in professional autonomy.

The case data shows how all six university libraries had been placed under pressure of various sorts to collect more performance information. In all but one case, academic and support departments (including the library) had been reorganized into cost centres. Most were also developing their own strategic plans and financial management systems, as now: 'college resources go direct to departments to spend as they see fit'. Linked to this was what most perceived to be a far more interventionist style of management at the university level. According to the librarian of one small teaching-led university, for example:

> It has become a lot more businesslike and ruthless you could say. They have a very efficient registrar and secretary and they make sure things don't get out of hand anywhere. They are beginning to talk about getting rid of people who don't provide research, giving them early retirement.

All six case libraries had come under closer financial scrutiny from university administrators and were under pressure themselves to develop strategic plans, improve efficiency and achieve greater control over internal organizational processes. As the librarian of another teaching-led university remarked, this pressure was likely to increase in the near future and:

> is going to require a bigger input from management. We have taken a small step here in strengthening the management team during the last year but I suspect we might need more, and some libraries, maybe

not here, but bigger libraries, ought to have an accountant on the staff, for instance.

In the case of one of the large teaching- and research-led university libraries, one person explained how 'running a library like a business is the main criterion of effective site performance'. There, the actual funding of the library was linked closely to its performance measured in terms of outputs such as stock turnover and utilization.

In all six cases, library staff had responded to pressure from university administrators by attempting to tailor their activities according to perceived 'customer' needs. One senior librarian in a technical university, for example, pointed out that, 'it was only good management practice to be able to spell out what you are going to do for your client'. In four out of the six cases, the library collection budget itself had been devolved to academic departments, a move which had given academic 'customers' a direct say in determining how the money was spent. In two cases, formal service level agreements (or contracts) had been set up. These set out certain standards of service, but also allowed individual academic departments to 'buy into' whatever library services they felt they most needed. Indirectly, this meant giving external users considerable power to decide how internal library resources were allocated and, consequently, to determine professional goals and priorities.

A variety of performance indicators measuring the efficiency of professional work were used to achieve greater internal control in all six cases. To a greater or lesser extent this had led, as described above, to the increased bureaucratization of professional work. A number of bureaucratic controls had been extended, including: greater emphasis on setting clear performance targets and objectives; efforts to measure costs and standardize work procedures; specialization of tasks and the use of more formal routines; increased hierarchy and differentiation between clerical and professional roles; and finally, efforts to give professionals increased managerial responsibility. Below, each of these 'controls' is discussed with reference to case data from the six 'old' university libraries.

Objectives and performance targets

An important element of bureaucratic control – and fundamental to performance measurement – is the setting of 'rational' targets and objectives for individuals and groups. In all six case libraries, we noted how professionals were under pressure to work according to measurable targets and objectives set by management, rather than to their own personal goals and objectives decided on a more *ad hoc* basis. In the technical library, for example, the librarian remarked on how her staff 'are responsible for organizing the commitment [to services] against targets, and for monitoring and submitting management reports'. Similarly, according to the librarian of the research-led library, 'we have to set each of our subject specialists a target . . . say, "This is the target we have set ourselves. Is it realistic? And at the end of the year, what have we achieved? How do we relate that back to our original objective?" '

Finally, the librarian of one of the teaching libraries talked about setting objectives for his professional staff working in 'subject teams':

> I am very keen that we set an agenda for them in general terms so that they know what they are doing and that they have got the job descriptions and tasks and objectives. They have got medium-term and short-term objectives as well which need assessing . . . I am very keen that having laid down those, that how they actually do the work is up to them.

This trend towards setting objectives helped ensure that certain levels of service were provided and that resources were not wasted. At the same time, however, it meant that management could assert greater control over professional work by formalizing it according to more open and transparent objectives.

Standardization

The desire to set clear objectives and targets was linked, in a number of cases, to achieving fixed 'standards' of service and relating these back to the actual 'costs' of providing those services. In the context of declining real-term resources, knowing what different activities cost is essential information for any library manager forced to make choices about service priorities. Some argued that only by quantifying these costs and systematically relating them back to desired standards of service could appropriate choices be made. In the research-led library, for example, the librarian described his plans to extend this principle even to areas such as professional enquiry work:

> We have a general enquiry desk in the building which is staffed on a rota basis by the subject specialists. Now, this takes them away from their primary activity. What I want them to look at is, "Do we need that level of person at the enquiry desk? What sort of public service

are we expecting to achieve? Is it necessary?" Because we are getting more things to do, it might be better to have a library assistant sitting on the enquiry desk and a proper system of referral. We want to say to people, "Should you be making yourselves available 100 per cent of the time just to receive the customer? . . . It sounds as if we are trying to be more bureaucratic, but it's in your own interest" . . . Managing their time.

Thus, allocating limited resources in a cost-effective way required the standardization of certain professional work routines; in this case setting up a 'proper system of referral'. In the other libraries, managements were also looking for ways of standardizing work practices which they found to be inefficient or wasteful.

Task specialization

Other aspects of the increased bureaucratic control in the libraries studied were attempts to specialize professional work roles and tie them more closely to fixed timetables and routines. Case data revealed a general trend towards specialization of job descriptions and an emphasis on managing time more cost-effectively according to bureaucratic routines. Staff in one of the smaller teaching-led libraries, for example, remarked on how their 'new librarian likes setting objectives' and that they now work within 'more tightly defined job descriptions with specific objectives and goals'. According to one professional there, an emphasis on time management and on specialization meant that:

> you become more closely identified with a particular function. We all had a particular function before, but it was a very flexible interpretation of it. You didn't say, "because I do this I don't do that". Now, because of the demands of the specialism, I think that will be more the case.

In this way, the freedom and autonomy to move from task to task, irrespective of bureaucratic routines and fixed job descriptions, had been reduced. In the technical university, staff also remarked upon how recently far 'stricter' job descriptions had been written and that their work was now more closely regulated according to bureaucratic routines. The same went for staff in one of the large teaching research libraries where recent developments had meant that, 'People have had to work more efficiently at managing their own and their staff's time'. Finally, in the research-led library, a junior professional remarked on how: 'I'm more conscious of juggling time, about how I manage things and the priorities for the day, the priorities for the week. I try to arrange my time around that.' In this sense, professional librarians were finding themselves more closely governed by bureaucratic routines and fixed timetables, with less autonomy to move around freely between tasks.

Emphasizing hierarchy

In some cases, management had formalized library organizational structures and, in so doing, greatly emphasized hierarchy and lines of command. This was seen by some professionals as a direct attack on their professional freedoms and collegiate status (which de-emphasized hierarchy). As one professional remarked about appraisals, for example, 'However you define appraisal there is an element there of "I'm being assessed, therefore I have to show willingness". That wasn't there before.' In one of the teaching-led libraries, staff reacted strongly against talk of 'quality' and 'cost-effectiveness'. There, professional staff regarded managerial efforts to standardize and monitor their work as a deliberate attempt to 'mould' them, and subject them to hierarchy, discipline and bureaucratic routines:

> The university . . . cannot think of the library in any other terms than the framework provided by the administration . . . This is a purely hierarchical structure . . . this is a non-hierarchical structure in the library and they are desperately trying to squeeze us into a mould which we will *not* fit. The hierarchy of the administration is absolutely straightforward – a real pyramid. It's all, "Yes sir, no sir, kiss my arse", all that sort of business. With us it basically isn't. There is the librarian and his deputy, then there is the rest of us and we are more or less on par.

Professional staff in that case opposed restructuring, which they saw as an attack on their professional autonomy. They also warned how, 'attempts to muscle in on what we are doing would be much resented'. In other libraries, not everyone held equally strong views, although all agreed that there was now more emphasis on the formal hierarchy.

Demarcations between professional and clerical roles

Increased scrutiny of professional costs and efficiency led some library managers to raise fundamental questions about the *value* of that work itself. This led some to evaluate more fully what constituted 'professional' and 'non-professional' (clerical) work. Increasingly, for professionals not to be seen doing professional tasks was regarded as wasting resources and as contrary to the objective of achieving value for money.

In all the libraries, professional staff occasionally got involved in clerical work, such as serving users or shelving the occasional book during periods of high turnover. In some libraries, however, these practices went further than in others. In one of the teaching-led libraries, for example, the librarian remarked on how, 'the lines between professional and non-professional staff are pretty wobbly here'. In the research-led library there also appeared to be some ambiguity between professional and clerical responsibilities. For the librarian there, making a distinction between these roles was necessary to achieve value for money, but at the same time:

> is turning out to be quite difficult in some of the small branches where they have always worked really as a bunch of equals . . . some of the longer-established people do find this difficult. They do not seem to appreciate the potential problems in terms of grading structure and claims for regrading. If your library assistants do all the same things that you do, and all you do is be in charge, how do you justify it?

In his view, turning each branch into a 'cost centre' would have a 'salutary effect', because 'making more explicit the cost of each operation . . . to our staff . . . will actually concentrate the mind'. A similar view was expressed by professional staff in the second teaching-led library where efforts had also been made to clarify professional and non-professional roles:

> if you are paying a senior person a fairly high salary, you would expect that their time is properly used. You wouldn't pay someone a high salary to shelve books all day . . . That seems a waste of resources. In that sense people are more aware of the importance of time and that time costs money.

This increased awareness of the 'costs' of professional work had reached the point where, as another professional remarked, 'We do feel guilty about things when we do unprofessional work, when we are forced into that situation . . . when your resources are far more suited to doing a managerial type job.'

In two cases – one of the large teaching libraries and the technical library – a very strict demarcation between professional and non-professional tasks had been established. In the technical library, for example, the librarian remarked, 'We have a very strong policy of not employing *over-qualified people* in clerical roles, so that everyone is reaching up as well as down a lot of the time.' There, a detailed 'skills audit' and evaluation of professional work had been carried out, the net result of which was a reduction in the number of professional posts as tasks were pushed down to an 'appropriate level'.

This process of clarifying professional and non-professional work was closely linked to the use of performance indicators which stressed the need for value for money and cost-effectiveness. It was also facilitated by managerial efforts to exert greater bureaucratic controls over the professional work. Changes in technology – especially in book cataloguing where on-line MARC (machine readable catalogue) records displaced the need for highly skilled professional experts – in turn, helped this process along. The result was that in all the libraries studied (except the research-led), the numbers of highly qualified professional staff had fallen, while the number of clerical assistants had increased.

Turning professionals into managers

At the same time as professional librarians were losing their autonomy and being subjected to bureaucratic controls, there was also a feeling that their jobs were becoming more 'managerial'. An emphasis on management was seen by some professionals as an opportunity to redefine their roles in order to dissociate themselves from clerical work. According to the librarian of the technical library, for example:

> The role of the librarian is changing from a person who has his pot of skills, to someone who is basically a manager, responsible for quality control, the organization and planning of an activity, as well as actually doing that activity.

In the technical library and in one of the large teaching–research libraries, professional staff at all levels had been given responsibility for decentralized budgets. The philosophy behind this was to integrate cost and quality concerns and, in so doing, pass the responsibility down to junior staff: 'We try to work on the basis that if people are responsible for delivering the service, then they've got to have the resources to do it. Therefore, they are responsible for staff and the money.'

In other libraries, the language of managerialism was also used quite extensively, although fewer efforts were made to give professionals control over their own budgets. Some still held the view that budgets should remain centralized in the hands of senior managers to allow them a strategic overview.

As well as budgetary responsibilities, professional staff in all the libraries were being given greater responsibility for supervision and control over specific functions, such as book acquisitions, on-line searching and technical services work. This in itself represented a greater incorporation of professional work with managerial concerns, heralding a further reduction in the traditional modes of professional autonomy. At the same time, this meant that some professionals (especially senior staff) were able to exercise greater discretion (as managers) than they had done previously. Some therefore regarded this as a positive improvement, giving them more scope to make decisions and take the initiative. Despite this, however, even with new managerial responsibilities, the end result was that professional librarians were forced to work within a tighter framework of financial and bureaucratic control. This is perhaps similar to what Hoggett (1991) describes as 'regulated autonomy'.

In all six cases, bureaucratic controls were being applied to professional work in order to achieve greater internal efficiency. A range of performance indicators, aimed at measuring the effectiveness of various professional activities, both facilitated and provided the justification for these bureaucratic controls. Another justification was provided by the use of discourses which stressed the importance of being responsive to (external) 'consumer' needs and demands. This emphasis on external 'consumers' led to increased calls for more bureaucratic control and therefore helped further reduce professional autonomy. Just as librarians could no longer afford to do work which was not cost-effective, it was argued, neither could they afford to concentrate solely on professional tasks independently of perceived external 'consumer' needs and demands.

CONCLUSION

This chapter has argued that notions of 'quality' in British higher education have focused primarily on measuring the value for money and efficiency of universities. To a lesser extent, the government has talked about making higher education services more responsive to 'consumer' needs and demands. The key issue has been one of how to increase university 'performance' in a context of declining *real*-term resources. To support this, national performance indicators of university teaching and research activity have been established and used by external funding bodies to allocate limited resources selectively .

These external pressures have forced university managers to address the issue of performance measurement and value for money in their own institutions. Following the recommendations of the Jarratt Report (1985), many have reorganized their institutions along the lines of cost centres. Increasingly, academic departments and university support services are being evaluated in terms of their own efficiency, and cost-effectiveness. Within this context, academic libraries have done especially badly, suffering a marked decline in resources. This has, in turn, forced library managers to respond to pressure from above by implementing their own performance indicators in order to demonstrate their accountability and to strengthen claims for additional resources.

External pressure on academic libraries to demonstrate value for money led some library managers to scrutinize their own staff's activities (Line 1986). One result of this has been the use of performance indicators as a justification for introducing greater bureaucratic controls. A key element of this bureaucratic control was its effect on professional work. For professional librarians, it implied greater formalization of tasks, increased hierarchy, more standardization, and a loss of their traditional autonomy to organize time and work priorities independently of management. Such bureaucracy it seems is a far cry from the claims of *In Search of Excellence* (Peters and Waterman 1982) and other management texts which link 'quality' to greater decentralization and the empowerment of street-level staffs.

Data from six 'old' university libraries suggest that greater bureau-cratization was a general trend, although subject to uneven development. In different institutions the *nature* of the change varied as managerial efforts to control professional working practices were locally contested and negotiated. Despite this, we argue that the overall trend is towards a slow reduction in professional autonomy.

We are not suggesting that librarians will be completely deprofes-sionalized as a result of these changes (although some argue that this is the case). Rather, what we have argued is that the balance of power between professional and managerial interests has shifted in favour of the latter and that performance indicators have had much to do with this. Professional librarians *have* lost much of their workplace autonomy. However as Lipsky (1980) reminds us, it may never be possible completely to standardize and monitor all the activities of a 'street-level' professional bureaucrat. Some level of discretion and scope for inde-pendent decision making will always be necessary, simply in order to respond to changing circumstances and implement agency policies during each unique service encounter. What we are suggesting, therefore, is not that professional work is now completely subject to detailed bureaucratic controls, but that the general trend is in this direction.

There are numerous ways in which discourses of 'quality' have been used (politically) in British higher education (Barnett 1992b). In this chapter we have focused on only one aspect and have suggested that, so far, both the government and university managers have favoured approaches to quality which emphasize efficiency, value for money and performance measurement. This is not to say that alternative notions, in particular those which focus on the role of consumers, have been excluded altogether, only that they have been less central in the government's project of transforming higher education. Likewise, we are not arguing that all professional occupations in higher education have been subjected to the same levels of bureaucratic control as have librarians. Clearly librarians represent a special (albeit interesting) case which demonstrates quite well the potential of performance indicators as a technique of control. Other groups with greater institutional resources at their disposal may be more successful in resisting managerial incursions into their workplace autonomy. Only further research on the uses of performance indicators in higher education will reveal more about this.

REFERENCES

Abbott, C. (1990) 'What does good look like? The adoption of performance indicators at Satan University library and information services', *British Journal of Academic Librarianship* 5(2): 79–94.

Barnett, R. (1992a) 'The idea of quality: voicing the educational', *Higher Education Quarterly* 46(1): 3–19.

Barnett, R. (1992b) *Improving Higher Education: Total Quality Care*, The Society for Research into Higher Education, Milton Keynes: Open University Press.

Becher, T. (1992) 'Making audit acceptable: a collegial approach to quality assurance', *Higher Education Quarterly* 46(1): 47–66.

Booth, C. and Roper, B. (1992) 'A new framework for quality', *Higher Education Quarterly* 46(3): 227–42.

Boreham, P. (1983) 'Indetermination, professional knowledge and control', *Sociological Review* 293–318.

Brindley, L. (1989) 'Performance measurement: can you manage without it? Summing up', *British Journal of Academic Librarianship* 4(2): 121–6.

Burrows, T. (1987) 'Funding and governance of British university libraries', *British Journal of Academic Librarianship* 2(3): 165–76.

Carter, N. (1989) 'Performance indicators: "backseat driving" or "hands off" control?', *Policy and Politics* 17(2): 131–8.

Cave, M., Kogan, M. and Hanney, S. (1989) 'Performance Measurement in higher education', *Public Money and Management* Spring: 11–16.

Committee of Vice Chancellors and Principals (1985) *Report of the Steering Committee for Efficiency Studies in Universities* (Jarratt Report), London: CVCP.

Committee of Vice Chancellors and Principals (1993) *University Management Statistics and Performance Indicators in the UK*, London: CVCP.

Cronin, B. and Davenport, E. (1988) *Post-Professionalism: Transforming the Information Heartland*, London: Taylor Graham.

Davies, A. and Kirkpatrick, I. (1995) 'Face to face with the "sovereign consumer": service quality and the changing role of professional librarians', *Sociological Review*.

Davies, A., Kirkpatrick, I. and Whipp, R. (1993) 'Management and professional change in the U.K. public sector', paper presented at the 'Professions and Management in Britain' conference, University of Stirling.

Enright, B. (1990) 'Concepts of stock: comprehensive vs selective', in Line, M. (ed.), *Academic Library Management*, London: Library Association.

Ford, G. (1989) 'Approaches to performance measurement: some observations on principles and practice', *British Journal of Academic Librarianship* 4(2): 74–87.

Gunson, N. (1990) 'Will sophisticated computer systems replace professional librarians or complement their skills?', *Computer Systems and Librarians* Nov/Dec: 303–11.

Henty, M. (1989) 'Performance indicators in higher education libraries', *British Journal of Academic Librarianship* 4(2): 177–91.

HMSO (1991) *Higher Education: A New Framework*, Cmnd. 1451, London: HMSO.

Hoggett, P. (1991) 'A new management in the public sector?', *Policy and Politics* 19(4): 243–56.

Howarth, A. (1991) 'Market forces in higher education', *Higher Education Journal* 45(1): 5–13.

Hunt, C. (1990) 'Staff structures', in Line, M. (ed), *Academic Library Management*, London: Library Association.

Kerr, C. (1987) 'A critical age in the university world: accumulated heritage versus modern imperatives', *European Journal of Education* 22(2): 127–32.

Lee, R. and Piper, J. (1988) 'Organizational control, differing perspectives: the management of universities', *Financial Accountability and Management* 4(2): 113–28.

Line, M. (1986) 'The survival of academic libraries in hard times: reaction to pressures, rational and irrational', *British Journal of Academic Librarianship* 1(1).

Line, M. (1990) 'Current issues in academic libraries', in Line, M. (ed.), *Academic Library Management*, London: Library Association.

Lines, L. (1989) 'Performance measurement in academic libraries – a university perspective', *British Journal of Academic Librarianship* 4(2): 111–26.

Lipsky, M. (1980) *Street Level Bureaucracy: Dilemmas of the Individual in Public Services*, New York: Russel Sage.

McElroy, A. (1989) 'Standards and guidelines in performance measurement', *British Journal of Academic Librarianship* 4(2): 88–98.

Mann, P. (1990) 'University expansion, library contraction', *Library Association Record* 92(2): 115–17.

Middlehurst, R. (1992) 'Quality: an organizing principle for higher education?', *Higher Education Quarterly* 46(1): 20–38.

Munn, R. (1968) 'The bottomless pit, or the academic library as viewed from the administration building', *College and Research Libraries* 29(1): 51–4.

Murphy, R. (1990) 'Proletarianization or bureaucratization: the fall of the professional', in Torstendahl, R. and Burrage, M. (eds), *The Formation of Professions*, London: Sage.

Pearson, R. (1990) 'Doubling student numbers – what are the prospects?', *Higher Education Quarterly* 44(3): 215–29.

Pollitt, C. (1988) 'Bringing consumers into performance measurement: concepts, consequences and constraints', *Policy and Politics* 16(2): 77–8.

Pollitt, C. (1990a) 'Measuring university performance: never mind the quality, never mind the width?', *Higher Education Quarterly* 44(1): 60–81.

Pollitt, C. (1990b) *Managerialism and the Public Services: The Anglo-American Experience*, Oxford: Basil Blackwell.

Prince, B. and Burton, R. (1988) 'Changing dimensions in academic library structures: the impact of information technology', *British Journal of Academic Librarianship* 3(2).

Roberts, N. (1991) 'A profession in crisis', *Library Association Record* 93(7): 450–3.

Rodger, E. (1988) 'Progress in documentation: British university libraries 1977-87. Some observations on the challenge of declining resources', *Journal of Documentation* 44(4): 346–78.

SCONUL (Standing Conference of National and University Libraries) (1992) *Performance Indicators for University Libraries: A Practical Guide* (Doc. 92/204), London: SCONUL.

Sizer, J. (1988) 'British universities' responses to events leading up to grant reductions announced in July 1981', *Financial Accountability and Management* 4(2): 79–97.

Smith, P. (1993) 'Outcome-related performance indicators and organizational control in the public sector', *British Journal of Management* 4: 135–51.

Tannock, J. and Burge, S. (1992) 'A new approach to quality assurance for Higher Education', *Higher Education Quarterly* 46(1): 108–23.

Thompson, J. (1991) *Re-direction in Academic Library Management*, Library Association: London.

Trow, M. (1992) 'Thoughts on the White Paper of 1991', *Higher Education Quarterly* 46(3): 213–26.

Watson, E. (1978) 'The concept of the steady state library – whose definition?', in Searle, C. (ed.), *Steady-State, Zero-Growth and the Academic Library*, London: Clive Bingley.

Witzel, M. (1991) 'The failure of an internal market: the Universities Funding Council bid system', *Public Money and Management* Summer: 41–8.

Chapter 5

Quality and social housing
Irreconcilable partners?

Alf Fitzgeorge-Butler and Peter Williams

INTRODUCTION

In popular perception there is little to link the current social housing
sector with issues of quality. Social housing, in the form of both local
authority and housing association rented accommodation, has been seen
to become the home of the most deprived and marginalized members of
the population (Page 1993). Through policies such as the Right to Buy
(RTB), the promotion of home ownership and curbs on new building,
the local authority sector in particular has been residualized and increasingly set apart from the mainstream of housing provision (Forrest and
Murie 1988; Cole and Furbey 1993). RTB Sales have been concentrated
in the best and most popular stock of housing (i.e. terraced and semi-
detached houses on suburban estates) and the overall size of the stock
has diminished by around 1.2 million. Perhaps most strikingly the social
composition of council housing has changed fundamentally. It now
houses a much narrower spectrum of the population. This is the low
paid, the unemployed, the retired and single parents. Partly this is as a
consequence of sales and tenants leaving the sector with their homes,
partly it is a product of reduced availability and the tighter targeting of
the allocation of local authority tenancies. These changes are almost
irreversible. As the older generation of tenants dies, it will be replaced
by younger tenants drawn from a narrower social base and they will
occupy a smaller and less desirable housing stock.

This residualization has had major impacts on the management of the
sector and raised doubts as to its long-term future (Audit Commission
1986: Forrest 1993). But the quality of the fabric of public housing stock
is also a factor since there is considerable evidence to suggest that there
is substantial and mounting disrepair in this sector (Department of the
Environment 1993; Welsh Office 1988). It is, therefore, within the

context of both a general residualization process and the quality of both the housing stock and housing management that the emergence of a range of quality-related initiatives must be viewed. There is a sad irony that concerns with quality are now alive within a sector which has sold its best housing and has already lost its least impoverished tenants.

This chapter begins by setting out the political and ideological context to our analysis of changes in the social rented housing sector. It then moves on to trace the range of initiatives taken to support and sustain social housing through what must have been its most difficult decade since the inception of this form of housing provision. Then, having examined the broad components of quality-related initiatives, we offer a detailed analysis of, and comparison between, different quality improvement systems: British Standard 5750 (BS5750), Total Quality Management (TQM) and Investors in People (IIP). There have also been different strands to the current pressure for change of which quality improvement has been but one aspect and an overview will be offered of these pressures within both the local authority and housing association contexts. Next, specific examples are provided of the application within the sector of the various quality assurance systems which tend to illustrate both the systems themselves and the differing approaches to quality adopted by contrasting housing organizations, which, in turn, reflect differing internal needs and politics. The chapter concludes by relating the experience of the housing sector back to the main themes of the book and reflecting upon them.

POLITICAL AND IDEOLOGICAL CONTEXT

The advance of the New Right ideology within the Conservative Party in the late 1970s can be seen as the beginning of an increasingly critical and antagonistic approach to the provision of public services by local authorities (Hall 1986). It also heralded an ever tighter rationing of scarce resources through 'free market' mechanisms, which, in turn, accentuated the divisions between those who have and those who have not (see Cole and Furbey 1994: chapter 7 for a useful review). As local services proved more resistant to change than might be expected, the government has now speeded up the process of exposing many hitherto exclusively public services, including public housing, to compulsory competitive tendering (CCT). This initiative is providing considerable opportunities for private sector companies to extract profits from these services.

This process can be linked to the growing fiscal crisis which a number of governments have been facing. The pressure to reduce public spending was first commented upon in the early 1970s (O'Connor 1973) when tax raising had difficulty keeping pace with burgeoning government expenditure, and thus led to an increasingly monetarist approach to the financing of public services and, specifically, to considerable cuts in housing investment. The rationale for such an approach is due to the need to reduce public expenditure, and to concentrate scarce fiscal resources on supporting the core economic structure and infrastructure. It is, therefore, possible to argue that there has been an ideological conjunction between the more overtly market ideology of the New Right, the need to resolve the fiscal problems facing western states and the need for governments to better manage the more unstable economies.

Accordingly, the first Conservative administration in 1979 moved quickly to reduce housing investment further and at the same time to promote owner occupation through the Right to Buy for council tenants. Although the sale of council houses had been permitted previously, the new government developed a much more aggressive approach to the promotion of home ownership via this route (Murie 1993). This was paralleled by a sustained critique of the ability of local authorities to manage council housing effectively. Councils were portrayed as incompetent and ineffective and seen to be an inappropriate mechanism for the direct provision of housing services (Black and Stafford 1988), while housing associations were promoted as a better and more appropriate vehicle for such provision. In adopting this stance to local authorities, the government was pinpointing weaknesses which certainly did exist in a number of authorities but which had been overcome, in part at least, in many more. In other words, it was recognized that local authority housing provision was not without its deficiencies, and through the late 1970s and the 1980s major improvements had been made in the running of 'council housing'. At the start of the decade it was difficult to find any recognition of these changes and the government was able to promote housing associations as a better non-political and community-based alternative. It was only later in the decade, and even more so in the 1990s, that the weaknesses of housing associations became more evident and they then became a target of government criticism.

The late 1980s and early 1990s have seen a change of emphasis in the approach to public housing. The suspicions of and antipathy to local authorities remain, and continuing economic problems have reduced still further the capacity and willingness of the state to fund public housing. There has been a further intensification in the commodification and commercialization of public housing (Forrest 1993). This time, it is through the extension of the more general requirement within local government to contract out services to the housing management function. At the same time, housing associations are encouraged to seek ever increasing amounts of private capital to fund their development programmes. According to Whitehead :

> What started as a relatively simple policy concentrating on the sale of local authority housing assets to their occupiers has become a highly complex range of instruments, all of which interact to achieve, at least in principle, greater choice for consumers, prices more in line with costs, and a better utilization of the stock, but not in general higher levels of investment in housing.

(Whitehead 1993: 117)

Along with these privatization initiatives, a great emphasis has been placed by the Audit Commission (1989) and the Citizen's Charter initiative on the publication by housing organizations of key performance indicators. The emphasis on performance indicators and targets, however, represents a 'top–down' attempt by government to improve the quality of public housing through the publication of, albeit rather crude, measures of quality. There is also a continuing uneasy relationship between this insistence on service improvements with respect to housing management and the poor condition of much council housing. The new financial regime introduced for local authorities under the Housing Act 1988 has meant that authorities have had to reduce substantially their own repair and maintenance expenditure funded from capital receipts. Thus, service improvements are being achieved against a backcloth of underinvestment in the public housing stock. This clearly cannot continue and so some authorities are being forced to move down the road of transferring their housing stock to another organization.

Although the government has made clear its concerns to see council housing operate as effectively as possible, considerations of quality are clearly somewhat secondary in relation to the desire to reduce state expenditure and the wish to encourage tenants to purchase council property as part of the more general commitment to home ownership. These are not totally incompatible aims, in that improved quality might also mean greater efficiency. However, this must be set against an overall reduction in investment in public housing by successive governments (Wilcox 1993) and a growing scarcity of available public rental tenancies. Only further investment will ultimately resolve such problems of access and repair and improvement to the stock. But this spiral of decline is partly masked by the rhetoric of quality improvement and the pressures to meet performance targets.

In addition, it can be argued that government interventions aimed at manipulating the market to counteract the effects of continuing economic disturbance, while at the same time fostering wealth-creation opportunities, have fed a growing legitimation crisis. The more they intervene, the more obvious their support role is, and the more apparent their failures are in attempting to stimulate and manage economic growth. Governments thus tend to lose the support and confidence of the 'ruled'. Habermas has argued that this is partially managed by encouraging the passivity of the citizenry through 'systematically distorted communication' which denies citizens understandable and accurate information (Habermas 1970: 205–18, 1976: xiii–xiv). Broadly, 'systematically distorted communication' points back to systematically distorted social structures, and so to the effect of power on individuals (Pusey 1987: 72). These tactics effectively reduce the opportunities for democratic expression of displeasure by curtailing the activities of local government, encouraging the creation of quangos or bodies, such as the committees of management of housing associations, who are not accountable to any electorate.

A further factor in the equation arises from the difficulties government has in allocating scarce resources, which tends to be a conflictual process, especially in relation to the limited resources available for public housing. Dear has argued that the reallocation of governmental functions to non-elected agencies:

> represents a purposeful conflict-diversification strategy, which shifts the effects of a structural crisis to community and local levels. The financial, rationality and legitimation crises are *regionalised*, thus temporarily removing the burden from the central state and implicating the local state in the genesis of the crises.
>
> (Dear 1981: 14)

This conflict-diversification process seems to depend upon a mixed strategy of permitting the status quo to persist (local autonomy over the allocation of council housing is a good example of this), where responsibility for the rationing of scarce resources has been located at local level, and setting up new agencies to bypass local democratic structures and public scrutiny. Local government, being more accessible to public pressure and complaint, therefore finds itself in the unenviable position of having to ration the diminishing stocks of council housing in the face of increasing demand but with no control over the total resources available.

The relevance of the above discussion is to connect clearly the 'discourse' of quality-cost savings, value for money, economy, efficiency and effectiveness with the macro-level activities of governments since 1979 (Stewart and Walsh 1992). It has led to the partial dismantling of the system of local democracy and, more specifically, to the entire dismantling of the monolithic edifice of council housing by a series of separate but connected initiatives. There is, therefore, a 'mismatch' or communication distortion between the publicly stated quest for service improvements in the public sector (which are only partial anyway), through quality initiatives, and the attachment of successive governments to cutting public expenditure. The public housing sector is an example of such a mismatch as well as being the victim of the government's preference for, and promotion of, home ownership (though this is also a public preference). The increased expenditure for housing associations can also now be seen to have been a short-term palliative to offset the run-down of council housing. In short, it could be argued that for quality improvement in public sector housing read cost saving and the restructuring of the tenures.

CURRENT PRESSURES FOR CHANGE

Although local authority housing services have faced a decade or more of continuing pressure, demand for their services has increased. This is due to a range of factors including continuing household formation and unemployment, increasing incidence of homelessness, the lack of new building during this period and the introduction of potentially wide-ranging changes such as community care. This increase in demand is not being met by housing associations, despite their rapid growth. The government has recognized these problems and has announced a review of access to social housing. This may well result in more restricted/ targeted access as one way of controlling demand, though where the displaced demand will go is difficult to foresee. Demographic change may come to the rescue in the medium term because it is predicted there will be a fall in the numbers of new households being formed but this might be offset by a fall in the number of lettings becoming available within the existing council housing stock.

The pressures upon local authorities are thus intense and are likely to remain so. Both officers and elected members have wrestled with ways of improving the situation. A radical solution has been to transfer the stock (and the service) out of the local authority sector via a 'large scale voluntary transfer'. This has been the chosen mechanism for around thirty authorities (involving 150,000 properties), and the new housing organization then has access to both private borrowing and public funds.

This solution is not readily available in all authorities and in these we have seen a renewed focus on the best ways to organize themselves, i.e. to become more efficient and effective.

A recent survey of organizational change within local government has shown that almost all housing departments have been reorganized within the last three years. Despite that, the survey (Young and Mills 1993) also revealed that only 45 per cent of authorities have 'stand alone' departments. As a consequence, in the majority of departments important services such as housing benefit continue to be managed outside such departments. This has important implications for the management and control of such services and assumes a crucial significance if quality improvements are sought.

Authorities in general and larger authorities in particular have also decentralized their services as part of a process of bringing them closer to the public they serve (Common *et al.* 1993). Housing has often been in the forefront of these initiatives. While decentralization can be considered to have been a success, it does raise issues concerning the consistency of the policies and procedures as applied to council clients. It should be noted that such questions of uniform conformity to specifications are vital elements in achieving quality improvements. The extension of CCT to housing management will move authorities further down this path through both standard-setting in the specifications and monitoring outcomes.

Whilst local housing authorities are responding to the changed circumstances, there is evidence of reduced morale amongst 60 per cent of senior managers and that tenants do not have an influential role in policy formulation or management (Young and Mills 1993). Elected members were also not seen as particularly significant 'change drivers' in the change process. Thus, in spite of the legislative and ministerial pressure to encourage increased participation of, and management by, tenants much has still to be achieved. There is also evidence of reluctant consultation with other agencies such as housing associations, their regulatory bodies (Housing Corporation and Housing for Wales), and the private and voluntary sectors, though this partly reflects the hostile setting in which authorities have been operating. Housing authorities seem, therefore, to have a continuing tendency towards closing themselves off from their environment and real involvement with their customers (Stewart 1988), raising questions about the capacity for achieving real change within their organizational cultures. This, again, has significant implications for the substantial and lasting cultural changes required by BS5750 and TQM certification.

Although many authorities have moved towards a performance culture, the evidence from the LGMB survey reveals that 44 per cent of authorities do not have performance management systems in place. There is, thus, much still to do (Bines *et al.* 1993). Although target setting and performance monitoring have become more commonplace under governmental pressure, the way these have been introduced might not result in the pursuit of excellence-striving for ever higher standards. In conjunction with the criticisms outlined earlier, quality certification may not necessarily lead to high standards for customers.

There is, therefore, considerable pressure for change both from government in terms of achieving their ideological and political objectives and from the need for local authorities to find effective organizational answers to the policy changes forced upon them – for example CCT, Community Care and Local Government Review. Frequent organizational changes, the involvement of other departments in core services, the impact of decentralization on central control, a continuing subordinate place for the relatively powerless customer, and the lack of performance review and measurement systems all indicate the pressures on local authorities and the difficulties they face in introducing quality systems. Such problems must be tackled if an effective culture of quality is to be created within a housing organization. When poorly understood or resolved, quality improvements may become no more than a token paper exercise of reviewing policy and procedures, meaning that organizations are considering, or have already taken the mechanical BS5750 path rather than the more difficult, but ultimately more effective, route of TQM and/or IIP.

THE NATURE OF QUALITY SYSTEMS

In order to consider the nature of quality systems with respect to social rented housing, it is first necessary to consider the nature of the housing management task and then analyse the key concepts which are related to the differing emphases within the various quality assurance systems on offer.

HOUSING MANAGEMENT

There are two particular points to be made about the work content of the housing task. First, there are considerable elements of officer discretion built into the management process. For example, housing officers essentially decide who gets what in a somewhat subjective manner. This is the case irrespective of the particular letting procedures which happen to be in force in given authorities. There is also a considerable interpretative element to housing officers' work when they come to apply given policies and procedures to individual housing cases. Second, there are considerable interpersonal elements to housing work with officers dealing with individual problems. It is therefore important to recognize the nature of the housing task and to understand that 'how things are done' may be just as important as the housing activity being undertaken. Taken together, these two points demonstrate the difficulty of applying relatively inflexible quality assurance systems to subjective and interpersonal decision making and relationships with housing customers. It is also likely that the motivation of housing staff to handle complex personal issues sensitively is just as important as the policies and procedures to be followed and applied.

It is also important to remember that housing managers are relatively inexperienced when it comes to applying management techniques to housing work. It is only in the last few years that National Vocational Qualifications have been developed for housing managers. These competences stress the importance of gaining knowledge and understanding quality issues but this will take some years to work through into the training of existing housing managers (Housing Sector Consortium 1993). This is not to say that some authorities and housing associations have not tried to apply quality systems, but they are in a minority.

The extension of CCT to housing management (HMCCT), however, is encouraging housing managers to adopt a more business-oriented approach to housing work, but it is problematic as to whether this process will lead to quality improvements in the housing service. It is suspected that HMCCT is yet another attempt to cut housing management costs since to insist that contractors have achieved quality standards will probably be considered anti-competitive.

It is therefore possible to argue that quality may be a potentially diversionary issue given the negative organizational climates within which they are being applied. These organizational climates can be typified by demotivated and demoralized managers and housing staff struggling to provide adequate services with inadequate resources. This position is unlikely to change in the near future since it is the lack of both capital and revenue resources, to build, maintain and manage public housing, which remains the central and dominant issue.

Finally, it should be recognized that there are important definitional difficulties in specifying housing management. Although local authorities and housing associations have been operating as landlords for over seventy years, there have been varying interpretations of the housing management task. This was perhaps best exemplified by the existence of two professional bodies: the Society of Women Housing Managers and the Institute of Housing. The two bodies (which subsequently merged) adopted contrasting approaches to the task. The former focused on a people-centred and intensive management approach, the latter on a property-centred and highly centralized approach. In recent years there has been considerable debate on these and related issues. Housing management has been decentralized to get services closer to the users while at the same time there has been a blurring of the property management and tenant support roles. For government this has proved to be an issue of particular significance because it has an impact upon the justifiable levels of subsidy in the form of management and maintenance allowances. It is also crucial in terms of the way government sets out the specifications for putting housing management out to contract under CCT. What all of this indicates is that there continue to be major problems with specifying the housing management task and this, of course, has implications for the adoption of quality systems.

QUALITY SYSTEMS

Most definitions of quality are related to exhortations to attain excellence in the production and provision of high-quality goods and services. It is also related to the notion of 'fitness for purpose' which is interpreted as providing services which customers need and want – 'conformance' to customer requirements to reduce the possible adverse effects of customer dissatisfaction. This is achieved through a review of, and improvements to, the customer–supplier chain which may involve many indirect links between the ultimate customer and sometimes distant suppliers which make up the complete system of product or service provision.

British Standard (BS) 5750 is the best-known quality assurance system in the UK and is also accepted as an European and international system (EN29002 and ISO9000). With respect to the provision of housing *services*, and indeed any service, the relevant British Standards Institute (BSI) specification is BS5750 (BSI 1987) which sets out the requirements of a quality system:

> where a contract between two parties requires demonstration of a
> supplier's capability to control the processes that determine the

acceptability of product (service) required . . . (and) are aimed primarily at preventing and at detecting any nonconformity during production and installation and implementing the means to prevent its recurrence.

(BSI 1987)

Such a definition clearly illustrates a common criticism of this standard in that the language and methodology, when attempting to apply it to service industries, is too rooted in engineering and production terminology and systems.

The specification does not in itself set standards for individual firms or institutions but sets out the mechanism by which given standards are maintained. This has led to further criticism in that certification does not necessarily lead to higher, but merely the maintaining of existing, standards and may lead to confusion between quality certificates and quality *itself*. It may also be a relatively expensive process, especially for small firms (some of whom have been forced to seek it by larger customers), to gain certification.

Attempts to apply the above specification to housing services will therefore meet a number of potential difficulties. First, many housing organizations, particularly the smaller, have poorly developed policy and procedural systems. There is, therefore, a great deal of work to be done before a 'quality policy' can be said to be effectively in place. It is therefore a relatively expensive process to set up and monitor. Second, it is extremely difficult to define 'nonconformity' in the context of the provision of housing services, which by their very nature have a high degree of interpersonal interaction as an essential element of the work (Housing Sector Consortium 1993). Third, the capacity of a service supplier to control the process of service provision, which is sometimes decentralized, certainly under-professionalized and frequently provided by individual housing workers without reference to managers or policy/procedure manuals is limited. Such 'control' can only be provided by intensive training of all managers and staff (in often large housing organizations) to ensure that they all take personal responsibility for the provision of consistently high-quality services. Verification procedures in such circumstances are difficult to implement. This also applies to inspection and verification to ensure that the 'documented quality system' is consistently applied. Likewise, the purchase of service products is fraught with similar verification problems in the case of housing, legal, accountancy, architectural and other such service products. There are, therefore, considerable difficulties with the implementation of BS5750 to housing organizations, difficulties which come back to the distinctions to be made between manufacturing and industrial contexts, and firms and institutions which provide a service.

Walsh has typified services as being 'not tangible', involving customers in their production as well as making them 'users', 'often consumed as they are produced' and more difficult to 'control.' He further states that: 'the straightforward application of BS5750 will lead to an insensitive emphasis on a quality bureaucracy and a proliferation of paper' (Walsh 1988: 3). Total Quality Management, however, sets out to ensure that organization structure, management and quality systems meet given organizational objectives by maximizing human and material resources. It also promotes *continuous* quality improvement, affects the ability of organizations to compete, and encourages its members to contribute, grow and excel. This is achieved by integrating organizational activities 'to achieve a common goal by developing a culture in which the customer is paramount' (Catterick 1992: 4). The significance of the TQM approach is that, by attempting to change organizational culture, a lasting commitment to quality is brought about which will, it is argued, lead to consistently high-quality service provision which meets customer requirements and is free from deficiencies.

There are, however, difficulties with the concept of supplying customers' needs and wants at the best possible level of service, since the customers of social landlords rarely have any *effective* choice to purchase or consume another similar product in the market-place if quality standards are found to be unacceptable. The reason for this is that council housing in particular is tenanted by some of the poorest and most disadvantaged members and citizens of our society. There is also considerable dependence by such on housing benefit and other social payments, and often, if they were to obtain a privately rented home, they would be unable to pay market rents. Even those who successfully overcome the secrecy, hurdles and obstacles which typify access to council housing and housing association tenancies will find it difficult to challenge poor quality service since such organizations are often 'judge and jury in their own case' – credible (and fair) complaints or appeal mechanisms are infrequent.

It has already been pointed out that housing organizations are simply not in a position to provide customers with what they need and want – a home, at an affordable rent, in a location they want, at the time they want it. Indeed Stewart and Walsh set out sixteen possible dimensions of quality with respect to local government service providers (Stewart and Walsh 1989: 10). Timeliness was their first dimension, reliability of provision was their second. There are also considerable problems associated with other dimensions on their list, as indicated below:

- Accuracy of information; some councils and housing associations break the law with respect to the information they provide (notably section 106 of the Housing Act 1985)
- Choice; there is little choice
- Barriers to access; there are linguistic, physical and social barriers of which the most notable is institutional racism
- Redress; a lack of complaints and appeals procedures
- Understanding the needs and problems of customers; it will be demonstrated that local authorities in particular do not tend to be close enough to, or involve, their customers
- Credibility; the scarcity of social housing presents a severe legitimacy problem for local government.

These dimensions represent serious obstacles to the implementation of both the above quality assurance systems.

However, our analysis so far would suggest that the most profitable path for housing organizations which wish to promote lasting change and improvements in service provision (within the overall constraint of scarcity) is TQM rather than the more narrow BS5750 approach. TQM addresses the need to change organizational cultures rather than just review policies and procedures, even though the latter will still ultimately be necessary. There is, however, one further initiative which has been sponsored and promoted by Training Enterprise Councils, funded by the Department of Employment. This is Investors in People (IIP) which has also been called 'the BS5750 for people'. It is accepted as an integral part of a TQM system. The requirements are as follows:

- A public commitment to develop *all* employees of an organization
- Explicit business objectives communicated to, and understood by *all* staff
- Efficient and straightforward planning for training and development
- Necessary action to ensure the above *actually* happens
- Evaluation of the outcome.

Organizations are therefore seeking to concentrate on the skills and abilities of those people who must make quality management systems and policies work for the benefit of their customers. IIP also requires the statement of explicit goals and a sense of direction for the organization. In some ways, this initiative represents a more logical method of progression towards quality assurance, since strategic planning and business plans are part of the process. These must precede the provision of reliable systems for the delivery of the plans. IIP is also linked to objectives of both the National Council for Vocational Qualifications and the Management Charter Initiative to improve the competencies of managers and staff, and it is envisaged that BS5750 will be an ultimate goal for which it paves the way.

It can be argued that, given the difficulties of the environment which local housing authorities and housing associations are operating in and the sheer scale of the changes required to the policy, procedures and practices are not capable of being attained simply through the imposition of crude performance indicators. A wholesale change of organizational culture is required.

QUALITY IN PRACTICE

One example of the BS5750 route to quality improvements is provided by the Housing Department of Alyn and Deeside District Council in North Wales, which successfully achieved accreditation for its client side housing repairs service. The stated targets of its quality programme were the meeting of pre-agreed targets in a key part of the housing service not under its direct control; getting it right first time; the need for competitive services; and ensuring customer satisfaction. Small incremental improvements are now being sought to raise the level of existing standards, and plans have been made to extend the process into other parts of the department.

There were, however, several assumptions underlying these objectives. First, although the needs for real and lasting commitment to the 'philosophy of quality' and for cultural change were recognized, it has already been found that BS5750 does not necessarily deliver these. The council clearly conducted its initial analysis of relevant information, briefed external consultants, appointed its quality representatives and drew up its revised procedure manuals on the basis of achieving accreditation. There was an opportunity to pursue culture change through the staff consultation exercise, but the processes or culture change were not clearly articulated, nor were other key factors such as how BS5750 might precisely 'aid management', how strategic objectives might be achieved by accreditation, and what contribution it made to helping plan and manage change more effectively. It is argued that the opportunity to involve all managers and staff in this somewhat mechanical process might have been a key lever in achieving cultural change instead of voluminous procedure manuals. It is also significant that the need to become more competitive was also cited as an objective.

There are clear connections here with the need for authorities to produce operational manuals (covering revised policies and procedures) in order to comply with the requirements of CCT. But there was no attempt to provide information which might have measured the effectiveness of service delivery. This would have required more emphasis on work measurement techniques and a thorough analysis of service costs. BS5750 simply measures the effectiveness with which organizations can generate new policies and procedures and, maybe, give crude measures of quality through certain specified targets. It was also stated that customers might have alternatives to council housing but it can be seen from the discussion above that this is not a powerful argument. Whilst not wishing to detract from the commitment to improve quality, it can be seen that opportunities to make lasting change were missed.

Coventry Churches Housing Association in the Midlands undertook a quality programme for different reasons. Their primary objective was to seek greater efficiencies within their growing organization in the face of a new financial regime. A training programme introduced the concept of quality to all staff, whilst emphasizing the need for teamwork and for the application of other techniques such as data gathering and problem solving. 'Gap analysis' was used to identify objectives, standards, output and performance measures with which to compare existing performance. It was stated that the development of a problem-solving capacity was one of the main achievements of the programme. Again, it can be noted that the initiative only went so far to bring about permanent cultural change, with the emphasis being rather upon short-term efficiency and cost-saving advantages.

Milton Keynes Borough Council has set up a number of Quality Audit Teams comprising customers, councillors and council officers which investigate customer satisfaction in a range of services. These teams use both questionnaires and face-to-face interviews to gather information to investigate agreed areas of study. Such teams complement customer guarantees made by the council in respect of frequency and standard of services in areas such as reception services and development control.

These three examples give some sense of how social housing organizations have sought to approach quality issues. It is clear this is still a relatively novel process within social housing organizations although there can be no doubt it is gaining momentum (AMA 1991a, 1991b;

Catterick 1992). It is masked, at present, by the activity generated by CCT and local government reorganization, and by continuing adjustments to the housing finance system. Combining the turbulence of the policy arena with the pressures brought about by the complexity of the housing management task itself means that full-blooded quality initiatives remain the exception rather than the rule. However, they are emerging, not least as part of other reorganization plans.

RELATIONSHIP BETWEEN QUALITY AND PERFORMANCE STANDARDS AND TARGETS

Section 167 of the Local Government and Housing Act (1989) places statutory requirements upon local housing authorities in respect of published performance indicators for tenants, but such indicators are of wider relevance to all housing organizations. This is because it is useful for customers, staff, committee members and senior management to have some visible measurement of what is being achieved by housing organizations. It should, however, be pointed out that these are much more useful to tenants/residents when an organization's performance targets have been published beforehand, enabling customers to judge whether services have come up to expectations. It may also be possible to compare the performance of their landlord with others but only where organizations are comparable – similar type of location, size and housing stock, for example. If such indicators are broken down by ward or by area/neighbourhood office, it might also be possible to test for issues such as consistency across an authority's area of operation. Such indicators have tended to be of both input (the resources provided to run the services) and output (the outcomes, or the actual service provided) types. The latter are more useful in terms of determining the quality of service provided. The full range of such information may be of considerable value in seeking quality improvements year by year, and provide yardsticks by which to set challenging but realistic targets for housing managers and staff.

The Audit Commission also has a statutory obligation (Local Government Act 1992) to develop measures of performance against which each local authority will be required to monitor its performance. Such indicators are to enable comparisons to be made by reference to the criteria of cost, economy, efficiency and performance achieved by comparable organizations within a financial year, and standards of performance achieved between different financial years. There are, however, performance measures which are not directly related to quality improvement, such as those which are volume based, for example the number of people using a given service, and the input type statistics referred to above.

There has, to date, been insufficient emphasis by the Audit Commission on qualitative indicators such as rectifying errors or the number and nature of complaints. Such measures may be harder to collect but there is a danger that organizations will be swamped by the requirement to collect data which has little qualitative value. It may also be argued that insufficient attention has been paid to central needs of citizens – what do they want to know about given services? There is also a close relationship between the explicit values and stated objectives of housing organizations and the qualitative data to be collected – particularly important since behaviourial values and objectives will be a significant component of performance measurement, given the high degree of interpersonal interaction in housing work. It is, however, noticeable that such measures are conspicuously lacking. This aspect of performance standard setting will be important to customers since it is not only necessary to have a service delivered but for it to be delivered with appropriate behaviour. The development of customer care codes was an attempt to provide guidance as to behavioural objectives but few satisfactory measures, if any, were developed. Standards must, therefore, meet customer expectations and cover the full range of service outputs, including behaviour. Both the targets and the results must be published.

It is useful to review briefly the Audit Commission approach since it clearly demonstrates that the government's approach to performance standards and to quality improvements is closely related to cost-effectiveness. This accounts for the emphasis placed on the volume of inputs, since such information concerning the cost of a service is part of a calculation of economy, effectiveness and efficiency, and only partially related, as stated above, to considerations of quality. Indeed, this is part of the Citizen's Charter initiative which sets out the clear relationship, for government, between quality, standards and value for money. Although it is clearly stated that such performance and quality standards should be comprehensible to citizens, it is apparent that behind the rhetoric, the central concern is one of cost. The Audit Commission has already spent considerable time and effort in specifying suitable indicators, which demonstrates that quality is inherently hard to define or measure (Audit Commission 1989, 1992(a), 1992(b), 1993). Such indicators will only be fully developed over the coming years.

SUMMARY AND CONCLUSIONS

It is clear from the above analysis of quality and housing that the government faces a continuing problem of paying for public services, especially in times of recession and economic down-turn. This also causes legitimation problems both for national and local government, the latter being subject to 'conflict-diversification'. Within the framework of this chapter, the answers provided by the government have included the commodification of housing (Right to Buy, market pricing, CCT), more broadly based critiques of local authorities and council housing, in particular focusing upon political dimensions, as well as attempts to 'systematically distort communication' concerning fiscal problems. The latter are reflected in reductions in local democratic control over local services and more recently by introducing cost-saving measures under the guise of quality improvements and improved choice for the customer. At the same time, by taking a closer involvement in local housing services, the government does run the risk of bearing greater responsibility for the outcome.

Paradoxically, not only has the government provided a wide range of wealth-creation opportunities within the public services, it has created similar opportunities for quality consultants, since the costs of implementing quality systems can be very large. Like CCT, the costs and benefits of quality remain somewhat uncertain, not least because we have had little time to see the impact work through (Walsh 1991; Walsh and Davies 1993). The emphasis on gaining accreditation via BS5750 may also deflect housing organizations from the need *actually* to improve quality. Looking at the overall context and the future prospects for social housing organizations, the objective of cost savings looms far larger than real quality improvement within housing services. While quality issues are not unimportant, the lack of resources and the pressure to reduce and otherwise limit the role of the social housing sector provide the central focus of activity and debate. This is unfortunate because, in reality, social housing would provide a real test of the quality industry and the power of consumers actually to influence the services they receive.

REFERENCES

Association of Metropolitan Authorities (1991a) *Quality Services: An Introduction to Quality Assurance for Local Authorities*, London: Association of Metropolitan Authorities.

Association of Metropolitan Authorities (1991b) *Housing Repairs: The Search for Quality*, London: Association of Metropolitan Authorities.

Audit Commission (1986) *Managing the Crisis in Council Housing*, London: Audit Commission.

Audit Commission (1989) *Managing Services Effectively – Performance Review*, Management Papers No. 5, London: Audit Commission.

Audit Commission (1992a) *Citizen's Charter Indicators: Charting a Course*, London: Audit Commission.

Audit Commission (1992b) *Citizen's Charter Performance Indicators*, London: Audit Commission.

Audit Commission (1993) *Staying Course – The Second Year of Citizen's Charter Indicators*, London: HMSO.

Bines, W., Kemp, P., Pleace, N. and Radley, C. (1993) *Managing Social Housing: Summary and Recommendations*, London: HMSO.

Black, J. and Stafford, D. (1988) *Housing Policy and Finance*, London: Routledge.

British Standards Institution (1987) *British Standard Quality Systems: BS5750: Part 2: Specification for Production and Installation*, London: BSI.

Catterick, P. (1992) *Total Quality: An Introduction to Quality Management in Social Housing*, London: Institute of Housing.

Cole, I. and Furbey, R. (1993) *The Eclipse of Council Housing*, London: Routledge.

Common, R., Flynn, N. and Mellon, E. (1993) *Managing Public Services: Competition and Decentralisation*, Oxford: Butterworth-Heinemann.

Dear, M. (1981) 'A Theory of the local state', in Burnett, A. and Taylor, P. (eds), *Political Studies from Spatial Perspectives: Anglo-American Essays on Political Geography*, New York: Wiley.

Department of the Environment (1993) *English House Condition Survey 1991: Key Facts*, London: HMSO.

Forrest, R. (1993) 'Contracting housing provision: competition and privatisation in the housing sector', in Taylor-Gooby, P. and Lawson, R. (eds), *Markets and Managers: New Issues in the Delivery of Welfare*, Milton Keynes: Open University Press.

Forrest, R. and Murie, A. (1988) *Selling the Welfare State: The Privatisation of Public Housing*, London: Routledge.

Habermas, J. (1970) 'Systematically distorted communication', *Inquiry*, 13: 205–18.

Habermas, J. (1976) *Legitimation Crisis*, London: Heinemann.

Hall, S. (1986) 'Variants of Liberalism', in Donald, J. and Hall, S. (eds), *Politics and Ideology*, Milton Keynes: Open University Press.

Harden, I. (1992) *The Contracting State*, Milton Keynes: Open University Press.

Housing Sector Consortium (1993) *National Occupational Standards for Housing*, London: LGMB.

Murie, A. (1993) 'Restructuring housing markets and housing access', *Social Policy Review* 5, London: Social Policy Association.

National Federation of Housing Associations (1993) *BS5750: A tool for improve- ment*, London: National Federation of Housing Associations.

O'Connor, J. (1973) *The Fiscal Crisis of the State*, New York: St Martin's Press.

Page, D. (1993) *Building for New Communities: A Study of New Housing Association Estates*, York: Rowntree Foundation.

Pusey, M. (1987) *Jürgen Habermas*, London: Tavistock.

Skelcher, C. (1992) *Managing for Service Quality*, London: Longman.

Stewart, J. (1988) *The New Management of Housing Departments*, Luton: LGMB.

Stewart, J. and Walsh, K. (1992) 'Change in the management of public services', *Public Administration* 70: 501–18.

Walsh, K. (1988) *Quality and Competition*, Luton: LGMB.

Walsh, K. (1991) *Competitive tendering for local authority services*, London: HMSO.

Walsh, K. and Davies, H. (1993) *Competition and Service: The Impact of the Local Government Act, 1988*, London: HMSO.

Walsh, K. and Spencer, K. (1990) *The Quality of Service in Housing Management*, Birmingham: Institute of Local Government Studies, Birmingham University.

Welsh Office (1988) *1986 Welsh House Condition Survey*, Cardiff: Welsh Office.

Whitehead, C. (1993) 'Privatizing housing: an assessment of the UK experience', *Housing Policy and Debate* 4(1): 101–39.

Wilcox, S. (1993) *Housing Finance Review 1992*, Papers in Housing No. 3, Research Centre for Housing Management and Development, Cardiff: University of Wales, College of Cardiff.

Young, K. and Mills, L. (1993) *A Portrait of Change*, Luton: LGMB.

Chapter 6

The quality of mercy

The management of quality in the personal social services

Ian Shaw

INTRODUCTION

The idea of a 'mixed economy of welfare' in which the statutory agencies are no longer the sole or even primary service providers received its first sharpened statement in Britain in the mid-1980s. Norman Fowler, then Secretary of State, reasoned that the state has not, cannot and should not monopolize the personal social services. He argued for a strategic view of all the sources of care in any area, and for the recognition that the direct provision of services is only one aspect of local provision and that other forms of care are also available. He pressed for a new 'enabling role' for local authority social services which promoted the fullest possible participation of other sources of care. This initiative was a relatively late flowering of the Conservative government's commitment to rolling back the frontiers of the state, and part of central government's programme to control local authority spending and promote cost-effectiveness. With this flagging of government intentions, the lead vehicle for the introduction of quality management in the personal social services in the United Kingdom was on the road.

The government's initial targets were services providing care in the community for the elderly, people with physical or learning disabilities and those with mental health problems. Since then, the objectives of a mixed economy of welfare and cost-effective services have been extended to all personal social services in the United Kingdom. Care in the community reforms, the Children Act 1989, a beefed up Social Services Inspectorate within the Department of Health, new local authority inspection units for social services departments, national standards and performance measures for the Probation Service, strategic plans and successive versions of performance expectations for supported housing projects, and a government-led scrutiny, succeeded by new departmental policies and guidance for relations between government departments and voluntary organizations, have followed hard upon one another's heels. Education and training for the personal social services has also been reformatted by these service changes and by the rapid introduction of quality management into higher education.

The languages of cost-effectiveness, service user satisfaction, empowerment, commercial models of quality management, monitoring and evaluation, service contracts, partnerships, staff supervision, financial decentralization and outcome assessments have permeated the planning, management and delivery of British social services.

In this chapter we pursue the central theme of this book, by seeking to deconstruct the concept of quality, showing how it is actually used in the personal social services. The core of the following argument is that the rhetoric of quality in the personal social services is politically and managerially driven. It entails an argument about partnership which is pursued as a way of managing a shift in state/voluntary sector relations, a rational managerialism which may threaten the professional role in social welfare, and a rhetoric about choice and satisfaction which paradoxically hinders the effective voice of the service user. We will show how quality arguments are used in the personal social services by different people for different purposes, and that the rhetoric of quality is justified on grounds as varied as risk protection, staff control, customer satisfaction or user empowerment, managerial control of the voluntary sector, cost-effectiveness, the need for decentralization, and various forms of partnership.

However, while the politics of policy agenda setting are important, we also need to appreciate the difficulties which arise when policy agendas are implemented. In the course of this chapter we question – along with Reed in chapter 2 – whether quality does indeed act as a 'relay device', 'linking government "mentalities" and policies with everyday organizational realities' as a way of introducing organizational change. We will illustrate that quality policies in the personal social services are implemented imperfectly for a variety of reasons. Agreement about appropriate service outcomes is often more apparent than real, and employees responsible for service delivery will bring their own lay explanations of policy to bear when evaluating or planning services. As a result, agreement about quality and standards becomes the subject of social negotiation, thus making standards partly contingent on their immediate service contexts.

The growth of supervision and surveillance of street-level staff has been a hallmark of these recent changes. This leads to one of the unresolved questions about the effects of quality management. Will it lead to a change in the nature of the professional task in welfare services? However this question is answered, we will argue that those who implement quality management usually have not recognized the extent to which risk management and discretionary behaviour constrain the extent to which new management practices can take root.

Finally, the case for a new customer/provider/purchaser relationship in which 'everything we do is driven by you' has not prevented service users from remaining marginalized. This is because a quality culture may not increase user choice, measures of customer satisfaction within the personal social services are problematic, customer satisfaction initiatives are paradoxically usually management-led, and the extent of user involvement is likely to remain variable, ambiguous and, on occasion, minimal.

QUALITY INITIATIVES IN THE PERSONAL SOCIAL SERVICES

Pfeffer and Coote identify four broad approaches to quality, according to whether the purpose is to convey prestige (the 'traditional' approach), meet standards set by experts (the scientific approach), measure customer satisfaction (the managerial or 'excellence' approach) or make the customer more powerful (the consumerist approach) (Pfeffer and Coote 1991).

Accounts of quality developments in the personal social services have often been limited to specific segments. However, the following map of quality initiatives throughout the personal services demonstrates the broadly comparable trends and arguments which characterize and buttress quality management in this field. To summarize, somewhat pessimistically and oversimply, politicians are primarily interested in quality as cost-effectiveness, managers aim for organizational and staff performance controls, and welfare professionals welcome quality as a mechanism that will guarantee professional survival in an uncertain world.

In consequence, the meaning of quality remains elusive, because it is made to service different purposes both by different people and by the same people at different times. Quality becomes fought over in both the macro- and micro-political battles of welfare provision. The definition of quality is also difficult because quality is often used to refer to a process of quality assurance, whether it be through user involvement, inspection, joint objective setting, new forms of service management or compulsory competitive tendering. The final benchmark of quality must be the outcome of services and not only the process by which quality of service is assured.

LOCAL AUTHORITY SOCIAL SERVICES

In 1986, the Audit Commission, which is charged with monitoring the effectiveness of local government financial arrangements and value for money, produced an influential critique of care in the community. The commission identified key financial problems around a mismatch of resources and services, and a lack of bridging finance to fund the transition to community care, together with organizational fragmentation and inadequate staffing arrangements. It also gave emphasis to the existence of 'perverse incentives' within the benefit system: 'Social Security policies appear to be working in a way directly opposing community care policies' so that 'the more residential the care the easier it is to obtain benefits and the greater the size of the payment' (Audit Commission 1986: 44). The commission argued that this tempted providers to go for residential rather than community care. The report provided a benchmark for later reforms and an actuarial, value for money orientation to the direction of those reforms.

Government proposals for reform of community care gained momentum during the late 1980s. The Griffiths Report (1988) introduced the proposal that local authorities should design and purchase community care services rather than be the major providers. The government moved with speed. A White Paper *Caring For People* (HMSO 1989) was followed by legislation (Community Care and National Health Service Act, 1990). This Act required social services departments to prepare Community Care Plans covering a three-year period. Plans were to include arrangements for quality assurance and systems for safeguarding service standards, including complaints procedures. Contracts between purchasers and providers were required to include monitoring systems and break-out clauses – a theme which continues to be reiterated by government departments.

In the White Paper, quality control systems were clearly viewed as a necessary adjunct of the proposed 'move away from the role of exclusive service provider to that of service arranger and procurer' (HMSO 1989: 5.6). To this end, the Social Services Inspectorate (SSI), based in the Department of Health (DH), was given a substantially strengthened role. Local independent inspection units accountable to each director of social services were set up to inspect local authority, voluntary and private residential homes, although the independence of these local inspectorates from local providers is not entirely clear. The Chief Inspector now reports annually to the Secretary of State on the effectiveness of these arrangements. Driven by the Citizen's Charter, the 1993 SSI report, through its new Chief Inspector, adopted a bullish, up-beat tone, advocating 'more explicit standards, openness, full and accurate information, choice, accountability and non-discrimination' (Social Services Inspectorate 1993a: 3.1).

The range and influence of the inspectorate's work is growing noticeably. Employing more than one hundred inspectors and still growing, global reviews of whole departments are now being undertaken jointly with the Audit Commission. The SSI is also augmenting its output through buying in work from major charities such as the Nuffield Foundation. There are several themes and aspirations in the work of the national inspectorate. Emphasis has been placed on 'the involvement of users and carers in planning and conducting inspections, defining the criteria to be applied, and reporting the findings' (SSI 1992c: 5.4), and satisfaction has been expressed at the extent to which this is taking place (SSI 1993a: 2.7). Recurrent anxieties have also been voiced over the need to improve managerial supervision of staff in personal social services. Thus, 'the variable quality of professional supervision is worrying . . . deficiences in supervision appeared in inspections of all services' (1992c: 13). The Chief Inspector has also supported a shift to managerialism, in which 'no individual fieldworker should be regarded as self sufficient' (SSI 1992c: 13). This managerialism is mirrored in the recurrent pleas and plans for a partnership of 'jointly agreed policies and practices, and fully agreed and understood interdisciplinary working arrangements' (SSI 1993a: 3.4), which will lead to a shared position among all interest groups.

In contrast, the commercially led route to quality accreditation ('kite marking') of services that satisfy the British Standards Institution (BSI) has as yet had a slight and patchy influence on the personal social services. Some privatized residential units have been accredited, and also a number of privatized services within the welfare sector. Discussions between the BSI and representatives of social work services have yet to produce much in the way of specific guidance, although a major voluntary organization, the Pre-School Playgroups Association, has recently promoted a process that leads to an accreditation of individual pre-school playgroups (British Standards Institution 1993). At least one local authority social work Inspection Unit – the Highland region in Scotland – has received the BSI mark of accreditation.

Quality concerns have also been demonstrated in the plethora of guidance and good practice documents flowing from the Children Act and the Care in the Community legislation. Standards in residential care and day care have been disseminated through the SSI's Caring for Quality series, now Inspecting for Quality, (e.g. SSI 1989, 1990a, 1990b, 1992a, 1992b, 1993b). Guidance for social workers carrying out the recently designated care management and assessment role has been produced both for managers and for practitioners (SSI 1991a, 1991b). The corresponding Guidance and Regulations for the Children Act runs to ten volumes, to which must be added an influential review of residential child care by the retiring Chief Inspector of the SSI and guidelines for working with child sexual abuse (Utting 1991; Department of Health 1991). The SSI also commissioned a more reflective assessment of the meaning of quality and its assessment (James *et al.* 1992).

THE VOLUNTARY SECTOR

The plans to introduce purchaser/provider relationships into the organization of community care through a mixed economy of statutory, voluntary and private care was paralleled by a Home Office scrutiny of funding and departmental links with agencies and projects in the voluntary sector. The consequent report, published in 1990, was liberally sprinkled with complaints that 'Departments were not agreeing objectives and targets with core funded bodies by which the success of the grant could be measured', that there were 'rarely any plans against which performance could be compared' and that, while monitoring of projects was often more intensive, there was 'very little rigorous evaluation of core funding' (Home Office 1990: 3.5.8, 3.7.6, G21, G28).

Familiar themes of quality management permeated the report's recommendations. Value for money and cost-effectiveness were seen as central to the role of government funding. 'We think that Departments should look for added value whenever they decide to give a core or project grant' (Home Office 1990: 3.4.6), by which it is meant that grants should carry commitments to additional fund-raised monies, service charging and volunteer input. The perceived need to strengthen partnership between voluntary agencies or projects and government departments also figured largely in the scrutiny. The most important aspects of partnership were regarded as joint objective setting between the department and the voluntary body, monitoring requirements, user feedback and three-yearly evaluations of all larger long-term grants. 'Strategies expressed through objectives' encapsulates the aim (*ibid.*: 3.3.15).

These recommendations were complementary in purpose to the wider restructuring of personal social services outlined above. The report paralleled the purchaser/provider split in community care with its proposal that 'Departments should look actively at the scope for using voluntary bodies as agents to deliver services which are currently provided by statutory authorities' (*ibid.*: 3.5.24). This efficiency scrutiny led immediately to a government action plan and subsequent departmental strategies, and was also followed by the establishment of Charities Evaluation Services, intended as a nationwide resource for charity evaluation.

However, departmental strategies seemed on occasion to be significantly more tentative than the original proposals. For example, the Welsh Office version of joint objective setting was that 'these objectives are set wherever possible (sic) in consultation with the appropriate voluntary organizations' (Welsh Office nd: 8). Anecdotal evidence suggests that some government departments may be highly selective in engaging in systematic joint formulation of objectives. Charities Evaluation Services has had a rather patchy impact, with large areas of the country still without a regional base.

SUPPORTED HOUSING AND HOUSING ASSOCIATIONS

We have illustrated that the introduction of quality management into the care in the community field cannot be viewed in isolation, but must be seen in the context of parallel government thinking for the voluntary sector. Likewise, thinking regarding the voluntary sector ties in closely at several points with Department of the Environment guidance and regulations for supported housing funded through housing associations via the London-based Housing Corporation, and with recent developments in Home Office policies for the Probation Service. The government provides an estimate of approximately £2 billion in annual grant to the voluntary sector. Of this, more than 50 per cent goes to housing associations, although the majority of this funding is spent on the development and management of general needs housing, rather than supported housing for people with special needs. The costs of employing staff to provide care and support in supported housing projects are provided from outside this budget.

The 1980s witnessed a sustained reaction against traditional large-scale hostel provision, with its shared eating, sleeping and catering facilities. Capital and revenue funding systems for housing associations changed radically, and housing associations have been part of the wider shifts towards a planned rather than an incremental approach and the stress on consumer involvement in service provision. Performance monitoring and quality assurance policies have increasingly taken root as the preferred tools of funding agencies for developing and appraising supported housing.

The Housing Corporation continues to feel its way in this area. It replaced its Performance Expectations guidance with a Performance Criteria handbook which concentrates on the basic minimum requirements rather than covering good practice recommendations as well (Housing Corporation 1989, 1992a).

Changes in the revenue funding system have also served to sharpen the preoccupation of housing associations and agencies with financial performance indicators for management. Guidance from the federal bodies representing housing associations has also encouraged the development of explicit housing management performance indicators (National Federation of Housing Associations 1987). User satisfaction and tenant participation are increasingly pursued as a key criterion for appraising special needs housing association performance, and agreed guidance is appearing in this field (e.g. Housing for Wales 1993a, 1993b).

PROBATION SERVICE

Following the establishment of national standards for the supervision of offenders in the community (Home Office 1992c) and the introduction of internal monitoring and inspection, the Home Office embarked on an annually revised Three Year Plan which sets quality targets for the Probation Service deriving from the Citizen's Charter. The 1994–7 plan introduced for the first time a series of key performance indicators against which the work of probation officers was to be measured. Intended to 'help assess the performance of the Probation Service, both nationally and at area level', 'the indicators are designed . . . to be of use at local level and to support good practice and the effective and efficient use of resources' (Home Office 1994: 14, 15). For example, the performance of each service will be measured against 'predicted and actual reconviction rates for persons subject to community orders by type of order' (ibid.: 14). The first quality objective for 1994–5 was 'to monitor and evaluate the introduction of performance indicators'. The consequences of this initiative will unfold through the mid years of the decade. However, it is worth emphasizing that quality measures here, and throughout the personal social services, have tended to be limited to those most easily obtained and those easily measured. Only one of the ten Home Office key performance indicators requires a qualitative measure.

Part of this Home Office strategy involves the establishment of partnership arrangements on the basis of either competitive tendering or joint planning with both the voluntary and the commercial sectors. This is to be funded by a top slicing of 'around 5 per cent' of each probation area's revenue budget (Home Office 1992b: 28). However, given the tentative nature of local accommodation strategy planning, the continued, uncertain Home Office murmurs about the role of the independent sector and the talk of parcelling out areas of work that are not within the 'core' of probation practice, the balance of power between the Probation Service and the voluntary sector remains weighted to the managerial interests of purchasers.

SOCIAL WORK EDUCATION

We indicated at the beginning of this chapter that social work education and training has been reformatted to service the quality concerns of government departments. The Central Council for Education and Training in Social Work (CCETSW) developed the rules and regulations required of all accredited social work courses, and set learning outcomes of knowledge, skills, values and competences (Central Council for Education and Training in Social Work 1991). These detailed regulations require structures for student assessment, internal and external monitoring systems, review and inspection arrangements, and new powers for providers.

The CCETSW received much negative public attention during 1993, which led the government to appoint a new chair committed to reviewing and changing CCETSW structures and policy. The interested departments also conducted a wide-ranging policy and financial management review of the organization, which charged CCETSW with the requirement to discover and respond to customer and user views, strengthen its arrangements for enforcing standards and ensure quality in training programmes. Heavy warnings were also made about the implications of public spending deficits for the funding of CCETSW in the next five years, and the subsequent demand that it develop improved systems for demonstrating that it is making cost-effective use of its annual revenue budget of £32 million (DH, 1993b). It remains to be seen how far the newly revised social work training regulations (CCETSW 1995) weaken or change the elaborate apparatus of quality management in social work education.

The recurrent themes in this brief survey are cost-effectiveness, joint objective setting between interested providers, strengthened account-ability of welfare professionals, explicit standards and performance monitoring, and customer satisfaction. This suggests that quality initiatives in the personal social services are, in Pfeffer and Coote's (1991) terms, a mixture of expert approaches intended to meet agreed standards, and a managerial or excellence approach designed to measure customer satisfaction.

It is our view that relations between the state, statutory welfare and the voluntary sector, the accomplishment of managerial control, and a determination to incorporate the customer's voice comprise the basic agenda of these quality initiatives. The extent to which a satisfactory resolution of these themes has been accomplished will be the focus of the second part of this chapter.

THE RHETORIC OF QUALITY

The question of whether this rhetoric of quality reflects what happens on the ground is to miss a central point. Indeed, we would argue that there is no way that the rhetoric could 'work' in some unambiguous, instru-mental manner, if only because different interest groups arguing for quality have different and possibly incompatible objectives. This di-lemma is occasionally recognized in official documents. For example, in the Department of Health guidance on the training implications of the NHS and Community Care Act 1990, the countervailing tendencies behind political drives for quality were neatly recognized in the warning that pressures for training 'are likely to be internal (the desire to raise throughput and quality while holding or reducing costs) and external as a result of user empowerment and possible resource constraints/ competition' (DH 1993a: 17).

Not that debates about quality should be rejected as irrelevant or misleading. There are several instances of public good arising from quality concerns within the personal social services. Citizens' concerns about standards of service are drawn into the public arena, and channels are provided for earlier disclosure of unacceptable practices. Quality management has stimulated some instances of good practice involving practitioners, managers and service users (James *et al.* 1992: 2.4, 2.7). The ENQUIRE system of quality assurance developed by the King's Fund is a further example of quality management which offers a more positive experience. It includes the establishment of Quality Action Groups, where professionals, users, carers, volunteers and others work together to evaluate the impact of different types of service, and in which information is presented in a way that is more likely to facilitate participation by users (Richards and Heginbotham 1992). These positive developments demonstrate that good service standards are not only a matter of obtaining good resourcing.

Yet quality management has not been accepted wholesale in the personal social services. For example, market forces and quality control mechanisms do not always sit side by side comfortably. This is because sustaining quality management often entails a costly quasi-governmental apparatus. Thus, the government has been caught back-pedalling sharply on some aspects of quality control. Tim Yeo, a minister at the Department of Health, wrote in 1993 to directors of Social Services urging them to be less assiduous in registering day care services under the 1989 Children Act – a circular that caused acute anxiety and opposition from groups such as the Pre-School Playgroups Association in England and in Wales (DH 1993c). This was followed later in the same year by a letter from the same government department indicating that the government was considering softening the requirements which they introduced in 1984 for the regulation of residential homes for the elderly.

Since April 1993, the implementation of the new community care requirements has been marked by a significant number of bulk purchase agreements between Social Services departments and existing providers whereby, for instance, all housing association contracts to provide places in residential care for elderly persons are renewed *en bloc* without competitive tendering and sometimes at existing prices. This seems to be a euphemism for the abandonment (temporarily at least) of significant features of the 'excellence' culture.

However, despite the positive benefits of quality mechanisms, and the limited degree to which quality management has permeated the personal social services, reflection on the developments discussed in the first part of this chapter suggests that, on balance, the public good has not been demonstrably served. First, the promotion of partnership marks a major and worrying shift in relations between the state and the voluntary sector. Second, quality management in the personal social services is marked by a rational managerialism which may threaten the traditional professional role in welfare activity and lead to a marginalization of the service user. Finally, talk of customer satisfaction and choice often hinders rather than promotes real attention to the voice of the service user. We develop each of these themes in the remainder of this chapter.

PARTNERSHIP, THE STATE AND THE VOLUNTARY SECTOR

Partnership language has been used to describe collaborative arrangements between purchasers and providers, statutory and voluntary or private agencies, central government departments and local departments, agencies or projects, and between service providers and users. Our case in the following paragraphs is that partnership arrangements threaten to establish a disturbing shift in relationships between the state and the voluntary sector.

The split between local authorities as service purchasers and a wider spread of agencies as service providers opens the way for a disaggregation of services and creates for the state a newly sharpened problem of how diverse voluntary, statutory and private providers can be integrated within a common government strategy. In response to this, it appears clear that quality control measures have been viewed by the government as a mechanism for managing these fissile tendencies. The review of quality measures sponsored by the SSI partly recognized this in its conclusion that the community care reforms placed the tensions between central and local, diversity and uniformity under strain. 'Quality assurance can be seen as one mechanism to manage the tension between uniformity and diversity' (James *et al.* 1992: 2.7.2). The mechanism is not straightforward. For example, the Home Office is encouraging the development of partnerships between Probation Services and the independent sector. Yet, as Smith has pointed out: 'The paradox is that the more probation work is "hived off" or contracted out to the independent sector the harder it is to achieve the levels of accountability the Home Office now expects' (Smith *et al.* 1993: 34).

This tension is managed, in part, by government emphasis on a culture of working together through jointly negotiated and shared objectives – a strategy that we noted in our examination of the Home Office scrutiny of the voluntary sector. This is one of the main mechanisms used by the government to achieve an attempted depoliticization of quality. Partnership talk provides the rhetoric of depoliticization. The managerialism that we illustrate below provides the vehicle through which this depoliticization takes place.

Studies of informal and voluntary care in the 1970s provided a point of rejuvenation for sociological work (Offer 1990). Philip Abrams – the most influential contributor to what Offer has aptly termed 'the sociology of morals' – warned about the dangers that could occur when government or local authority departments colonized the voluntary sector (Abrams 1984).

Partnership policies pose precisely this risk. There are two associated dangers. First, the values of the state sector may penetrate the voluntary sector – the phenomenon of colonization. As a result, the major voluntary organizations – for example, the Children's Society, National Children's Home, Barnardo's and the major special needs housing associations – may come to dominate the sector, lose their independence and critical edge, and unwittingly elbow out the smaller voluntary organizations. The diversity of the voluntary sector could be lost. Second, with this radical shift in relations between the central state and the local state, the new commercially oriented private sector will prove best equipped to take advantage of the welfare economy, to the disadvantage of smaller voluntary groups.

A rather different solution to this development is proffered in a research report which received widespread attention for its author's proposal that voluntary organizations should have their charitable status withdrawn and split into either non-profit service providers or traditional campaigning and innovatory bodies (Knight 1993). In the first category would be the big voluntary agencies already bidding for contracts in the health, education and social services markets.

A similar risk exists in the sphere of influence of the Probation Service – the 'risk of a loss of genuine independence in the independent sector as it becomes colonized by a probation service concerned to demonstrate efficiency, effectiveness and economy in the achievement of its core tasks' (Smith et al. 1993: 34).

Valuable grass-roots work accomplished on developing partnership between service providers and service users (Marsh and Fisher 1992) will be vulnerable to the neutralizing tendencies of these macro-political developments.

THE NEW MANAGERIALISM

The work carried out through the SSI and the enormous growth of guidance documentation from government departments assume that a new and strong management style – both at senior and middle management levels – will provide the vehicle through which quality management will be made part of the warp and woof of services. This managerialism drives the aspirations for partnership and functions to increase supervision of professional staff. Managers in social work have traditionally been in a powerful position relative to the professionals who deliver social work services (Howe 1990), unlike medicine, where managers have until recently been relatively weak in relation to doctors. Social work managers almost always come up through the professional ranks and are not usually introduced from outside the profession as management specialists. This, paradoxically, may strengthen their position by giving them dual claims to both managerial and professional authority.

The introduction of quality measures into this equation creates an additional complication. The risk exists that social work management will be moulded into a rational straitjacket, which sets an impossible agenda for welfare agencies by requiring that the organizational core should control the periphery and that all staff should know what to do in all circumstances.

What consequences are likely to follow for the role of professionals in the personal social services? Those who received a social science education during the 1960s and 1970s probably accepted without too much question a critique of professional power – a critique of excessive claims and limited achievements, failures of professional responsibility, absence of professional neutrality, trampling on citizens' rights, lack of accountability and so on (Wilding 1982: 85–128). In the policy climate of the 1980s and 1990s when the government has said 'precisely so' to this battery of criticisms, there have been few commentators willing to ask whether a damaging transformation of professional roles may be occurring. The question is raised elsewhere in this book in relation to the NHS, by Kitchener and Whipp (chapter 9), and to university libraries, by Davies and Kirkpatrick (chapter 4).

There are three important related questions. First, has the widespread introduction of quality management weakened the professional role in social work, or is professional power in the process of remaking the role and retaining power? Second, are operational professional values – the actual values inherent in day-to-day practice – being transformed? Third, is there a shift towards either increased indeterminacy or greater rationality in the carrying out of the professional task?

It is too early to make firm generalizations regarding the impact of recent changes in public sector management on professional power, and rather contrary interim conclusions have been reached by different contributors to this book. There are, however, several straws in the wind that suggest social work professionals may be in a weaker position, and Pfeffer and Coote are in no doubt that 'one of the main effects of the changes has been to begin to limit the power of the "caring" professionals' (Pfeffer and Coote 1991: 12).

It seems plausible to suggest that a significant minority will become quasi managers through taking on a care management role, whereas the introduction of quasi-professional tasks will weaken professional influence. If the welfare task comprises market commodities, local authority social workers may become 'welfare traders' where, for example, debt collecting skills rival the importance of counselling.

The shift should probably not be overstated. The grass-roots reality of social work management and practice is probably rather different from the rhetoric of planning, analysis, standards, evaluation and so on. For example, in research currently being undertaken by the writer, a Principal Social Services Officer (PSSO) in a Social Services department child care team described her role in supervising social workers' assessment tasks in a way which underscores the ambiguity of assessment, discretionary judgements, and risk taking:

> Assessment is very broad . . . we use it to cover a lot of things. Everything is seen as needing assessment. Assessing risk and assessing service requirements are needed throughout. A senior practitioner may be involved. The concerns that decide this are maintaining independence, the protection of the social worker, and my judgements about people's expertise . . .
>
> The senior practitioner acts as a filtering system. The PSSO will use discretion, and the PSSO/senior practitioner relationship is very crucial. Senior practitioners are not meant to be line managers . . . a contentious issue but that's the structure.
>
> Each social worker and social work assistant has two-weekly diaried sessions with a senior practitioner . . . but they often have to be cancelled. Planned supervision sessions are constantly at risk because of the overriding claims of having to respond to crises.

This extract illustrates the way in which quality assurance can operate as a managerial device to ensure safety and risk protection (cf. Pendleton, chapter 10; Bull and Shaw 1992), and in reality departs from the managerial model officially advocated for work in child protection cases where social work is regularly appraised against objectives, standards and operational criteria (SSI 1993b; Pithouse 1987).

Managerialism is also growing rapidly in voluntary organizations. Line management structures are being adopted throughout the voluntary sector. While this may give voluntary organizations greater credibility with funders, it is likely to lead to a loss of volunteer involvement. The language of governance is in the air. Commercial models, strengthened by the publication of the Cadbury Report on the financial aspects of corporate governance (Cadbury 1992), are being transferred to voluntary organizations. Additional incentive has followed from the Charities Act 1992, which has heightened preoccupations with accountability among trustees of voluntary organizations (Charities Commissioners 1993).

Yet again, experience at the street level of service delivery is likely to be somewhat different, and be marked by management practices leading to indeterminate outcomes. Recent work in the supported housing field has shown how the negotiation of definitions of need at the point of referral, the brokerage of rule making and breaking during people's stay in projects, and the chronic ambiguity surrounding move-on as a goal of supported housing all underline the extent to which goals are, to a significant degree, socially constructed from the point of entry, through daily living in the scheme, to leaving such projects (Shaw and Williamson 1992).

Evidence for the 'distortion' of quality indicators at the level of day-to-day implementation can also be illustrated from the social work education field. A study of methods, skills and knowledge used by social work practice teachers to evaluate the competence of social work students demonstrated that practice teachers tended to rely on intuitive 'gut feelings' in assessing students. The extent to which underlying models of competency outcomes were shared by the interested parties was thrown into doubt by this research (Williamson and Jefferson 1989).

THE USER AT THE MARGINS

The new managerialism is not only rational and inimical to professional autonomy, but may lead to the marginalization of the consumer.

In one of the most thorough reviews of quality assurance practices in social services departments, the pessimistic conclusion was reached that:

Again and again we found definitions of Quality Assurance in use and evidence of standard setting which overwhelmingly represented the view of managers and professionals rather than those of service users. We found these systems had in general at least as much to do with achieving bureaucratic efficiency and good professional practice as improving outcomes for users.

(James *et al.* 1992: 2.1.3)

Unless a heavily cynical view is adopted, this potential marginalization of the user is not what was intended by the framers of the Children Act and the community care reforms. 'Both aim to replace systems dominated by professionals with approaches based on partnership with service users . . . The focus . . . has been on ways to make it easier for children, parents, users and carers to participate and be heard' (SSI 1992c: 5.2, 5.3).

There are several reasons why, at the very least, the jury must remain out on the impact of this alleged culture change in the personal social services. The central issues are the extent to which service users have real choice, the question of whether it will prove possible to reach a partnership of views with service users on appropriate and desirable outcomes, and the ambiguity and even conservatizing effects of drawing on user assessments of satisfaction as a basis for managing service developments.

Policies of choice for service users are not a guarantee of quality for many customers of the personal social services. There are three reasons for this. First, the sovereign consumer is a far cry from 'most dependent people whose needs come within the remit of the personal social services . . . (and who) are tied because of frailty, illness, fear, handicap, low income or habit to their local area' (Barclay 1982: 220). Second, welfare clients who believe they are in receipt of an unsatisfactory service often cannot choose an alternative because they are involuntary users. The emphasis on providing exit options for welfare clients frequently chooses to ignore this obvious reality. Third, this inability to shop around often may be compounded by the fact that the need for given services may be confined to a small number of people in the population and alternatives, therefore, will not be available in any given area. For example, specialist drugs and alcohol units or day care facilities for people with certain disabilities are likely to hold a monopoly in any one area. This may be exaggerated following the introduction of local government reform, leading to smaller unitary authorities.

There is already some evidence that the introduction of contracting may serve to increase the likelihood of this problem occurring. For example, early evidence from a study of the development of relationships between purchasers and providers through the process of contracting suggested that, in the majority of contracts the authors had studied, 'the existence of the contract did nothing to increase user choice of services'. A common reason for this was that 'services provided through the contract became the only service meeting a particular need for a particular client group in a particular locality' (Common and Flynn 1992: 35). Choice becomes a reality for purchasers, not for service users.

> Restructuring may have been advanced as a way of enhancing choice – and thereby quality – but in practice, in health and personal social services, the right to choose falls not to individual patients and clients, but to those who hold the purse strings.
>
> (Pfeffer and Coote 1991: 22)

Pfeffer and Coote point out that users are both citizens – interested in services as members of the community – and customers who are interested as individual users. They are also frequently providers of care. 'We are interested as citizens in planning and as customers in delivery' (*ibid.*: 26). If users are to exercise influence and choice then they must be empowered in both their customer and citizen roles.

The problematic nature of user choice has to be viewed in the light of difficulties in interpreting user judgements of services they receive. For example, it is well documented that user statements of satisfaction with a given service may have a conservatizing effect on policy developments. There is ample evidence that high satisfaction levels can co-exist with high problems or poor service (Shaw and Walton 1979; Shaw 1984; Ste Croix 1992).

There are several reasons why this may be so. For instance, service users may have low expectations of service quality arising from previous experience of these services or wider life experience. Also, when asked to suggest how existing services can be improved, they may find it difficult to grasp a wider framework of services than that with which they are already familiar. More generally, responses to service users' evaluations must take into account the impact of the power differential between users and providers. Satisfaction thus has a rather tenuous relationship to meeting needs. 'Meeting needs is not the same as satisfying tastes or wants' (Pfeffer and Coote 1991: 13).

It may appear trite to observe that a person's satisfaction with the outcomes of a service will depend on their prior assumptions regarding the aims of a service. Yet we still have limited evidence regarding the kinds of criterion which citizens will adopt in appraising a service. In a recent evaluation of supported housing schemes, debate about move-on, integration into the community and policies of normalization underlay many of the attempts by participants to make sense of their daily and working lives (Shaw and Williamson 1992). For example, in one housing scheme for people with learning difficulties, a woman had recently left and was now living in a nearby local authority housing development, newly married to a partner who also had learning difficulties. When scheme staff and others were asked what they would regard as a measure of success or failure, this event was often raised: 'I don't know whether they've settled where they are now . . . We may have made a mistake, we altered her life completely, we relieved her of too much.' This committee member's doubt was expressed still more strongly by a staff member who cited the incident as an example of where the home had failed. Both of these respondents interpreted this particular outcome in a negative light because they believed the project's goal was the provision of a permanent home. However, another staff member, who was emphatic that the project should aim to provide rehabilitation to permanent housing, quoted the same example as evidence of where they were succeeding.

The implications are clear. Instances of people moving out of the project were interpreted as quite contrary evidence for success or failure depending on the views that each person held regarding project aims.

A rational, actuarial approach to performance measures of outcomes, based on an assumption of shared service objectives, is also at risk from processes of lay theorizing and policy making. Such processes appear to be part of the way both service employees and users typically endeavour to make sense of guidance from above (Bull and Shaw 1992).

Normalization polices in supported housing schemes provide an illustration of this process of lay policy construction. A staff member in a scheme providing for people with learning disabilities was asked about the aims of her project:

'Normalization . . . as far as you can go. For example, I say "Go and change your shirt", and John complains, "Don't talk like that", and I say, "It's normalization, John". He asks me to shave him and I tell him to shave himself . . . he wanted me to insert pessaries for his haemorrhoids!'

Government and academic statements of normalization policies are relatively elaborate, and based on general values and statements. In contrast, street-level staff fashion ways in which guidance from above can be made understandable and feasible in day-to-day work.

This brief discussion of service outcomes and day-to-day policy implementation illustrates that agreed practices of care, support and management over matters as central as major house rules or as apparently mundane as gardening are kept in place as the uncertain outcomes of negotiated realities between residents, paid employees, outside professionals in housing or welfare networks, and purse-holders from provider agencies and organizations.

CONCLUSION

We have argued that the implementation of a culture of quality within the personal social services is likely to remain at risk because it does not recognize the contingent, socially negotiated characteristics of much street-level management practice. A rational, quality-control model of management demands major behavioural changes on the part of social workers. The difficulties of these changes tend to be underestimated and their desirability taken for granted. The service user can easily become marginalized. Quality culture may not increase customer choice, and the apparent liberal values behind advocacy of user satisfaction as a criterion of quality compete with several inbuilt tendencies to conservatism. Quality cultures typically fail to recognize the power differentials between providers and users.

Yet the rhetoric of quality management has some way to go before it burns out. It provides a convenient catch-all forum within which competitive political, managerial and professional interests are played out. It will continue to function as one of the central managerially led mechanisms in an attempt to unify social service provision under a disaggregated, purchaser/provider split, and it will continue to provide an impetus for the partially achieved shift in relations between the state and the voluntary sector.

Pfeffer and Coote (1991) advocate an alternative approach to defining and assuring quality, designed to achieve common goals and meet individual needs – a democratic approach, which acknowledges the differences between commerce and welfare. Such an approach, they believe, must pursue equitable opportunities for all, a responsiveness to individual needs, and a commitment to making the public more powerful, both as citizens and as customers.

Tensions between these goals will remain, for reasons we have discussed in the later part of this chapter. It is our conviction that an undue preoccupation with quality process is not the way forward, but rather a determination to place quality outcomes centre stage. Gatehouse has suggested six tests of whether quality has been achieved. Does the service meet the needs of the individual client or carer? Are services available to people irrespective of location, race, gender, belief or ability to pay? Are consumers satisfied and is their distress or difficulty reduced? Are the expectations of consumers, providers and tax payers satisfied? Are no more resources than necessary used to achieve the stated aim? (Gatehouse 1992). Squaring the circle of these tests, of relevance, equity, effectiveness, social acceptability and efficiency will never prove easy. But it is the real quality agenda facing the personal social services.

REFERENCES

Abrams, P. (1984) 'Realities of neighbourhood care', *Policy and Politics* 12: 413–29.
Audit Commission (1986) *Making a Reality of Community Care*, London: HMSO.

Barclay, P. (1982) *Social Workers: Their Roles and Tasks*, London: Bedford Square Press.

British Standards Institution (1993) Correspondence.

Bull, R. and Shaw, I. (1992) 'Constructing causal accounts in social work', *Sociology* 26: 635–49.

Cadbury, A. (1992) *Report of the Committee on the Financial Aspects of Corporate Governance*, London: Gee.

Central Council for Education and Training in Social Work (1991) *Rules and Requirements for the Diploma in Social Work*, London: CCETSW.

Central Council for Education and Training in Social Work (1992) *Setting Quality Standards for Residential Child Care*, London: CCETSW.

Central Council for Education and Training in Social Work (1995) *Requirements for Qualification in Social Work*, London: CCETSW.

Charities Commissioners (1993) *Charities: The New Law*, London: Charity Commissioners for England and Wales.

Common, R. and Flynn, N. (1992) *Contracting for Care*, York: Joseph Rowntree.

Department of Health (1991) *Working with Child Sexual Abuse*, London: Department of Health.

Department of Health (1993a) *Training for the Future*, London: HMSO.

Department of Health (1993b) *Policy and Financial Management Review of the Central Council for Education and Training in Social Work*, London: Department of Health.

Department of Health (1993c) *The Children Act and Day Care for Young Children: Registration*, LAC (93)1, London: Department of Health.

Gatehouse, G. (1992) 'Ensuring quality in the new culture', in Allen, I. (ed.), *Purchasing and Providing Social Services in the 1990's*, London: PSSI.

HMSO (1989) *Caring For People: Community Care in the Next Decade and Beyond*, London: HMSO.

Home Office (1990) *Efficiency Scrutiny of Government Funding of the Voluntary Sector*, London: HMSO.

Home Office (1992a) *Partnership in Dealing with Offenders in the Community*, London: Home Office.

Home Office (1992b) *Three Year Plan: 1993–1996*, London: Home Office.

Home Office (1992c) *National Standards for the Supervision of Offenders in the Community*, London: Home Office.

Home Office (1994) *Three Year Plan for the Probation Service 1994–1997*, London: Home Office.

Housing Corporation (1989) *Performance Expectations*, London: Housing Corporation.

Housing Corporation (1992a) *Performance Criteria*, London: Housing Corporation.

Housing Corporation (1992b) *Tenant Participation Strategy*, London: Housing Corporation.

Housing for Wales (1993a) *Making it Work: A Guide to Tenant Participation for Housing Associations*, Cardiff: Housing for Wales.

Housing for Wales (1993b) *Measuring Tenant Satisfaction*, Cardiff: Housing for Wales.

Howe, D. (1990) 'Knowledge, power and the shape of social work practice' in Davies, M. (ed.), *The Sociology of Social Work*, London: Routledge, 202–20.

James, A., Brooks, T. and Towell, D. (1992) *Committed to Quality: Quality Assurance in Social Services Departments*, London: HMSO.

Knight, B. (1993) *Voluntary Action*, London: CENTRIS.

Marsh, P. and Fisher, M. (1992) *Good Intentions: Developing Partnership in Social Services*, York: Joseph Rowntree.

National Audit Office (1989) *Control and Management of the Probation Service in England and Wales*, London: HMSO.

National Federation of Housing Associations (1987) *Standards for Housing Management*, London: NFHA.

Offer, J. (1990) 'The Sociology of Welfare', in Davies, M. (ed.), *The Sociology of Social Work*, London: Routledge.

Pfeffer, N. and Coote, A. (1991) *Is Quality Good for You? A Critical Review of Quality Assurance in Welfare Services*, London: Institute for Public Policy Research.

Pithouse, A. (1987) *Social Work: The Social Organisation of an Invisible Trade* Aldershot: Avebury.

Richards, H. and Heginbotham, C. (1992) *ENQUIRE: Quality Assurance through Observation of Service Delivery*, London: King's Fund College.

Shaw, I. (1984) 'Consumer evaluations of the personal social services', *British Journal of Social Work* 14: 277–84.

Shaw, I. and Williamson, H. (1992) *Management and Welfare: Evaluation of Special Needs Housing in Wales*, Cardiff: Housing for Wales.

Shaw, I. and Walton, R. (1979) 'Transitions to residence in homes for the elderly', in Harris, D. and Hyland, J. (eds), *Rights in Residence*, London: Residential Care Association.

Smith, D. Paylor, I. and Mitchell, P. (1993) 'Partnerships between the independent sector and the probation service', *Howard Journal* 32: 25–39.

Social Services Inspectorate (1989) *Homes are for Living In*, London: HMSO.

Social Services Inspectorate (1990a) *Inspecting Home Care Services*, London: HMSO.

Social Services Inspectorate (1990b) *Guidance on Standards for Residential Homes for People with a Physical Disability*, London: HMSO.

Social Services Inspectorate (1991a) *Care Management and Assessment: Practitioner's Guide*, London: Department of Health.

Social Services Inspectorate (1991b) *Care Management and Assessment: Manager's Guide*, London: Department of Health.

Social Services Inspectorate (1992a) *Guidance on Standards for the Residential Care Needs of People with Specific Mental Health Needs*, London: HMSO.

Social Services Inspectorate (1992b) *Guidance on Standards for the Residential Care Needs of People with Learning Disabilities/Mental Handicap*, London: HMSO.

Social Services Inspectorate (1992c) *Concern for Quality: The First Annual Report of the Chief Inspector, Social Services Inspectorate 1991–1992*, London: HMSO.

Social Services Inspectorate (1993a) *Raising the Standard: Second Annual Report of the Chief Inspector, Social Services Inspectorate*, London: HMSO.

Social Services Inspectorate (1993b) *Evaluating Performance in Child Protection*, London: HMSO.

Ste Croix, de, R. (1992) *Can Quality be Assured in an Uncertain World?*, Bristol: School of Advanced Urban Studies.

Utting, W. (1991) *Children in the Public Care*, London: HMSO.

Welsh Office (nd) *Welsh Office Funding of the Voluntary Sector: A Strategic Statement*, Cardiff: Welsh Office.

Wilding, P. (1982) *Professional Power and Social Welfare*, London: Routledge.

Williamson, H. and Jefferson, R. (1989) *Assessment of Practice – A Perennial Concern?*, Cardiff: University of Wales.

Chapter 7

Quality, competition and contracts in general practice fundholding

Robert Harris

INTRODUCTION

The aim of this chapter is to discuss 'quality' in the context of the restructuring of the British National Health Service (NHS) from an integrated service to a service based on contracts. From its birth in 1948 to the beginning of the 1990s, the NHS was an integrated service financed mainly by general taxation which provided health care to patients mainly through publicly owned and managed providers. This model was abandoned early in the 1990s in favour of a model based on contract and competition.

This restructuring of the NHS, which is part of a Europe-wide political project of disengagement from the commitments of the welfare state and towards a 'contract' or 'enabling' state, was first presented as government policy in the White Paper *Working for Patients* in 1989 (Department of Health *et al.* 1989). The 'linchpin' (Paton 1990) of the proposals in the White Paper is the idea of internal markets in health care. Internal markets were to be created in the NHS by distinguishing between organizations, or parts of organizations, which purchased health care and those which provided it. The underlying argument of the White Paper is that competition between health-care providers for the custom of purchasers will bring greater efficiency in the use of NHS resources and improvements in the quality of service to patients.

Restructuring the hospital and community services (HCHS) involved splitting the parts which bought services from the parts which provided them. These latter parts remained 'directly managed' by purchasing parts unless, and until, they opted for 'independence' as NHS trusts which they have been encouraged to do by government. A wide range of health services is involved, including secondary and tertiary hospital care, ambulance services and community-based nursing and associated medical services.

Primary medical care was restructured by providing general practices, which met the required criteria, with the option of a new form of general practice in the NHS. Under this form of practice, general practices with lists of 7,000 or more registered patients can apply for practice budgets with which to purchase a defined range of hospital and community health services, prescribed drugs and practice staff. The hospital services include 'cold surgery', or elective surgical procedures, outpatient services and diagnostic investigation of patients and specimens.

Fundholders may purchase these services from NHS providers and/or the private sector, in the UK or outside it. GP fundholders are permitted to spend money from one budget head (e.g. hospital services) in other areas. In addition, any net savings they make on their total budget can be reinvested in developing the services offered by the practice. Savings cannot be retained as income. Non-fundholding general practices are bound by the contracts set by their parent purchasing or 'commissioning' authority. Their freedom to refer is constrained by contracts in whose making they have very little say.

While fundholding provides incentives for GPs to search for less costly forms of care for their patients in order to make savings, the search for alternatives is to take place in a market in which there is competition between general practices for patients. Practices which attract most patients receive the most money (DH et al. 1989: 48: 6.2): 'the money follows the patient'. This, it is argued, ensures that fundholders have incentives to become more efficient at delivering 'high quality, cost-effective care' to their patients, relative to competitors, in order to attract and keep patients (DH et al. 1989: 5). Competition between general practices for patients, who are free to choose another practice, is, therefore, the guarantor of 'quality' in that it prevents GP fundholders from making savings at the cost of a deteriorating service. In a similar vein, Saltman and Von Otter argue that the freedom of choice of doctor, 'transforms the patient into an agent of quality control at the heart of the resource allocation process' (Saltman and Von Otter 1992: 126).

Clearly, within this discourse, patients are construed as active, well-informed and rational consumers of health care, who need only be 'enabled' or 'empowered' by the state to exercise their right to choose one general practice over another. Thus, as part of the 1989 reforms of the NHS, the right to change their GP, which patients have always had within the NHS, has been made easier to exercise by removing the necessity for patients contemplating a change to inform their existing GP of their intentions. It is a classic liberal measure of market deregulation.

However, the idea of consumer sovereignty in health care has to contend with the fact that, in the internal market, health care is bought on behalf of patients, or consumers, by NHS purchasers making contracts with providers. To this extent, patients follow contracts. Contracts include a variety of 'quality' standards to be met by the provider. These standards are examined from the point of view of monitoring and modifying the performance of providers in relation to the standards set. Purchasers and providers negotiate different types of contract, each of which carries different 'perverse' incentives. The problems of monitoring the effects of these incentives on the 'quality' of the service is also discussed.

It is argued that the assurance of 'quality' by these means contains formidable and underestimated problems arising, in part, from inherent 'information deficits' between providers and purchasers, and also from lego-administrative features of general practice which prevent its corporate or general management and hence prevent an 'order' from being imposed within it. This theme is developed through a discussion of the GP contract paying particular attention to the 'out of hours responsibility' for which it provides. It is argued that the standardization and measurement of 'quality' – the bureaucratization of 'quality' – through contracts can occur only at the expense of this universalist feature of the NHS with consequent detrimental effects on the 'quality' of people's lives.

DEFINING 'QUALITY'

As the Welsh Office and the NHS Directorate acknowledge, ' "quality" can mean different things to different people' (Welsh Office, NHS (D) 1990: 10). Diverse and possibly conflicting definitions of 'quality' as in, for example, 'a quality health service', render management in terms of 'quality' impossible. 'Quality' can only become an object of management if it is defined in terms of sets of standardized procedures which, ideally, embrace everything that everyone does in the organization (Welsh Office, NHS (D) 1990). The 'quality' of a service, as a whole or in its parts, is inferred from measurements of individual performance in relation to the standards. By these means, 'quality' is reduced to individual performance and rendered quantifiable. Thus, 'quality' becomes a means by which the behaviour of individuals in organizations is disciplined and manipulated by management. The pursuit of 'quality' by these means is a form of power in the sense that it constrains what can and cannot be said about 'quality'.

For example, in their discussion of 'quality' in the health service, Harrison *et al.* argue that 'quality', although used in a variety of ways, is 'closely related' to the concept of 'effectiveness' (Harrison *et al.* 1992: 118). They provide, as an example, the surgeon who makes fewer mistakes than an 'average surgeon'. 'The high-quality surgeon is slightly more effective in a slightly higher proportion of similar cases' (*ibid.*: 118). Another of their examples is the receptionist who manages 'to help and/or reassure 80 per cent' of the people who present themselves at the desk, while the 'average receptionist' manages to help and/or reassure 70 per cent.

The problem with this way of conceptualizing 'quality' is that it says nothing about the kind, or 'quality', of mistakes surgeons and others may make, or of the kind, or 'quality', of help and/or reassurance offered by individual receptionists. Some mistakes are more serious than others, and some help and/or reassurance is more effective than others. A surgeon may make a small number of large mistakes or a large number of smaller mistakes. A receptionist might help and/or reassure, for example, only 40 per cent of the people s/he sees, but the help and/or reassurance s/he provides might be much more helpful to the people helped than that provided by colleagues who help and/or reassure 80 per cent of the people. Hunter and his colleagues are attempting to derive measures of 'quality' from measures of quantity. The implication of their conceptualization is that 'quality' means compliance with standardized ways of doing things. For example, the quality of reception might be judged on the basis of the extent to which receptionists comply with given standards of dress, address, the length of the exchange with customers and its closure.

To get round this difficulty, Harrison and his colleagues define 'quality' as denoting, 'how appropriately a particular feature of the care process is carried out'. The 'appropriateness' of care is determined by the extent to which 'it meets the needs and wishes of the consumer' which they refer to as 'fitness of purpose'. This, they say, 'opens up the question of *whose* purposes are to count, and since the mid-1980s much of the debate on quality (at least in Britain) has been concerned with enhancing the influence of the consumer' (Harrison *et al.* 1992: 119). However, while, during the 1980s, 'a large number of consumerist initiatives had been spawned . . . many of them had a superficial "charm school" air about them, and few appeared either to empower the consumer with genuine choice or to trespass on the sacred turf of doctors' discretion and clinical freedom' (*ibid.*: 125).

As I have pointed out, the 'needs and wishes of the consumer of health care' are not registered directly in the internal market (even assuming that we know what we need when we are ill, and that our wishes and our needs are not incompatible) but are mediated through NHS purchasers, including GP fundholders making contracts with providers.

SETTING 'QUALITY' STANDARDS IN CONTRACTS: THE POLITICAL MANAGEMENT OF THE TRANSITION TO THE MARKET

In the internal market, GP fundholders make contracts with health-care providers for specified services to be provided to patients, at agreed prices, over a given period, usually a year. Apart from 'extra contractual referrals', patients can only be provided with the range and amount of services contracted for. If the amount of a service contracted for on their behalf is delivered before the end of the contractual period, patients either wait until the service becomes available to them through a subsequent round of contracts, or obtain the service, on their own behalf, from the private sector unless the practice is able and willing to overspend its budget.

During 1990–1, making contracts was an entirely new activity for general practice. GPs in the 'old' NHS defined the health-care needs of individual patients, as they presented at their surgeries or in their homes, and treated or referred them within the NHS as they deemed 'appropriate' in the circumstances. Since making and monitoring contracts is a highly technical area with which GPs had not the slightest familiarity, the potential for a deterioration of 'quality' through a disruption in the flow of services to patients and patients to services, when the new system was put into 'contract mode' was, to say the least, very high. In the event, services were not disrupted. What were the reasons for this?

First, during the 1990–1 preparatory year, the Welsh Office, like the Department of Health in England, impressed upon the new NHS purchasers, including fundholders, the need to maintain a 'steady state' in the service. In practice, this meant that purchasers were encouraged to obtain more or less the same volume and mix of hospital services from the same providers as they had the previous year but to obtain them under contract, or in the 'contract mode'.

The preferred form of contract, at this stage, was the block contract. Under block contracts the provider agrees to provide a defined range of services for a given sum, usually payable in twelve equal monthly instalments. The main advantage of these contracts is that their information requirements are minimal and, therefore, such contracts were more common at the outset of fundholding when management information systems (MISs) were underdeveloped. Their disadvantages are that purchasers do not know the number and value of treatments they actually receive and, hence, they have an incentive to 'over-refer'; providers will not receive extra funding if the volume of activity increases above the anticipated workload and, therefore, have an incentive to 'undertreat'. These are known as 'perverse' incentives. Both over-referral and undertreatment imply that the 'quality' of the service is less than it could or should be. While undertreatment/overtreatment by hospitals can, in principle, be monitored by GP fundholders, under/over-referral requires self-monitoring within practices since patients do not, by definition, know what is wrong with them and how it should be treated and, therefore, they cannot act as their own monitoring agents. The problems of monitoring are discussed in the next section.

Second, contract negotiations occurred within an established social context, or network, in which participants usually already knew at least some others through personal or working relationships and, not infrequently, both. The people involved – GPs and practice managers, hospital managers and consultants, Family Health Service Authority (FHSA) and District Health Authority (DHA) officers – had often developed working relationships over many years. Frequently, they shared a common commitment to the maintenance and development of 'local services' and the 'local hospital'. While GPs wanted to improve the quality of care through their contracts with providers, they did not wish to undermine their local hospital's viability or damage their relationships with local consultants on whom they had to continue to depend for non-fundholding work such as emergency admissions. Glennerster *et al.* report similar findings for England (Glennerster *et al.* 1992).

Third, the Welsh Office had provided fundholders with a variety of sample agreements, originally designed by Peat Marwick, the international management consultants for Trent Regional Health Authority, which fundholders might use, modifying them where necessary. These agreements covered, *inter alia*, services contracted for, where services were to be provided, volume and mix, price, procedures for billing and payment, substance of communications between practice, provider and patient, and a number of quality standards. Use of this 'model agreement' as the basis for the usual block contracts meant that there was considerable standardization in the early contracts set in Wales.

Finally, the Welsh Office played a consensus-building role through the meaning it gave to contracts. Unlike contracts in the private sector, the contracts between NHS purchasers and providers are not legally binding. Officially, they may be referred to not as 'contracts' at all, but as 'service agreements', and are regarded 'above all (as reflecting) the developing new *relationship* between the primary and secondary care sectors which will for some years to come be evolutionary and dynamic owned and developed by the NHS and GP fundholders' (Welsh Office 1992: 2.1.2). Parties to these agreements were bound to them, and to each other, by joint ownership. As joint owners each had a responsibility to see that the other gained from them. Welsh Office officials spoke of reaching 'win-win' outcomes from contract negotiations. This approach to contracts assumes and represents the figure of economic man, rationally pursuing his own self-interest and securing, thereby, the interests of all. As long as parties to buying and selling act rationally, there will be no losers. The ideological effects of this are clear. 'The developing new relationship between primary and secondary care' in the NHS is reflected in the contracts which are made between them. Through these contracts both sides win. Contracts reflect the fact that the NHS, in its primary and secondary care, is a winner.

While these factors contributed to the smoothness of the transition to 'contract mode', they were not, of course, fixed. 'Steady state' slipped into 'phased change'; more cost-and-volume contracts were made; relations with 'local' hospitals, always a 'negotiated order', became increasingly subject to economic considerations with subsequent effects on the 'win-win' ideology.

Cost-and-volume contracts specify the number of cases to be treated during the contracted period, at what cost, and the charge for additional cases, 'marginal costs'. These demand more information than block contracts and are most suitable where there is a regular pattern of referral to a provider unit. Under these contracts, providers have an incentive to 'over-treat' and purchasers an incentive to 'under-refer' both of which affect 'quality'.

A third kind of contract is the cost-per-case contract. Under these contracts, purchasers are charged separately for each item of service. Purchasers may be able to obtain services at marginal cost by utilizing providers' spare capacity. However, an effect of purchasers holding back substantial sums in the hope of obtaining services at low marginal costs is that the cost of services to other purchasers would rise and providers would be destabilized. In general, block contracts benefit hospitals most and GP fundholders least. Cost-per-case contracts benefit

GP fundholders most and hospitals least. Cost and volume contracts are negotiated compromises between these competing positions.

From the point of view of GPs, the 'quality' standards in contracts amount to 'good practice'. However, not only are the standards unenforceable in the sense of constituting legally binding contractual obligations on the part of provider units, but many of them are qualified by such phrases as 'where appropriate', 'where possible', 'in normal circumstances' and the like. These qualifiers relate to notions of reasonable behaviour in the circumstances obtaining at the time. Here are some examples:

> The unit will inform the patient of the date of an inpatient or day case admission with a minimum of two weeks notice *where possible*.

> On admission, any patient of the Practice should not wait an *unreasonable* period before being accommodated in a bed. Medical and nursing assessment should similarly take place *soon* after admission.

> All cases will be seen by the consultant or senior registrar at least once during an inpatient stay (*in normal circumstances*).
> (Extracted from more than one contract. Emphasis added)

Such formulations of standards create a problem for purchasers arising from their dependency upon providers' accounts of the circumstances. Purchasers have no independent way of validating the accuracy of the information they are given. There is an inherent 'information deficit' between providers and purchasers which, except in the gravest cases, cannot be rectified. To this extent, providers are in a notably more advantageous position than GP fundholders should the 'quality' of service received by their patients ever become an issue between them.

Other standards are more precise. For example:

> The patient and his/her relative/carer will be informed with *at least 8 hours'* notice of time of discharge.

> The practice will be informed *within 5 working days* of the patient's discharge.

> The unit will supply a *minimum of 7 days' supply* of take home drugs and dressings. Where discharge occurs over a bank holiday the supply will always cover the bank holiday.
> (Extracted from more than one contract. Emphasis added)

However, for 'quality' to become more than a description of 'good practice' in unenforceable 'service agreements', contracts have to be monitored and means of dealing with underachievement of 'quality' objectives have to be created. The relations of power between GPs, hospital consultants, NHS managers and patients in the internal market may be traced through an analysis of these 'quality' monitoring and assuring sets of practices.

MONITORING 'QUALITY' STANDARDS IN CONTRACTS

As a general point about monitoring, it seems evident that the more general the 'quality' standard in contracts, the more difficult it is for purchasers and providers to monitor the extent to which the standard has been achieved. For example, monitoring the extent to which 'the optimum clinical outcome' has been achieved in particular cases, and across cases as a whole, is much more difficult than monitoring the rate of compliance with standards relating to the timing and content of discharge reports from consultants. Nevertheless, there are formidable problems not only in monitoring the simplest of these standards but in creating the means of rectifying matters when standards are deemed not to have been met. For example, purchasers are not in a position directly to monitor providers' performance in respect of standards which relate to issues of timing in relation to the treatment of patients. In order to find out such matters as what proportion of their patients actually had eight hours' notice of discharge and the like, purchasers must ask the patients or be told by the hospital. As GPs, GP fundholders are clearly in a somewhat better position to do this than District Health Authorities (DHAs) since they have direct contact with patients both before and after an inpatient, outpatient or day-case episode. However, there are two problems here.

First, by no means all episodes are followed by a consultation with the GP. Second, questioning the patients on a number of specific details of their contact with the hospital (how much notice of admission did you get, how long did you wait before being allocated a bed, were you kept informed, etc.?) is a time-consuming addition to the more clinical kinds of questioning and examinations which are, arguably, more proper to GP follow-up contacts with patients. Moreover, the results of such interviews between individual GPs in a practice and individual patients would require centralized collation and analysis which fundholding general practices are not, as yet, set up to do.

GP fundholders can only be told by the hospital if the hospital knows. There are no technical reasons why MISs in hospitals could not collect and provide information of hospital performance against these kinds of 'quality' standards, eventually. Moreover, there are obvious commercial reasons for doing/not doing so. For example, a hospital which kept records of hours of notice of discharge given to patients, might wish to publicize its performance if it had hit some target set by itself or others.

However, for information to be of use, fundholders need to know the performance of the hospital in relation to *their* patients, not patients as a whole. In order to provide this information, hospitals must not only have the MISs which can trace individual patients by referrer, but must produce two sets of performance data, one in respect of non-fundholders and the other in respect of fundholders. Such data, if it existed, would relate to the highly contentious and politicized issue of equity of access and treatment as between the patients of fundholders and non-fundholders. The more successful fundholders were shown to be in purchasing a higher 'quality' of care for their patients (as measured by these standards), compared with other NHS purchasers, the more fund-holding could be criticized for creating a two-tier service. If fundholding were less or no more successful it could be regarded as failing.

Perhaps of greater importance than the difficulties of monitoring specific 'quality' standards is the difficulty of monitoring for the effects of the incentives created by different kinds of contract: the incentive for hospitals to 'undertreat' and for GPs to 'over-refer' under block con-tracts, and for hospitals to 'overtreat' and for GPs to 'under-refer' under cost-and-volume contracts, as mentioned in the previous section.

The incentive to 'undertreat' arises from the fact that, under block contracts, the provider receives the same payment whatever level of diagnostic investigation and active treatment is performed on patients. Thus, there is an economic incentive for questions to be asked, from somewhere in the provider organization, concerning the 'necessity' for the next additional test or treatment. While GP fundholding purchasers are aware of this possibility, in monitoring for it they must rely upon the provider for the information which such *clinical* monitoring implies and, of course, they must have the necessary expertise to be able to interpret the information provided. In practice, the problems of block contracts become increasingly academic as GP fundholders make more cost-and-volume and cost-per-case contracts.

Under cost-and-volume contracts there is an incentive for hospitals to 'overtreat' since they gain no financial benefit from providing a total volume of service less than the volume contracted for. They may, in fact, gain financially from exceeding the volume contracted for in so far as purchasers may be in a position to pay for the extra services provided. Moreover, a provider which delivers its volumes contracted for before the end of the contractual period is in a position to sell its spare capacity at discounted prices to purchasers with money still to spend. The more successful providers are at this, the greater their profitability. This explains the bizarre state of affairs in which patients whose health care is bought by DHAs are not admitted to hospital while patients whose health care is bought by GP fundholders, and whose needs are no greater, are. The same problems of monitoring by GP fundholders, arising from the 'information deficit', occur here as under block contracts.

Clinical monitoring by GP fundholders is clearly not as simple a matter as has recently been implied by Le Grand, who argues that GP fundholders 'have the best information concerning the quality of care: they can assess a patient's health before he or she goes into hospital and reassess it when he or she comes out' (Le Grand 1994: 5). Before-and-after clinical assessments by GPs cannot, except in extreme cases which, by definition, are rare, tell GPs whether or not something was not done when, perhaps, it should have been done (undertreatment) or whether something was done when, perhaps, it should not have been (over-treatment). By 'perhaps' I mean to suggest that such decisions are rarely clear-cut and the party with the most information (the provider in this case) is in a better position than the purchaser to get its version of events accepted as the most reliable.

All of this indicates formidable problems in monitoring even the simplest standards of 'quality' set by GP fundholders in their contracts. Precision and measurability are seldom built into them, and where they are, the practical difficulties of measurement and interpretation are substantial and underestimated.

However, the 'quality' issue is not simply, or even primarily, technical and to be dealt with through such means as marketing in the NHS (Sheaff 1991). The conceptualization of 'quality' as conformance with norms policed through various forms of monitoring and 'feedback mechanisms' can take effect within institutions, whilst 'quality' in some other sense(s), deteriorates as a result of those effects. The 'quality' of a health service could, after all, be evaluated from within discourses entirely different from those within which 'quality' is bureaucratized as an effect of a desire to assure it.

GP FUNDHOLDING, COMPETITION AND THE GP CONTRACT

In the academic literature on health services, the 'politics of health' is most often conceptualized in terms of a struggle between the contending interests of health professionals, especially doctors, and a rising group of managers (the classic statement is Alford 1975). Whilst the existence of another interest – the patient's – is recognized, this interest is increasingly represented as a 'consumer interest'. Other forms of representation of the patient interest have to contend with this. For example, the representation of the patient interest as a political interest, within the discourse of consumerism, restricts the politics of health to struggles over the rights of individual patients as consumers of health care.

However, the 'quality' of a health service may not rest upon the rights individuals possess whilst consuming it but, rather, from the security it provides them when not consuming it. In the NHS, this security has its lego-administrative basis in the contract that the GPs who are principals hold with their FHSAs. Under their contract, each individual GP has, among other obligations, a twenty-four-hour responsibility to provide health care as 'appropriate' to each of the named patients on her or his list. The contract implies a relationship between government, GP and citizen in which the government agrees to meet the cost of the health care deemed 'appropriate' by the GP for the individuals for whom s/he is responsible.

While their contract brings many benefits to GPs (it is, after all, the basis not only of their autonomy at the workplace, but of their remuneration, which remains high relative to other groups of professional workers), it also gives the patient the benefits of a named individual, uniquely responsible, both professionally and legally, for dealing with her or his health-care needs as and when 'appropriate' to that patient in those circumstances for twenty-four hours of every day of their lives. The benefits of this for the 'quality' of patients' lives cannot, in my view, be lightly dismissed and it should also be noted that no marketeer has suggested that such a service could be provided for *everyone* through the market.

The GP contract impedes the development of competition between general practices and, hence, the improvement of 'quality' through increased competition which is the basis of the reforms, since it prevents the imposition of any particular order within general practice. However, since competition between general practices would be accompanied by 'creamskimming' or 'adverse risk selection' (Wynand *et al.* 1992), it would reduce the 'quality' of the service for members of those groups which were not competed for, i.e. the old, the handicapped and the less favoured classes more generally, whose multiple morbidities are expensive to treat and difficult to prevent within the context of widening social inequalities.

The incentive to make savings, or the necessity to break even, provides the grounds for the emplacement of 'utilization controls', which may or may not be described as 'quality' controls, within fundholding general practice. Such controls attempt to standardize rates of referral, prescribing and other areas of work between the GPs. However, this form of order cannot be imposed within general practices since there is no agency, internal or external, with the necessary authoritative resources. The contract makes all GPs who are principals self-governing equals.

The GP contract does not fit GP fundholding and GP fundholding does not fit the GP contract. So what happens next? The history of the 'managed care' movement in the USA, which provided the models for GP fundholding in the form of Health Maintenance and Preferred Provider Organizations, suggests that the growth of such 'health-care delivery systems' depends upon the availability of doctors prepared, for whatever reason, to become salaried employees, working under contracts which specify the 'utilization controls' necessary for these organizations to remain in business. 'Managed care' proletarianizes doctors (McKinley and Arches 1985). As yet, there is not a supply of doctors waiting to be proletarianized in the UK where well over 90 per cent of GPs are principals.

However, the proportion is not fixed and neither is the contract. GPs might opt out of their contract if attractive alternative forms of practice developed. GPs themselves, at least GPs who are principals, are known to be unhappy about 'the twenty-four-hour responsibility' clause in their contracts and, according to a recent BMA survey, only 38 per cent of GPs believe that 'it should remain an integral part of general practice'. Among younger GPs, the proportion is even less. Only 31 per cent of GPs under thirty agreed that it should remain while 61 per cent believed it to be an 'outdated idea'. Overall, 82 per cent of GPs believed that it should be possible to opt out of the responsibility (BMA 1992: 37–8).

GPs who opted out could not be principals as presently defined. They could, however, be salaried employees of GPs who are principals. That is, they could become proletarianized with their responsibilities specified in their contract of employment. Existing responsibility for patients would, as a consequence, shift from individual GPs to a corporate body, namely the practice. The practice, not individual GPs, would define where work was to be done, what the task consists of and what are necessary/unnecessary tasks, as 'appropriate' (McKinley and Arches 1985: 161).

If there are possibilities for the growth of this form of salaried service on the supply side, what about the demand side? At present, the largest fundholding practices have around 20,000–22,000 patients. In the USA, the largest Health Maintenance Organization has 500,000 patients. The advantage in growth in fundholding is that the greater the number of patients, the less the budget is affected by unanticipated and costly expenditures. Financial planning is made more robust. Until now, general practices have grown larger by becoming bigger partnerships. Taking on more partners in fundholding practices is irrational since the practice would not control their contract. Under fundholding, practices are more likely to grow by employing more doctors. This will create a salaried service with 'physician employers' for doctors who would prefer a regular nine to five job. The importance of the existing contract to GPs would dwindle as more and more of them opted for service in the emerging super-practices.

These practices would compete with others for contracts with 'Health Commissioners' formed out of mergers between DHAs and FHSAs and would themselves make contracts with providers as 'appropriate', just as GP fundholders do now, though, no doubt, they would do it more efficiently. Residents of health commissioning areas would have to register with the organizations which had won contracts from their purchasing authorities and accept, as patients have always had to, at least while consuming it, the service provided.

The right to choose your doctor no longer appears to be the key to the door of a 'quality' health service if the doctor you can choose is employed to deliver a service designed by his or her employer to meet the minimum standards of publicly financed Health Commissioners. Both the patient and his or her doctor will have lost ground over the determination of 'appropriateness'. Whatever will assure 'quality' in this form of health service, it will assuredly not be patients.

REFERENCES

Alford, R. (1975) *Health Care Politics: Ideological and Interest Group Barriers to Reform*, Chicago: University of Chicago Press.

British Medical Association (1992) *Your Choices for the Future*, London: British Medical Association.

Department of Health, Welsh Office and Scottish Office (1989) *Working For Patients*, London: HMSO.

Glennerster, H., Matsaganis, M. and Owens, P. (1992) *A Foothold in Fundholding*, London: King's Fund.

Harrison, S., Hunter, D. and Pollitt, C. (1990) *The Dynamics of British Health Policy*, London: Routledge.

Le Grand, J. (1994) 'Into the quasi-market', *Community Care* 27 January: 4–5.

McKinley, J. and Arches, J. (1985) 'Towards the proletarianization of doctors', *International Journal of Health Services* 15: 161–95.

Paton, C. (1991) 'The Prime Minister's review of the National Health Service 1989 White Paper "Working for Patients", *Social Policy Review*: 118–40.

Saltman, R. and Von Otter, C. (1992) *Planned Markets and Public Competition: Strategic Reform in Northern European Health Systems*, Buckingham: Open University Press.

Sheaff, R. (1991) *Marketing for Health Services*, Milton Keynes: Open University Press.

Weiner, J. and Ferriss, D. (1990) *GP Budget Holding in the UK: Lessons from America*, London: King's Fund.

Welsh Office, NHS Directorate (1990) *A Quality Health Service in Wales*, Cardiff: Welsh Office.

Wynand, P. *et al.* (1992) 'How can we prevent cream skimming in a competitive health insurance market?' in Zweifel, P. and Frech, H. (eds), *Health Economics World Wide*, Dordrecht: Kluwer Academic Publishers.

Chapter 8

Professional cultures and paradigms of quality in health care

Philip Morgan and Christopher Potter

INTRODUCTION

The many changes resulting from recent legislation aimed at the National Health Service (NHS), which include allowing hospitals to 'opt out' and become self-governing NHS trusts with responsibility for their own budgeting and resourcing decisions, coupled with a new managerial culture emphasizing service quality, employee commitment and value for money have led to an increase in service monitoring and inspection. These include the techniques of quality assurance (QA) and total quality management (TQM) and encompass systems, procedures, facilities, materials and staff activity aimed at achieving prescribed standards of quality which necessitate commitment at all levels of an organization. In common with many public and private organizations, hospitals and other health-care organizations are now moving towards implementing many of these new quality initiatives.

This chapter is informed by ongoing research and is based on our experience working with various NHS groups at various levels. Specifically, it identifies conflict at both national and local levels as a result of recent NHS reforms. First, at national level, we perceive conflict between what the politicians want to achieve with the various reforms, and what the professional and various representative bodies, including the royal colleges, want for their members. Second, at local level, there is conflict between the various professional occupational 'subcultures' (nurses, doctors, professionals allied to medicine, etc.). Also at local level there is conflict between the various professional bodies and regulatory agencies and the 'new managerialism' culture embodied in recent NHS legislation.

Ways in which health-care professionals indirectly attempt to combat the culture of increasing 'managerialism' by regulating their membership in order to perpetuate their power are also explored. Finally, a model is presented of the basic dichotomy between the premisses of total quality management and quality assurance paradigms related to the health service.

NHS REFORMS

During the 1980s, the NHS underwent a series of reforms more fundamental and radical than any experienced since its inception in 1948. Starting with the Griffiths Report in 1983 and culminating with *Working for Patients* in 1989 (Department of Health 1989), these reforms have radically altered the management structure and delivery of health care in hospitals.

The Griffiths Report recommended the introduction of general managers at all levels (regional, district and unit) who would be responsible for making all decisions. The general manager's duties were to help achieve objectives, break down inappropriate professional boundaries, involve doctors more closely in management, improve the measurement of health outcomes, ensure devolution to unit level and to improve the sensitivity of the service to the views of the consumer (Department of Health and Social Security 1983).

The new system was based on systematic monitoring, a single chain of command, an integrated structure, the rule of generalists rather than specialists, greater devolution in addition to greater central control, flexible staff and flexible structures, and hybrid staff members who would know something of everyone's job.

However, as Pollitt *et al.* argue, the new managerialism was founded on distrust, in that the Griffiths model demands proof of performance reviews of Regional Health Authorities (RHAs) and District Health Authorities (DHAs). Individuals and authorities are called to answer if they do not produce according to plan. Pollitt concluded that the Griffiths Report failed to offer a convincing analysis of the relationship between the business of running the NHS and the workings of the political system in which the service is set (Pollitt *et al.* 1991).

Working for Patients had the objective of facilitating and providing better quality and greater choice of services for patients. The intent was to create a market in which hospitals, as the providers of health care, compete with one another to win contracts from DHAs. The contracts would enable districts to increase their control over the amount and quality of the health care they purchased, while the competition engendered was intended to encourage hospitals to provide low-cost services but of sufficient quality. Specifically, it proposed more delegation of responsibility to local level, self-governing hospitals, new funding arrangements, additional consultants, GP practice budgets, reformed management bodies and better audit arrangements.

Since the reforms were introduced, several major issues have emerged. First, the main reforms are to be achieved through incentives rather than through structural reorganization where control is through trust. Second, there must be a balance between freedom to compete and manage one's affairs and regulation to provide comprehensive and accessible services (Nichol 1989). Managers are required to monitor closely the cost and quality of their services, while doctors are expected to play a key role in management and budgeting. Competition is to be used as a stimulus to create greater incentives for efficiency. The most important quality needed is the ability to manage change. One of the key roles is for all managers to provide leadership in the creation of a positive climate.

However, Strong and Robinson argue that the NHS may expect a few problems of its own making. These include 'the integration of the trades within a service' (Strong and Robinson 1990: 187) which could prove difficult, especially with regard to internecine rivalries within the health service. Also, they suggest that achieving quality care could be difficult since 'the benefits of competition are premised on the assumption that purchasers possess serious information about the product' (*ibid.*: 190). However, this is next to impossible to accomplish in the NHS since most consumers operate on the basis of partial or complete ignorance of the quality of care they might expect to receive.

These two issues – internecine rivalries and the problems of introducing quality based on 'consumer ignorance' – are exacerbated by the fact that professionals and managers find themselves in direct confrontation with each other, primarily as a result of the recent changes in the NHS. Coupled with this is the fact that politicians appear to have a hidden agenda of their own that may not have been made explicit to the professionals and their representatives. For example, many feel that the reforms are motivated politically rather than by a desire to serve the needs of the public.

HOSPITALS AS NEGOTIATED ORDERS

At local or unit level, the conflict is also political. For example, hospitals are classic examples of what Strauss (1971) terms 'negotiated orders', since they represent political arenas in which different groups jostle for power and influence. These interest groups consist of various occupational subcultures within hospitals which embody different values, assumptions and orientations.

The recent emphasis on quality appears to draw the various parties together around common objectives because similar vocabulary and terminology are used. However, closer analysis reveals that, behind the words, very different sets of assumptions are operating. Identifying these assumptions helps clarify the different cultural values which exist between the various groups. The main interest groups can be broadly described as managerial and professional.

It is recognized that many managers have a clinical professional background and many qualified managers consider themselves 'professionals' in their own right. In fact, it is observable that managerially oriented professional bodies are adopting approaches to quality which favour clinical professionals by allowing them to define the standards of quality. This underlines the argument that some approaches to quality have more to do with professional values than managerial values, for example the emphasis on BS5750 (Pfeffer and Coote 1991).

It may also suggest that the quality aspirations of external stakeholders (politicians and public) may not be realized if the rhetoric of quality is sidelined into mere bureaucratic 'quality reassurance.'

The increasing use of clinicians and other technical professionals in marginal roles adds both to the confusion and the tension between managerial and professional staff. Before discussing these problems in detail, it seems appropriate at this juncture to define what is meant by professionalism, since this is one of the main issues around which much of the conflict revolves.

PROFESSIONALISM

Definitions of professionalism vary. One of the earliest was provided by Weber who linked it to the bureaucratic concepts of division of labour and functional specialization, well-defined hierarchies, systems of rules and procedures, impersonality of interpersonal relations and promotion and selection based on technical competence (Hall 1968). Intuitively, this model would seem appropriate to the health service since it could be argued that the NHS is a large bureaucracy. For example, the recent proposed changes to the health service can be seen as being an attempt to change the organization's culture in the broadest sense, from a role or bureaucratic culture to one based on task or goals (Handy 1988). However, despite this, many people feel that the NHS has become even more bureaucratized because of the new reforms (e.g. the new hospital board structure which adds additional layers of management required of hospitals which become NHS trusts). For this and other reasons, many health service institutions still operate very much like bureaucracies. Because of this, the bureaucratic model may still be appropriate in understanding the new managerialism.

More recently, several writers have noted the discrepancy between the demands of a bureaucratic managerial system and those of a professional system. For example, Raelin notes that 'there is perhaps no greater source of strain between managers and professionals than over the conflict between bureaucratic and professional standards' (Raelin 1985: 163). He points out that professionals 'are allowed to experience the purity of professional knowledge, without the contamination of bureaucratic conditions . . . and their objective is to meet and even eventually raise the standards of excellence in their discipline' (*ibid.*). By contrast, bureaucrats can rarely achieve the ideal standards espoused by professionals. As Scott notes, 'the bureaucrat, possessing only partial skills, is much more likely to receive on-the-job training, which will include some indoctrination as to the proper goals and objectives of his activities' and that 'he has relatively little basis or social support for questioning the appropriateness of these objectives' (Scott 1966: 272).

For Abbott, professionalism is very much identified with the degree of abstraction and codification of knowledge, since these are the ultimate 'currency of competition between professions' (Abbott 1988: 102). He maintains that only a knowledge system governed by abstraction can redefine its problems and tasks and defend them from interlopers and encompass new problems. He cites the example of medicine which has encompassed alcoholism, mental illness, hyperactivity, obesity and other peripherally related medical problems within its purview.

> Abstraction enables survival in the competitive system of professions. If automechanics had that kind of abstraction, if they 'contained' the relevant sections of what is presently the engineering profession, and had considered taking over all repair of internal combustion engines on abstract grounds, they would, for my purposes, be a profession.
>
> (Abbott 1988: 102)

Abbott equates the abstraction of knowledge with the theoretical and suggests that it is the degree of abstraction that distinguishes one profession from another. As professions become more abstract and theoretical we tend to accord them higher status. For example, he notes 'as social work and nursing have become collegiate professions, medicine has become postgraduate' (*ibid.*: 9).

Freidson (1970) maintains that the main aim or characteristic of a profession is autonomy and protection of independence. This tends, he continues, to form part of the ideology of professionals. Freidson further argues that professional ideologies are intrinsically imperialistic, claiming more for the expert's skill and broad jurisdiction than can be justified on the basis of professional practice (Boreham 1983).

The concept of the professional as 'knowledge worker' based on 'sapiential authority' gained wide acceptance in the NHS in the late 1960s and early 1970s (Salmon 1966; Grey Book 1972). Here, professionals are defined as occupational groups that provide services through drawing on their expert knowledge and specialized training, and who use their knowledge to control the work processes and achieve both operational and strategic autonomy (Raelin 1985). In certain service areas such as health care, this 'knowledge base' permits professionals to impose 'their own definitions of the producer customer relationship' (Johnson 1972), largely as a result of what Green (1984) terms 'consumer ignorance'. This concept of the 'knowledge worker' seems fairly well established.

Other writers on professionalism have tied it in with the concept of power and control over its membership and as a bulwark against bureaucracy. For example, Reed maintains that the basic power strategy of the 'knowledge worker' or 'symbolic analyst' 'is to monopolize and control, as effectively as possible, this abstract or universal knowledge and related tacit skills as they are applied to specific areas or domains of "professional work" and the occupational structures through which it becomes organized' (Reed 1992: 4). According to Reed, this group does this through 'effective occupational closure and control based on effective monopolization of defined operational domains are brought together within a hybrid organizational form consisting of elements of collegiality and hierarchy' (Reed 1992). Following the earlier lead of Strauss, Reed sees the conflicts that result as being resolved through a kind of negotiated order (Strauss 1971). These themes are explored in the next section.

In summary, and based on a selected literature review, we may list the characteristics of professionalism as consisting of a broad, theoretical and abstract knowledge-based expertise (Abbott 1988); one that deals with non-routine tasks and unprogrammable decisions according to ends decided for society or institutions within it, and supported by professional occupational groups where work is a central life interest. Professionalism also depends on meeting certain entry requirements into a career by means of extensive education and skill application that extend beyond the immediate work experience (Eliot 1972; Wilensky 1964).

NHS PROFESSIONAL OCCUPATIONAL CULTURES

As previously noted, hospitals and all health delivery organizations are the classical or archetypal examples of what Strauss (1971) terms 'professional locales' which are 'negotiated orders', with many professional groups and stakeholders who expect to be consulted about changes, and for whom changes may represent threats to what they consider their professional territory. Even in private hospitals in the USA, Chief Executive Officers do not have unrestricted power over professional staff, and debate about hospitals' missions and priorities continues. The more general managers in the UK try to influence quality in direct patient care areas, the more issues of professional versus managerial responsibility will arise. Negotiated order theory views organizations 'as temporal, emergent and contingent entities which consist of multiple locales where rules, contracts and codes are constantly being revised, renewed or revoked . . . whose order is maintained through a constant process of negotiation among shifting interest groups' (Chua and Clegg 1989: 104).

Professional occupational groups represent a major problem for NHS managers and may be one of the greatest challenges facing them in the near future, as occupational groups become increasingly 'tribalized' as a result of increased specialization among the professions. That is, hospitals and other health-care institutions are composed of various 'tribes' – midwives, nurses, doctors and professions allied to medicine – all represented or regulated by various professional bodies (the RCN, BMA, CPSM, UKCC, GMC, etc.) and all having slightly different goals and perceptions of what constitutes effective care. The result is that many of them may be pulling in different directions at national level. At local level, general managers, created after the Griffiths Report (1983), have experienced difficulty in bringing these various professional groups together in order to make them work as effective health-care teams. One of the strengths of the professions has been their ability to maintain nationally agreed terms and conditions of service for their members, maintaining the notion that all nurses or all doctors of the same grade are equally skilled and should be equally rewarded. This is clearly counter to the idea of effective local management by results and, to implement this, the 1989 White Paper and additional legislation have given general managers greater powers for making, appointing and rewarding NHS members. For example, under NHS trust rules, managers can now negotiate employees' salaries and working conditions outside those specified by Whitley.

These professional groups tend to form sub-cultures within the larger organization. That is, groups with common interests and beliefs band together in an attempt to give meaning to their work and to socialize new members. In the interests of preserving their identity and somehow differentiating themselves from other professional groups, they simultaneously reinforce and preserve the characteristics of the 'in-group' (the profession) and the 'out-group' (anyone who does not belong to the profession) by protecting, preserving and cultivating their own domain of expertise. This is accomplished by various means; some of the more obvious examples are dress codes (uniforms and insignia), use of esoteric language (Latinized names in diagnosis and treatment), professional qualifications and other 'tools of the trade' (Van Maanen and Barley 1984). Additionally, a shared sense of stress associated with health-care professions serves further to tie these occupational groups together and fosters an 'us versus them' attitude to any groups outside the professions.

These various professions are in constant movement, and even conflict, in relation to one another. At times, nursing seems to be moving into areas previously the domain of doctors or of physiotherapists, at other times the core nursing role is emphasized with a view to abandoning 'non-nursing duties'. Not surprisingly, with such large heterogeneous bodies, the views of members are often in conflict with their 'leaders' over what constitutes the proper role and training for professionals.

PROFESSIONAL AND REPRESENTATIVE BODIES

In addition to these various professions, the health-care arena is dominated by professional and representative bodies of these professionals. It is professional bodies which decide how the providers of services are to be trained. Their charters and legal machinery protect who can do what, and they can significantly affect the numbers and grades employed and in training, both directly by control of accreditation mechanisms, and indirectly by influencing and negotiating with policy makers.

The professions have very senior representatives within the various national departments of health (including the departments within the Welsh Office, Scottish Office and Northern Ireland Office). These high-level officers – the Chief Medical Officer and Chief Nursing Officer, for example – are able to influence greatly politicians and civil servants making policy. Although civil servants themselves, they can almost act as the chief representatives for their respective professions within the corridors of power. At regional level, and in all health authorities, trust boards, Family Health Service Authorities (FHSAs) and other boards and authorities, the professions are strongly in evidence, with guaranteed seats. Politicians are reluctant to take on the professional bodies. Not only can they not afford to alienate the professionals because of public sympathies and the sheer numbers of staff involved, but they depend on the professionals to mediate the difference between what services are funded and what is demanded. The medical profession, in particular, acts as the regulator, ensuring that perceived demand does not wildly outstrip supply. Without this tacit collusion, the NHS would not be as efficient as it is currently, in terms of the amount of services delivered for the relatively small proportion of gross domestic product spent on it.

The professions are largely left to monitor and audit themselves, which on the whole they do badly. Although there has been increasing audit activity, there is relatively little pressure put on doctors to conform to standards, control mechanisms are weak and there is a shying away from fixed-term contracts or direct sanctions. Salaries for consultants rely on a secretive merit system of awards, until recently managers were excluded from medical interviews and, as the Confidential Enquiry in Perioperative Deaths (CEPOD) reports make clear, much poor medical practice is left unchallenged.

Attempts to regulate the professions by external bodies are strongly condemned and resisted as unwarranted interference from people who simply do not understand their problems (Van Maanen and Barley 1984); witness the BMA's reaction to the many governmental reforms since 1948. For decades all reports that have attempted to amalgamate, restructure or integrate the training of professional groups within the NHS have been systematically shelved. By contrast, those reports which boosted the status and rewards of single professions have been embraced. For example, the Oddie (CPSM 1970), McMillan (DHSS 1973), Zuckerman (DHSS 1968) and Briggs (DHSS 1971) reports were all shelved; Salmon (1966) and Halsbury (1975) were accepted, and Project 2000 was accepted by the professions and almost succeeded as a *fait accompli*. Perceived external threats to the rights of professionals to regulate themselves and ways to avoid them become part of the rituals at national conferences held by the professionals (Van Maanen and Barley 1984).

To practise any of the technical and professional skills within the NHS, individuals must be registered with the UKCC (nurses, midwives and health visitors), GMC (medicine) or the CPSM (professionals supplementary to medicine). These bodies, and the supporting cast of Royal Colleges, societies and boards, have enormous influence in the way students are taught, the values that are inculcated and the techniques which are accepted as best practice. Their 'turf' is jealously guarded. The chiropodists trained by Scholl, for example, are not allowed to practise within NHS premises – it annoys the CPSM that they can practise at all. Despite the numerous working parties (listed above) which concluded over the years that there should be more generic training for many of the professions, such attempts have always ended in failure. There has been only one major change in recent years, when the physiotherapists finally merged with the remedial gymnasts. The professions even monitor the personal behaviour of their members, who can be 'struck off' for various reasons, and therefore effectively prohibited from plying their trade.

In addition to this, the professional bodies are sensitive to the image their respective professions present to the public. Above all else, they believe, the public's perception of the integrity and expertise of the profession must be jealously guarded and maintained at all times. Any perceived threat to undermine the public's trust in the profession is immediately dealt with severely. In many cases, degradation rites are invoked, i.e. scapegoats are identified (usually high-status people within the profession) followed by an investigative ritual to ascertain guilt which, if determined, is followed by swift removal from office.

POWER AND CONTROL OF THE PROFESSIONS

In many ways, the power and control of the professions is stronger than that of the employers and managers. The employers are on the receiving end of policy made elsewhere, their spokespersons are less well briefed and organized, there is less opportunity to put forward coordinated management responses or employers' points of view, because of the multiplicity of lines of accountability on the management side.

This became clear to one of the authors when he was chair of a national committee advising on the implementation of NVQs into the NHS. He was constantly approached and briefed by staff-side representatives and the professional bodies who were monitoring the developments, but ignored by the civil servants' and employers' side who failed to attend meetings, provide opinions or attempt to consider the strategic issues involved. Similarly, Whitley Council machinery is largely a sham, with the employers' side representatives badly briefed, if they attend at all, and the treasury, in fact, determining the employers' side's offers.

Tactically, and locally, managers may be more obviously in charge but in both the general shape and scope of the NHS and, at local level, in the precise way in which service is delivered, professionals are more significant. Even the advent of general management has not changed things greatly, as general managers are on short-term contracts (usually 3–5 years) and are often reluctant to become pulled into strictly professional matters – after all, most carry no personal professional liability insurance!

Given the power of professional bodies in health-care delivery, the values of the professions are clearly significant in the context of quality control in health care.

QUALITY AND PROFESSIONAL ATTITUDES

In their critique of the quality rhetoric being used in the NHS, Pfeffer and Coote (1991) list five different ways in which the term 'quality' is used. These are:

1 The traditional approach (which embodies the everyday usage) meaning some service or product deemed to be of high quality (e.g. Harley Street medicine, Harrods, Savile Row suits, etc.).
2 The 'scientific' or 'expert' approach where a product or service is considered to be of high quality if it measures up to standards set by experts, largely based on the idea of 'fitness for purpose' (e.g. the BS 5750 label).
3 The managerial or 'excellence' approach best exemplified by the work of Peters and Waterman (1982) where quality is based on customer satisfaction and the pursuit of market advantage, and where quality strategies emphasize consumer research, staff training in handling customer complaints, quality manipulation, etc.
4 The consumerist approach which challenges the notion that customer satisfaction is a sufficient criterion (especially if the client's knowledge base or choices are inadequate) and suggests that in order to provide better service the client must be given choice, power and appreciation of the way quality might be determined.
5 The democratic approach which perceives quality as a means of achieving common goals in the interest of the whole community, i.e. what is important is not individual needs or treatment outcomes but the democratically identified collective needs and outcome standards.

The organizational audit or quality assurance model, which is dominant as the expression of quality in health services in countries such as the USA and Australia (and increasingly in the UK with the development of the King's Fund Audit) are clearly of the second approach since they are based on expertise. The Prime Minister's citizen's charters are a mixture of the expert, excellence and consumerist approaches, while purchasing authorities now, and NHS planners in the past, have looked to combine the expert and democratic approaches. Patient action groups may be interested in the consumerist rather than the expert approach.

In other words, different stakeholders at different times will be using the term 'quality' to convey quite different ideas about the service being defined.

The Japanese approach to quality, usually talked about under the rubrics of TQM or CQI (continuous quality improvement), or even kaizen, adds another dimension. As well as looking closely at consumer preferences, it also emphasizes staff involvement to improve working conditions in making the product, and to improve the design or production methods (to lower customer costs/raise profits or to increase product reliability etc.). It also makes considerable use of deliberate and detailed monitoring using operational research techniques, enabling 'zero defects' or just-in-time management strategies, again aimed at improving customer satisfaction and cost control.

Maxwell's (1984) approach to quality in health services has been widely adopted and adapted. He was looking more specifically at whole health systems and suggested the following dimensions:

- Access to services
- Appropriateness of services
- Relevance to need (for the whole community)
- Effectiveness (for individual patients)
- Equity (fairness)
- Social acceptability (cultural appropriateness)
- Efficiency and economy.

In terms of a basic systems model as suggested by Donabedian (1980) (input–structure–output), each paradigm tends to focus on a different aspect of the model. The various quality approaches used in the past within the UK and USA can be characterized as being structure- or input-oriented in the former and process-oriented in the latter. In the UK, the professionals have adopted the attitude that if people are trained thoroughly, and equipment, drugs and buildings are of high quality, society, managers and politicians can assume that the outcomes will be satisfactory. In the USA, there was a much earlier emphasis on matters such as peer review, laying down standardized procedures and medical audit, i.e. if the processes are clearly defined and monitored, society *et al.* can assume that the outcomes will look after themselves. We see an example of this (admittedly overstated) difference in the way hospital doctors are employed in the two countries. To some extent, a British doctor can do what he or she wants to do and is prepared to defend in court. In the USA there are clearly delineated 'privileges'.

DIFFERENT PERCEPTIONS OF QUALITY

We can see from the different meanings of quality that the scope for confusion is considerable, and that politicians, clients, purchasers/ commissioners, and provider organizations may have quite contradictory ideas about what constitutes quality within health care. Even within health-care delivery there is scope for arguing whether one approach is more appropriate than another. It may make more sense to emphasize the expert definition of meeting expert criteria in the case of performance of neurosurgery than in the treatment of depression, for example, but even this can be argued both ways.

Health-care managers will be well aware that doctors have a different definition of quality than they do. The doctor is generally only interested in the best outcome for the patient sitting in front of him/her at that moment, regardless of cost. The needs of patients still on the referral list, and especially patients requiring the help of other specialists, are of relatively lesser importance.

We thus have different vocational specialities developing different paradigms of quality: medical profession versus planner or manager, for example. Using the Maxwell (1984) typology we have effectiveness for the individual in conflict with relevance, equity and efficiency.

The more profound conflict comes at the point where some of the Pfeffer and Coote (1991) paradigms, and those of the Japanese, contrast markedly with the whole ethos of professionalism.

Professionalism rests on the premise that some services require the work of specially trained experts who not only have an esoteric knowledge base derived from years of study, but are legally protected from non-members muscling in on their occupational turf. The idea that the patient/client could or should have anything useful to contribute in diagnosis or determining treatment regimes is difficult for many professionals to accept. For decades the professions and the politicians have broadly agreed the shape and scope of services to be offered in this country. It is centrally funded, and the public accepts the type of service offered. In reality, there is little choice of practitioner, little scope for selecting non-hospital-based, technical intervention-type packages of care. This is clearly changing but very slowly. (Ironically, the new 'internal market' is restricting patient choice rather than increasing it, because service agreements and contracts limit where a patient is likely to be referred.)

The idea that anybody other than members of the specific profession should be able to comment on quality is also often anathema to professionals. They dislike being managed by non-members, but equally find it hard to accept that what are perceived as lesser occupational groups could have anything valuable to contribute in discussions about quality. In their research and consultancy, the authors have seen numerous examples of doctors refusing to join quality circles with other staff; senior grades of nurses meeting separately from juniors; ancillary staff being ignored; and ideas from juniors and support staff ridiculed, trivialized or ignored by senior professionals. Yet often these are the very people who are interacting most fully and frequently with patients, and who are most aware of 'customer' perceptions (Potter, *et al.* 1994).

Professional attitudes have also profoundly affected the types of quality model which have become dominant in health care. Donabedian's (1980) distinctions between structure, process and outcome have become firmly established in the language of health-care quality. One of the earliest proponents of systematically monitoring and managing quality was an American surgeon named Codman. During the second decade of this century, he championed the idea that surgeons should look at the outcome of their activities in order to inform their selection of patients, clinical methods, etc. with a view to improving the profession's performance.

Although his influence led directly to the development of what is now the Joint Commission for the Accreditation of Health Organizations (JCAHO), it is perhaps ironic that the QA model that the JCAHO has developed over the years, and which has become the dominant approach, has until very recently been completely concerned with issues of structure and process.

The QA/audit model relies very heavily on Pfeffer and Coote's (1991) second quality paradigm. Experts (i.e. professionals) determine who can practise what skills (and can add a requirement for an extra year or two of experience, or a degree if it will improve their status and bargaining power); they determine the copious 'standards' and criteria which identify what constitutes best practice (i.e. offers best defence in court); and their members can act as the invigilators ensuring the system is maintained.

The QA model (i.e. experts determining what is 'fit for service') is highly congruent with the professionalism model. It reinforces the power of professions and it is little wonder that it is the approach both professional bodies and their members are most ready to espouse.

By contrast, quality paradigms that seek to empower clients, to draw on the insight of co-workers, or to take seriously the need to package services in ways which seek to maximize client satisfaction are least compatible with professional aspirations.

Within the British NHS, it has been the work of two individual doctors, Lunn and Devlin, who have pushed the annual Confidential Enquiries into Perioperative Deaths (CEPOD), which has shown an unacceptably high level of avoidable deaths during operations. But these enquiries are confidential, otherwise they would not be able to obtain the data. Medical audit is still considered a waste of time by many doctors and the great amount of time given to it has seen remarkably little change of behaviour.

The Royal College of Surgeons is now pushing the audit system, and in Australia it is the various Royal Colleges which are pioneering newer outcome indicators. But, generally, the professions need to take a much broader view of what constitutes quality, to be prepared to share information and ideas, and to be more active in promoting behavioural change among their members if their clients are going to see the improvements in quality they are coming to expect. Their current, late espousal of audit, BS5750 and QA approaches can be seen as a reluctant acceptance of the need to respond to quality issues, which in fact further protects their power. To the extent that managers and others want to press forward with staff suggestion-type strategies, customer first strategies, cost control and efficiency changes, they will continue to be faced by professionals whose cultural values are inimical to such approaches.

TQM VERSUS QA

Although there are various approaches to quality, two fundamental approaches dominate: quality assurance (QA) and total quality management (TQM) or continuous quality improvement (CQI).

Essentially, QA is based on standards, either statutory or agreed by experts in the field, which define the components of a service (e.g. staff qualifications, size of buildings, access to journals, etc.) and the processes to be followed (e.g. committees to be set up, data to be collected, protocols to be prepared, etc.). Under this approach, regular external inspections are performed to ensure that standards are being maintained. The assumption is that if standards are correctly defined and being adhered to, a high quality of service will follow. Examples of QA approaches are BS5750, the accreditation processes of various professional bodies, which determine whether training can occur at particular institutions, the USA's JCAHO accreditation system and the King's Fund Audit in the UK.

A major advantage to adopting a QA approach is that it is comprehensive and systematic. Major flaws and procedural omissions can be identified and minimum standards across a wide range of services and institutions are maintained.

However, QA by itself does not necessarily guarantee improved quality outcomes; it may even suppress the development of better quality by promoting complacency, or suppress improvement by stifling innovation ('the book says we must do it this way'). Consequently, its value in promoting continuous quality consciousness (except in the short term) to achieve accreditation is questionable. Moreover, in the USA and Australia there has been a major shift in emphasis towards outcome-oriented 'clinical indicators'. The reason for this is that after years of QA and accreditation there has been a general plateauing of standards which have not kept pace with public expectations.

The second major approach to quality is encapsulated in the terms TQM/CQI. Conceptually, the TQM/CQI approach is quite distinct from QA since quality inspection is counter to many underlying assumptions of professional bureaucracies. TQM/CQI requires continuous and relentless improvements in the total process that provides care, not simply in the improved actions of individual professions. Improvements are, therefore, based on both process and outcome. TQM/CQI requires an understanding of quality which includes the 'customer' (internal and external customers, i.e. other organizational members as well as patients) in addition to an appreciation of statistical measures of outcomes.

By contrast, quality approaches to the health sector in the UK have relied heavily on professional interpretations of what constitutes good practice and a somewhat 'laissez faire' attitude predominates. This attitude to patients can best be characterized as 'doctor knows best' and, if things go wrong, there is always recourse to professional disciplinary bodies and to the courts. More recently, much attention has been directed towards medical and nursing audit (and other professionals are being increasingly involved). However, there is still much suspicion among professionals and they often resent what they perceive to be an infringement of their clinical and professional freedoms.

These two factors – attitude to patients and suspicion of interference – make it difficult to orientate professionals, especially medical staff, towards quality matters. Such professionals tend to be dismissive of patients' concerns, pointing out that it is impossible to cut waiting lists when resources are scarce. They consider that the TQM/CQI injunction to treat patients as 'customers' is crass and demonstrates a complete misunderstanding and misinterpretation of the professional doctor–patient relationship. Moreover, doctors maintain, patients know too little about the technicalities of treatment for them to judge properly the quality of the service offered (Green 1986).

Professionals tend to perceive quality in purely technical terms; if the technical outcome is acceptable, patient or hospital visitor perceptions are irrelevant. If outcomes are unacceptable this is simply viewed as unfortunate. As one doctor put it to us, 'none of us sets out to deliver poor quality; we are all doing our best in what are often very trying circumstances'.

PROFESSIONAL PARADIGM VERSUS TQM PARADIGM

During the course of our research, we discovered the work of McLaughlin and Kaluzny (1990). Their work exactly parallels and reinforces our own findings. In reference to our quality strategy quadrant model, McLaughlin and Kaluzny present two contrasting models, the professional and the TQM, and discuss their various different principles. They argue that professionals may resist TQM since it empowers clients and other 'unqualified' or junior staff, and generally changes or even erodes their authority and occupancy of a central position in the organizational hierarchy. Medical professionals, therefore, find themselves at a crossroads as they are pushed and pulled in different directions while they struggle to redefine their roles. We also perceive a conflict between the attitudes of the various professional bodies and their members to the various paradigms.

The authors claim the QA approach is essentially static. Having identified standards, one then sets about detecting errors or gaps in the actual performance that fail to meet standards – after they have happened. It is an *ex post facto* system in that one has to wait for the effort to occur.

The underlying premise of QA has been to identify human errors in the process, to follow established protocols and to search for failures to meet the standards. TQM, by contrast, aims at error prevention and predetection. TQM emphasizes that any errors that occur are the fault of the system. Instead, the aim is continuous process improvements in the system. Moreover, all such improvements should be the responsibility of all staff, not simply those people designated as 'QA' personnel.

McLaughlin and Kaluzny (1990) argue that this approach constitutes a total 'paradigm shift' in health-care management and presents a series of potential conflict areas in the way health-care organizations are managed. For example, the basic paradigm shift required as a result of introducing TQM/CQI into health-care institutions tends to upset the balance. TQM/CQI emphasizes staff-related activity aimed at empowering staff and changing the culture through the introduction of group and team-related activities in the form of quality circles, focus groups and adoption of a customer focus through, for example, the Patient's Charter. These dichotomies have been well documented by McLaughlin and Kaluzny who noted that whereas the professional model emphasizes individual responsibility, professional leadership, autonomy and quality assurance, TQM emphasizes collective responsibilities, managerial leadership, participation, accountability and continuous improvement. McLaughlin and Kaluzny note also that while professionalism is primarily concerned with the application of independent judgement, management stresses teamwork, bureaucracy and empowerment of junior staff. All of these are antithetical to the clinical professional paradigm as they are perceived as further contributing to the erosion of the professionals' power base. (See Figure 1.)

Figure 2 summarizes our own findings in the form of a model encapsulating the two paradigms: quality assurance (QA) and total quality management (TQM). QA is the system preferred by the professionals since it allows them to set and maintain their power

Professional paradigm	versus	TQM paradigm
Individual responsibility		Collective responsibility
Clinician-led		Manager-led
Autonomy		Accountability
Administrative authority		Participation
Professional authority		Managerialism
Goal expectations		Process and performance expectations
Rigid (fixed)		Flexible planning
Retrospective IPR		Concurrent IPR
Quality assurance		Continuous improvement

Figure 1: The professional paradigm versus the TQM paradigm

Source: McLaughlin and Kaluzny 1990

	QA	versus	TQM/CQI
Preferred by:	Professionals		Managers
Standards based on:	Process and protocols either statutory or expert-based		Both process and outcome measures
Method of control:	Inspection (*ex post facto*)		Continuous assessment of both process and outcome
Belief, assumptions & rationale:	Professional expertise based on consumer ignorance		Customer-focused both internally and externally
Function:	Serves to protect the *status quo* of the professional and preserves their 'place in the sun'		Challenges professional *status quo* Diffuses power to junior staff levels
How quality is measured:	Technical outcome mainly		Both qualitative and quantitative
Nature of expertise:	Expert knowledge-based Abstract/codified		Multidisciplinary team-based Based on continuous improvement
Predominant culture:	Person- and/or role-based		Task-based

Figure 2: QA versus TQM/CQI

through standards set by them; TQM is preferred by managers and aims to empower all staff at all levels. QA standards focus largely on processes and protocols, either statutory or expert-based; TQM standards are based on both process and outcome measures. Inspection under QA is *ex post facto* outcomes (that is, after treatment is provided the patient is assessed in terms of the outcome); under TQM inspection is based on continuous assessment of both process and outcome. Rather than being based on the end result the whole system is audited for flaws. Thus, if a ward is not clean, it may not be the fault of the cleaner, it may result from the whole contracting process. The underlying assumption behind the QA approach is a belief in the expertise and infallibility of the professional as arbiter of the appropriate care. It is also based on the assumption of consumer ignorance in that it assumes that patients have little or nothing to contribute to the health-care process. TQM, by contrast, is customer-focused and recognizes both internal and external customers and that both groups have an important part to play in the quality chain. Patient questionnaires are recognized as having an important contribution to make to the quality process. The function of QA is to protect the *status quo* of the professionals and to ensure that they maintain their power and influences since they alone possess the necessary specialized health-care knowledge. TQM presents a challenge to this professional *status quo* since it seeks to diffuse the power and knowledge to fairly junior staff through such means as quality circles and focus groups. These groups, composed of various staff levels, identify problems and attempt to resolve them at group level. Under QA, quality is measured in terms of the technical outcome; TQM attempts to measure it qualitatively and quantitatively. Under QA, the expertise resides in the individual clinician or professional and is based on a highly abstract codified knowledge system; under TQM, the expertise is more widely diffused and resides in the collective expertise of a multidisciplinary team. Under the QA system, the predominant culture tends to be person-centred or even role-centred and leads to turf protecting. TQM encourages a task-based culture aimed at continuous quality improvement.

IS QUALITY A FAD?

Improvements in quality in industry, together with increasing litigation and criticism that much of the work carried out on patients is unnecessary (estimates suggest that as much as 20 per cent of clinical work is not beneficial) has caused health-care workers to appear patronizing and anachronistic in their attitudes. As a way of redressing the balance, many in the NHS have jumped on the quality bandwagon. From a situation in the 1970s when quality was simply not considered by anyone within the NHS in any serious way, it is now centre stage as one of the three contractual criteria on which purchasers are to judge providers. However, as we have demonstrated, quality appears to mean different things to different health service stakeholders.

An obvious question arises, therefore: 'Is the current emphasis on quality merely a fad?' Is it merely a trendy management buzzword destined to join the ranks of management by objectives, participative management, organization development, and probably business planning and performance engineering?

Perhaps the main problem is not that quality will become a mere fad, but that it will simply become bureaucratized and sanitized into a 'quality reassurance' system (as happened with the JCAHO quality assurance system in the USA and to some extent the BS5750 system in the UK). Once everybody has achieved the 'kitemark' the system is of little value, failing as it does to differentiate the good and bad, and inhibiting the motivation to do better.

'Quality care' has the potential of becoming a rallying point around which managers and clinical staff can unite. A point at which their different cultural values can come together to improve services, rather than allowing them to operate in a constant state of mistrust and misunderstanding. It can also serve as a means of breaking down the cultural barriers and practices which tend to foster traditional divisions between clinicians and managers and perpetuate the 'it's-not-my-problem' syndrome. But for this to happen, managers (and politicians) need to demonstrate their concern through resource allocation (including the provision of information systems); through consistent, maintained attention; through modelling their concern; and through identifying worthwhile standards of performance which are credible with clinicians as valid indicators of quality.

Quality is now institutionalized in the contracting process. It is being taught to managers and clinical staff alike, and understanding of its various facets is improving all the time. There is, therefore, little reason why it should prove to be a fad. However, to avoid this, there must be a sustained and deeply felt need to provide excellence in all its forms, if it is not to become a bureaucratized, empty genuflection or an occasional programme run by management consultants for the benefit of hospital staff.

CONCLUSION

The current emphasis on quality has implications for politicians, managers, clinical staff and 'quality professionals'. Politicians must adopt a 'hands-off' approach and allow the professionals (including the managers) to get on with the job. Rather than being politically driven, quality should be customer- and professionally driven. The temptation the professionals face is merely to talk about quality and to do just enough to reassure everyone that quality is high. However, as we have indicated, when even the words and concepts used by different stakeholders show quite variable understandings of what is being demanded of the NHS, the potential for conflict and confusion is great. A service with many lines of limited (or ill-defined) authority, where the political goal-posts are forever changing, where resources are limited and where emotions run high, is always going to find itself in conflict. In order to resolve some of the dysfunctional conflict it is necessary to find leaders who can inspire people with the desire to excel.

	Quality assurance		Management culture
Review mechanisms			Staff training
			Quality circles, systems and structure that facilitate staff contribution
Clinical audit			Communication up, down, across and with clients
Set and review appropriate standards			Cost control/value for money
Risk assessment			Clear goals, procedures and tasks
Written departmental objectives			Involved leadership
Focus groups	Proactive systems for identifying client needs	Monitoring systems	Clinical indicators
Questionnaires			Supervisory systems e.g. check lists
Patient representatives			Record keeping
			IT investment
Complaints and feedback mechanisms			Comparison of performance indicators

Figure 3: A multifaceted strategy for quality outcome-oriented management
Source: Potter *et al.* 1994

But a desire to excel must be coupled with a willingness to change. Despite all the activity on medical audit, the constant complaint of medical staff is that it is a waste of time, since people are unwilling to change their practices – and this extends to clinical management and interpersonal relations. Managers need to find more effective ways of motivating clinical staff to change. No doubt the realities of trust status and the internal market will assist this process. But clinical staff must realize that if they do not change themselves, others will force change on them, and it will probably not be in a form they would prefer.

Much more work is needed to ensure that quality management in all its aspects is better understood by all staff, and from an early stage in their career. Even many of the 'quality professionals' have a very limited outlook, having been promoted from within nursing or brought in from outside the NHS to introduce BS5750, or 'turned on' by a particular brand of quality taught at a programme run by a consultant cum salesperson.

It has to be recognized that different services need to emphasize different approaches to quality improvement at different times. No one approach is universally appropriate. QA can easily become a bureaucratic game, wasting time and resources and achieving little. Yet it has its place in consolidating minimum standards. TQM can also become a displacement activity, ending up with staff time being expended to achieve only minor changes. But it can also represent a powerful set of techniques to empower and engage staff attention, raise morale and provide a better sense of purpose.

Our research clearly showed that successful quality implementation can only be achieved when a multifaceted approach is adopted (see Figure 3). Such an approach should incorporate QA and an appropriate management culture coupled with monitoring and proactive procedures for identifying client needs (Potter *et al.* 1994). Above all, we feel, more attention is needed to devise better outcome measures which will help focus staff attention on the benefits to patients, rather than simply resulting in increasing professionalism and bureaucracy for their own sake.

REFERENCES

Abbott, A. (1988) *The System of Professions*, Chicago: University of Chicago Press.

Boreham, P. (1983) 'Indetermination: professional knowledge, organization and control', *Sociological Review*: 293–318.

Chua, W. and Clegg, S. (1989) 'Contradictory couplings: professional ideology in the organizational locales of nurse training', *Journal of Management Studies* 26(2).

Council for Professions Supplementary to Medicine (1976) *Report and Recommendations of Remedial Professions Committee* (Oddie Report), London: CPSM.

Department of Health (1989) *Working for Patients*, Cmnd. 555, London: HMSO

Department of Health and Social Security (1968) *Hospital Scientific & Technical Services* (Zuckerman Report), London: HMSO.

Department of Health and Social Security (1972) *Report of the Committee on Nursing* (Briggs Report), Cmnd. 5115, London: HMSO.

Department of Health and Social Security (1973) *The Remedial Professions* (McMillan Report), London: HMSO.

Department of Health and Social Security (1975) *Report of the Committee of Inquiry into Pay and Related Conditions of Service of the Professions Supplementary to Medicine and Speech Therapists* (Halsbury Report), London: HMSO.

Department of Health and Social Security (1983) *National Health Service Management Inquiry* (Griffiths Report), London: HMSO.

Donabedian, A. (1980) *The Definition of Quality: Approaches to its Assessment* No. 1, Ann Arbor: Health Administration Press.

Eliot, P. (1972) *The Sociology of the Professions*, London: Macmillan Press.

Freidson, E. (1970) *Profession of Medicine: A Study of the Sociology of Dominance: The Social Structure of Medical Care*, New York: Aldine.

Green, D. (1986) *Challenge to the NHS*, London: Institute of Economic Affairs.

Grey Book (1972) *The Arrangement for the Reorganised National Health Service*, London: HMSO.

Hall, R. (1968) 'Professionalisation and Bureaucratisation', *American Sociological Review* 3(1).

Handy, C. (1988) *Understanding Organisations*, London: Penguin.

Johnson, T. (1972) *Professionals and Power*, London: Macmillan.

Joint Commission on Standards for Hospitals (1989) *Accreditation Manual for Hospitals*, published by the *JCAHO Journal for Quality and Participation: Visions of Excellence in Healthcare* Jan/Feb. 1991.

McLaughlin, C. and Kaluzny, A. (1990) 'Total quality management in health: making it work', *Health Care Management Review* 15(3): 7–14.

Maxwell, R. (1984) 'Quality assessment in health care', *British Medical Journal* 13: 13–34.

Nichol, D. (1989) 'Working for patients: the role of managers implementing the White Paper', *Health Service Management* 85(3): 107.

Øvretveit, J. (1992) *Quality Health Services*, Brunel: Brunel Institute of Organisation and Social Studies.

Peters, T. and Waterman (1982) *In Search of Excellence*, London: Collins.

Pfeffer, N. and Coote, A. (1991) *Is Quality Good for You? A Critical Review of Quality Assurance in Welfare Services*, London: Institute for Public Policy Research.

Pollitt, C., Harrison, D. and Marnoch, G. (1991) 'General management in the National Health Service: the initial impact 1983–1988', *Public Administration* 68 (Spring): 61–83.

Potter, C., Morgan, P. and Thompson, A. (1994) 'Continuous quality improvement in an acute hospital: a report of an action research project in three hospital departments', *International Journal of Health Care/Quality Assurance* 7(1).

Raelin, J. (1985) 'The basis for the professional's resistance to managerial control', *Human Resource Management* 24(2): 147–76.

Reed, M. (1992) 'Experts, professions and organizations in late modernity', paper presented at the Employment Research Unit Annual Conference 'The Challenge of Change: The Theory and Practice of Organizational Transformations'.

Salmon Report (1966) *Report of the Committee on Senior Nursing Staff Structure*, Chairman B. Salmon, London: HMSO.

Scott, W. (1966) 'Professionals in bureaucracies – areas of conflict', in Vollmer, H. and Mills, D. (eds), *Professionalization*, Englewood Cliffs: Prentice-Hall.

Strauss, A. *et al.* (1971) 'The hospital and its negotiated order', in Castles (ed.), *Decisions, Organizations and Society*, London: Penguin.

Strong, P. and Robinson, J. (1990) *The NHS Under New Management*, Milton Keynes: Open University Press.

Van Maanen, J. and Barley, S. (1984) 'Occupational culture and control in organizations', in Straw, B. (ed.), *Research in Occupational Behaviour* vol. 6, Greenwich, CT: JAI Press.

Wilensky, H. (1964) 'The professionalization of everyone?', *The American Journal of Sociology*, LXX(2).

Chapter 9

Quality in the marketing change process
The case of the National Health Service

Martin Kitchener and Richard Whipp

INTRODUCTION: 'A REVOLUTION IN PROGRESS'

The election of the Conservative government in 1979 heralded a diversion from the postwar, Keynesian public policy model which envisaged incrementally expanding centrally funded service provision. Largely in response to mounting financial crises and building on earlier managerialist initiatives (e.g. Griffiths Report 1983), a new public sector management paradigm began to emerge at the beginning of the 1990s. This new paradigm, which was informed by the New Right's 'public choice theory' emphasized: fiscal reorganization, privatization, the separation of purchaser and provider roles within quasi markets, and the sovereignty of the customer (Butler and Vaile 1984; Thompson 1992). These ideological and structural changes are now recognized as a significant break with the past (Fitzgerald 1993) and John Major acknowledges the programme as a 'revolution in progress' (Major 1989: 1). The reformers have often ritualistically cast aside traditional, public sector and professional values (Hood 1991). In their place, a diffuse set of management ideas have been imported from the private sector. These have subsequently been aggregated and termed the 'New Public Management' by commentators such as Stewart and Walsh (1992).

The UK health sector is not alone in facing these paradigmatic shifts since they mirror 'hyperturbulent' changes in the Swedish and US health services (Meyer *et al.* 1991). Reporting on the American experience, Shortell *et al.* (1990) conclude that the enormity of the reforms requires 'executive mind-set reorientations', a shift towards market orientation and increasing emphasis on strategic as opposed to operational management. This chapter reports that similar responses are being required from UK hospitals and that a fundamental reorientation of hospital management is under way.

Using the findings of an Economic and Social Research Council (ESRC)-sponsored investigation of organizational change within the National Health Service (NHS), this chapter demonstrates how hospitals are increasingly adopting marketing techniques in the hope of surviving the competitive pressures within the quasi market (Sheaff 1991; Le Grand 1991). As part of the wider marketing change process, the chapter illustrates how quality initiatives are being used as 'bridges' between the development of market-oriented hospitals and the values of the still powerful health-care professionals. For example, some hospital managers have attempted to disguise initiatives aimed at reducing clinical autonomy and developing professionals as 'part-time marketeers' (Gummesson 1991) within new hospital mission statements laden with references to quality defined in terms of cost-efficiency and quality assurance. Consequently, quality in the NHS, which was previously associated with professional peer review of expert services, has now become a complex discourse involving multiple meanings to a variety of stakeholders. Overall, marketing change is shown to be an iterative and contested process. Above all, that process of marketing change is bound up with the social construction and negotiated order which characterizes organizations in the NHS (Reed chapter 2).

This chapter begins with a description of the study on which the chapter is based. Section 2 outlines the main organizational and market reforms, the professional service features of the NHS and their implications for the marketing change process. Section 3 discusses the nature of the current discourse on quality and locates it within the specific NHS context. Section 4 joins the earlier theoretical discussions with research data to reveal the subtly constructed interface between marketing and quality during the NHS marketing change process.

1 THE PROJECT

This chapter arises from a study which investigates how the problematic implementation of marketing into the NHS is handled in hospitals (McNulty *et al.* 1993). Previously, neither the marketing nor the management of change literatures had adequately explained this process (Ahmed and Rafiq 1992). Existing work suggested a limited conceptual understanding of process, rarely admitted failure and did not address the unique NHS context. What was required was the development of a processual understanding of the dynamics of NHS marketing change over time (Morgan and Piercy 1990: 956). This project was primarily concerned with the management of the marketing change process and its linkages with the distinctive features of the NHS. A central aim of the research was to investigate the processes by which a market orientation develops within hospitals as part of a broader process of NHS organizational change. The originality of this chapter stems in part from it being the first to explore the implementation of marketing into the NHS in Wales (Harrison 1990). Above all, the work's emphasis upon the problematic development of a market orientation as a process of organizational change avoids the more deterministic stance found in the marketing literature.

This first investigation into Welsh NHS marketing change necessitated the use of case studies to reveal this emerging process. The design choice in this study was to use the 'comparative-intensive' case method (Pettigrew and Whipp 1991). This has involved the systematic analysis of the marketing change process in relatively few NHS units over time, rather than more superficial analyses of a larger number. This holistic case study research represents a step beyond the prevailing questionnaire survey or incidental studies that have so far failed to provide a robust explanation of the way that units handle the marketing change process. Instead, this study emphasized the prior social influences on behaviour and the economic and social contexts in which the NHS has operated (Kitchener 1992: 4).

The chapter concentrates on the experience of one district in the NHS in Wales, Dinashire, and two of the three main hospital groups it contains (Tyfu, an NHS Trust and Marw, a Directly Managed Unit). The choice of Dinas District Health Authority (DHA) satisfied Schatzman and Strauss's (1973) 'casing criteria'. While the choice of units was in no way based on a search for typical units, both share the general features of many hospitals (and public sector organizations) such as goal ambiguity, diffused authority and centralized accountability mechanisms. Both Tyfu and Marw are classed as district general hospitals (DGHs) and were chosen because they displayed both similar and contrasting features that could be compared in terms of their implementation of the same government-imposed marketing change initiative. The similar features included: the wide range of services provided, the common DHA, an early indication of marketing awareness and their willingness to participate in the study. There were also obvious contrasts between the two units and these include the history, service-mix, age, man- agement structure, district-planned future and location (Tyfu is a city centre hospital whereas Marw is located on the edge of the conurbation). A broad comparison of the two units is made in the table below.

The data from over 100 main interviews conducted across the two

Table 1: The two major research sites

Factor	Tyfu	Marw
Age	170 years	60 years
Budget (1991–2)	£50m	£38m
No. beds	750	520
Status (1.4.94)	DMU	NHS Trust
Staff	2,300	2,000
Major depts	Trauma and orthopaeds	Maternity
	Accident and emergency	Care of the elderly
	Gen. surgery/medicine	Gen. surgery/medicine

sites have been triangulated with documentary examination, observation and a series of structured comparisons with other units in England and Wales (Todd 1979). As the chapter indicates, this methodological approach has allowed a more comprehensive, processual description to emerge, one which is sensitive to the nuances of both professional service contexts and the vagaries of marketing (Kitchener 1994: 15).

2 *WORKING FOR PATIENTS* 1990: RADICAL NHS MARKETING CHANGE

One of the most revolutionary of the recent public sector transformations is occurring in the 'professional service context' of the NHS (Heald 1990). Largely inspired by *Working for Patients* (Department of Health 1989), the enabling Act of Parliament and reform agenda, was conceived at a time when marketing's stock stood at an all-time high in the UK (Walsh 1991). The basis of the reform was that the role of the health-care purchaser and provider should be separated and the mechanisms of health-care provision should be largely governed through a quasi market (Le Grand 1991) rather than by central planning. Replacing the previous system of funding based on a district's catchment area, the government now funds purchasers (DHA and general practitioner fundholders who have negotiated their own budgets) to buy services on behalf of their population, from provider units. The provider organizations include both directly managed units and the newly created NHS trust hospitals. While both must now earn revenue from the services they provide within the quasi market, Trusts operate independently from DHAs. Although this structure falls far short of a free market, this quasi-market approach to public sector management has extended the theoretical principles of economy and efficiency to involve new 'trading relationships'. As a result, both purchaser and provider organizations are required to emulate commercial organizations and develop managerial and marketing competencies.

Although the development of market relations has been shown to be crucial to these centrally imposed NHS reforms, little attention has been paid to the problematic process of marketing change, either practically or empirically (Piercy 1991). Unit-level experience and responses to change have varied greatly. However, realizing that hospital survival has become increasingly dependent upon competition, many units now pay greater attention to the ideas and techniques of marketing (Sheaff 1991). Yet while marketing terminology is now heard on wards and in clinical meetings, early attempts to develop market-oriented (Kohli and Jaworski 1990) hospitals have been highly uneven in both approach and outcome (McNulty et al. 1993).

Using research across a number of units, this study contends that marketing change can be assessed initially by paying attention to three dimensions: marketing philosophy, marketing method and marketing function. First, marketing philosophy refers to the prescriptive commercial orientation for managing exchanges in the market-place and is typically rehearsed within debates concerning the marketing concept (Houston 1986: 85). Central to this dimension is the concept of market orientation (Kohli and Jaworski 1990; Narver and Slater 1990). The concept is framed as a social process rather than a technical exercise limited to the application of marketing ideas and techniques. Concerns over the ideological and prescriptive status of marketing indicate that the perceived legitimacy of the proponents, ideas and activities associated with a market orientation cannot be assumed within the NHS (Whittington and Whipp 1992).

Second, marketing method contains the range and sequence of activities which are used to operationalize the philosophy. This chapter, therefore, will suggest that the development of a marketing method in the NHS will require hospitals to become more aware of the idea of 'relationship marketing' (Yorke 1990; Dufour 1991) which stresses keeping customers as much as obtaining new ones (Christopher et al. 1992). Moreover, it allows for more adequate attention to the more intangible issues of 'quality' rather than strict adherence to the orthodox marketing mix variables (Sheaff 1991). Third, marketing function relates to the organization and allocation of marketing responsibilities throughout the hospital including the role of formal marketing departments.

Recognizing the simultaneous processes of production and consumption of NHS services, the following sections suggest that the development of a marketing function within hospitals relies greatly on securing the involvement and commitment of health-care professionals as 'part-time' marketeers (Gummesson 1991)

3 MARKETING CHANGE IN PROFESSIONAL SERVICE CONTEXTS

Attempted NHS marketing change is complicated by the involvement of organizational professionals within this service context (Raelin 1985; Gardner 1986). While the Conservative Party once viewed autonomous professions as a stabilizing and necessary element for the development of society, this view changed during the 1980s. Professional groups are now seen as a middle-class variant of trade unions and possibly more disruptive to the workings of markets. This major change in the perception of clinical roles led one commentator to state that, 'professionalism must now be practised only by consenting adults in private' (Phillips 1993). The ensuing process of professional deregulation and commodification is likely to continue, argues Raelin (1985), since professional interests are less likely to assert themselves in competitive environments such as the emerging NHS quasi market.

While the attempts to identify professional characteristics have been criticized for the lack of consensus achieved on either their content or relative importance, they have indicated some frequently underplayed features which affect organizational change (Roach Anleu 1990). These features include autonomy, the ability to use expert knowledge to achieve degrees of closure and professional monitoring of quality assurance through peer review (Pollitt 1990). However, as health-care professionals become increasingly viewed as pluralistic, task-oriented coalitions containing differential distributions of power, they are perhaps best understood through their development of client relationships (Walsh 1991: 12; Yorke 1990). This conception avoids the passive role ascribed in the traditional models and implies that professional change evolves through a slow, social process (Mintzberg 1983: 213).

The issue of clinical autonomy is important to NHS marketing change, not least because many have cited its role in the maintenance of the administrative–professional divide which acts as a barrier to organizational change (Anthony *et al.* 1992). Organizational domain theorists have attempted to clarify the relationships between interests within human service organizations such as the NHS, and have identified three pluralistic domains: policy, management and service. Early forms of this approach underestimated the importance of alliances, and viewed conflict between bureaucratic management and the semi-autonomous service or professional domain as almost inevitable (Alderfer 1987). However, more recent approaches have recognized that the dynamic relationship between hospitals' professional and management domains is often based more on dependence than conflict (Winstanley *et al.* 1992). Some have even viewed professionalization and bureaucratization as companion processes with similar custodial values (Ackroyd *et al.* 1989).

Partly as a result of the governmental project to have professional expertise 'on tap' rather than 'on top', clinical autonomy has been attacked on a number of fronts (Pollitt 1990). The first real challenge arose from the Griffiths Report's (1983) attempt to increase the numbers of clinicians in management and so render them responsible for rationing. Although largely unsuccessful, some converts were made. One of these, Dr David Owen, sought to spread the gospel to ex-colleagues: 'the constraints on total resources mean that doctors acting individually can constrain the clinical freedom of their colleagues and also limit the effectiveness of health care for other patients' (Owen 1976: 1008). More recent pressures on autonomy have included increased clinical work measurement through quality assurance, the subdivision of medical specialities and attempts to alter practice standards (Calnan and Gabe 1991). This shift has been from an emphasis on the production of 'internal goods', such as a self-defined, high-quality service, to the attainment of 'external goods', such as achieving cost-effectiveness. Moreover, attempts to subvert practice standards arise from clinical practices' vulnerability to hospitals' increasing emphasis upon 'external goods' within the quasi market-place (MacIntyre 1990: 187; McNulty *et al.* 1993).

These concerted attacks on health-care professionals' practice standards and values have left many fearing that the attempted development of market-oriented hospitals is merely another attempt to de-skill clinical tasks, make them 'sell' their services and reduce costs. Many staff at Marw, for example, equated marketing with the selling of private sector goods. Some expressed concerns regarding the amount of time and money that was being spent on commercial/marketing activities compared to medical issues. A union representative equated marketing initiatives with the new porters' uniforms and concluded that they were without substance and rather like the Health Minister, 'all fur coat and no knickers'. These views were further reinforced by staff's recent exposure to an alien commercial language and job titles, and the unsuccessful forays into income generation schemes elsewhere. For example, 1992 saw major changes in job titles such as the unpopular decision to replace 'sister' with 'ward manager'. Those affected felt that this move was indicative of a new managerial ideology based around a need for leadership, accountability and responsibility as opposed to the traditional coordination of professionals' roles. One sister returned from maternity leave to find a 'whole new language based around customers (whoever they are) and markets being used'. She felt threatened and wary of the developments.

A number of experienced managers, including the District Procurement Officer, recognized that the careful use of language was vital to ensure professional support for change:

> Marketing is foreign to NHS thinking and people don't like to think of marketing, it is a bad term to use in the NHS and where there are professionals . . . I would never call an initiative 'marketing' . . . in the NHS it conjures up the wrong mission . . . If ever there was a training need it is with the use of language.

Despite the attempts to marginalize clinical autonomy, the evidence from this study confirms that health-care professionals remain powerful precisely because of their functional monopoly of expertise during a period of organizational change (McKinlay and Stoekle 1988). This power continues to be displayed, for example, through the reshaping of NHS managerial initiatives to protect and further professionals' interests, in the way in which many resource allocation decisions have come to be regarded as a branch of medical ethics, and in the way in which 'chronic' and 'community' forms of care still generally enjoy less status, power and resources than the acute area (Strong and Robinson 1990; Glover and Kelly 1992).

Recognizing the contested legitimacy of marketing and the continued power of health-care professionals, it appears that management is obliged to script professionals into the marketing change process (Whittington and Whipp 1992). A *Health Service Journal* editorial commented on the pressing need to involve clinical staff in all areas of management in 1987: 'Management can be made to fail at any level; it can only succeed at the point of delivery' (*Health Service Journal* 1 January 1987: 4). It is clear that clinicians – whose decisions commit substantial resources – are vital to the implementation of the marketing process at the point of delivery. The ability of managers to develop professionals as 'part-time marketeers' (Gummesson 1991) and implement 'internal consumerization' (Gronroos 1990), in order to broaden ownership, distance marketing from pure selling and legitimate the transformation, will become a central issue in determining the success of hospitals' marketing initiatives. This process, while problematic, appears to have been aided by a number of factors. First, marketing is not entirely new to those clinicians who have operated private or regional practices. Second, some appear to be accepting role changes to include marketing responsibilities in order to preserve their privileges (or limit their loss), and to prevent or neutralize the impact of other changes (Harrison *et al.* 1992: 103). If the experience of the USA is followed in the UK then the development of market relations may in itself lead to some doctors resembling 'corporate clinicians' because, increasingly, 'the tie that binds Board Members, Medical Staff and Administrators is one of avid competition with another Hospital or Regulatory Bodies' (Schulz and Detmer 1977: 8).

4 THE DEVELOPMENT OF A LANGUAGE OF QUALITY IN THE NHS

'Quality' as an issue within the NHS is proving a difficult term to define as it increasingly becomes part of a discourse which arises from the exchanges between a variety of stakeholders (Ellis 1988). Prior to *Working for Patients* (1989), quality issues within hospitals were largely defined and monitored by health-care professionals using peer review techniques such as medical and nursing audit. This medical construction of quality had long been established as the prevailing one within hospitals, a legitimate professional concern and one which had important implications for change management. As Ham states, 'Any attempt to integrate doctors into management must acknowledge this conflict and recognise the significant personal commitment of most doctors to provide high-quality service' (Ham, *Independent* 15 September 1988).

During the 1980s, mirroring private sector initiatives, NHS management and the government began to develop an interest in transplanting the techniques and rhetoric of quality assurance and total quality management (TQM) into the NHS (DH 1990; Welsh Office 1991). As part of the government's political reform process, patients' needs had to be prioritized through quality initiatives such as universal medical audit (National Audit Office 1988). This form of quality, involving the identification and satisfaction of customer requirements, began to point to the links between the concepts of quality and marketing. Following governmental leads, hospital quality managers began to redefine health-care quality to resemble Rooney's definition of 'the totality of features and characteristics of a service that bear on its ability to satisfy stated or implied needs' (Rooney 1988: 46). These 'needs' have increasingly become determined by management, and sometimes patients, through quality assurance initiatives such as the King's Fund Organizational Audit which sets and measures conformance to standards (Ellis 1988). Even professionally determined processes of medical and nursing audit are increasingly adopting a quality assurance approach. This is exemplified by the Department of Health's attempt to define the process as 'a systematic, critical analysis of the quality of medical care' (DH 1989: 39).

Mirroring the experience throughout the public sector, these NHS quality initiatives are being used to justify increased management scrutiny of the costs and quality of formerly autonomous professionals. For example, although the Citizen's Charter has been criticized for its lack of teeth (National Consumer Council 1993), it does call for improved standards, access and information about professional services. One result is that many quality indicators relate to economy, and marketing-type information, such as purchaser satisfaction data, rather than to risk management or user satisfaction.

Whether or not the new approach to NHS quality was specifically intended to achieve this reduction in clinical autonomy, the legitimacy of quality initiatives has suffered as a consequence. Nonetheless, most hospitals are now engaged in the practice of developing quality assurance initiatives which involve the generation of considerable market data. However, given the continued strength of health-care professionals and the fragile state of marketing in the NHS, the contested nature and form of quality initiatives is by no means secure. As the next section will demonstrate, the attempts to dovetail marketing and quality since 1991 have been as extensive as they have been unpredictable.

5 LINKING THE MARKETING AND QUALITY PROCESSES

There is a measure of agreement between organizational theorists that change processes are unlikely to be successful unless the values and assumptions underpinning the philosophy of change are perceived as legitimate by organizational stakeholders. Failure to recognize the importance of legitimacy 'finds its way straight to the bottom line' (Plant 1987: 14). However, the marketing discipline's myopia regarding the political and contextual aspects of organizations has led to implementation problems within the professional service context of the NHS (Webster 1988; Wong et al. 1991). The following section demonstrates that the health-care professional's view of marketing change is dependent not only upon the perceived legitimacy of the change pro- ponents but on their methods, the core ideas and the specific change activities (Quinn 1980). Drawing on local experience through case study data this section demonstrates how, in attempting to develop market- oriented units, some NHS managers have been able to link clinical quality and marketing initiatives as a means to legitimate marketing change to professionals. This activity is readily apparent across the three dimen- sions of marketing: philosophy, process and function.

Philosophy

The imposition of the quasi market ensured that formal consideration of mission statements was placed on hospital management board agendas as early as 1990–1 (Welsh Office 1991). Previously, most units had never made their mission formally explicit. The nearest equivalent had been through the evolution of a more or less discernible set of hospital values which involved the desire to maintain existing services within a professional collegiate structure. Moreover, both of the main units in this study complained that, prior to 1991, their unit philosophy and strategy development was largely constrained by those of the 'painfully cumbersome District Health Authority'.

By the end of 1992, it became apparent to one experienced external management consultant that most NHS unit managements were attempt- ing to move away from the 'philosophy of the throw-away 1960s and 1970s' which he illustrated with the following example of waste:

> In those days (before the present reforms) each of six or seven surgeons would have a favourite make of prosthesis and would demand that a supply be kept of all relevant sizes . . . As and when the technology changed, a shed full of obsolete appliances would be left at about £750 a throw.

As early as 1991, there were indications that the concept of 'money following the patient' was leading managements to reconsider a whole portfolio of issues including cost control, service-mixes, quality assurance, its customers and its managerial style. Indeed, the Marw Management Board was quick to realize that: 'we potentially stand to lose £10.14 million worth of business if other authorities no longer choose to send their patients to us for treatment' (Marw 1990: 4).

The emergence of a formal unit philosophy at the Marw unit was precipitated by work on a 'Quality Strategy'. As part of the search for a balance between fundamental general surgery and marketable specialties, the precursor to a transformation in guiding principles for the hospital was outlined:

> A programme for developing profiles for specific elements of the service will be embarked on, particularly focusing on specialist services where there is the potential to win market shares in the contracting market . . . We must identify existing and potential markets and competitors . . . examine our competitiveness . . . decide whether to adopt a strategy of service diversification or specialisation, target identified 'gaps' in the market, market our products . . . A Unit profile must be the first step in working towards a more comprehensive marketing strategy . . . particularly focusing on specialist services where there is the potential to win market shares in the contracting market.
>
> (Marw 1991: 8)

At Tyfu, the unit management began to consider the mission of the hospital and the unit's first business plan was produced in 1991. The previous unidimensional hospital motto of 'commitment through quality and quality through commitment' was replaced with the first unit mission statement: 'To provide the highest quality of care for patients, to motivate and develop staff in a caring environment, to meet health contracts and respond imaginatively to change, and to exceed customer expectations' (Tyfu 1991: 5). This statement clearly indicates that, even at this early stage, top management was clear about the need for marketing to inform the new philosophy but not to the total exclusion of quality, as this senior accountant realized: 'We have a very strong vision of contracting as the way forward . . . We have majored on quality as an issue, it is the one thing we have always tried to make sure that's part of our marketing vision.'

As these examples suggest, whilst management realized the need to introduce marketing to their mission considerations, it was not a totally marketing-oriented philosophy that emerged but rather a marketing–quality hybrid. This lack of total commitment to a market orientation has resulted in many health-care professionals maintaining that their customer is the patient, not the purchaser (i.e. the GP fundholder or the health authority).

Process

Images of the methods used by proponents of marketing change also impacted upon its perceived legitimacy. For example, much of the BMA's early opposition to the reforms was based on its perception that there was not sufficient scope for consultation between proponents of change and the professional bodies. This was mirrored at the Marw unit where much of the opposition to the organizational changes could be traced to the occasion when many of the staff read of the hospital management's decision to apply for trust status in the local evening newspaper.

During the marketing change process, the management of Tyfu unit displayed a consciousness of the need to legitimate the reforms to health-care professionals in the realization that their support and involvement was vital to securing marketing implementation. It was the Director of Business and Planning who first realized the potential in the use of quality initiatives as a method of introducing and legitimating marketing ideas to professionals 'through the back door'. He openly admitted this sleight of hand:

> I was personally moving marketing to clinicians through quality, there is no question about that . . . we were using quality as the vehicle . . . some of the clinical directors are now talking in marketing terms. So I can now switch to actually becoming much more open in my marketing approach.

This linking of quality and marketing initiatives was achieved through a variety of projects. For example, a board member explained how one 'unit quality initiative' had involved prioritizing 'shop window-type training'. Under this scheme, approximately 60 per cent of the non-medical staff had attended some form of customer service training. The unit quality coordinator explained how she felt that her role and that of the Unit Quality Council became inextricably linked to two main projects that had been embarked upon for their marketing elements. First, she felt that the primary reason for becoming the first Welsh hospital to take part in the King's Fund Organizational Audit was the board's desire to use the results as a marketing tool and attempt to measure professional work. Second, she felt that the drive to obtain the views of the hospital's clients was predominantly a PR tool for use during the contracting process.

Many senior clinicians involved with market-weak, 'cinderella' services such as geriatrics began to believe that a combination of marketing and quality could help their departments survive. Management encouraged departments to improve the quality of their service to purchasers by making them aware of potential avenues for future development and therefore a ward sister stated:

People are saying we can improve the quality of our service by developing our ability to market the service . . . Our professions have always been the ones that nobody understood what we do so we have been very keen to get out there and say, 'Look this is what we do.' We want to improve our profile and we see marketing as a means to an end.

The success of this management project to legitimate marketing to professionals, is also illustrated by some of the more commercially minded clinical directors' use of this process in their own departments. One senior clinician explained how she used a 'service quality initiative' to introduce her idea of marketing to professional radiology staff:

we even type the notices for the notice board now as a result of the King's Fund Audit and patient satisfaction questionnaire feedback . . . the reception area staff have now been trained in customer service elements like friendly greetings . . . my (professional) staff like this and see the point of this type of marketing.

Work on receptive contexts for change indicates that the *status* of proponents of ideas is a determinant of successful change (Pettigrew *et al.* 1992). In the units where marketing change was most advanced, the change champions tended to have had health-care professional backgrounds or were visibly supported by prominent medical professionals. For example, at Tyfu, the UGM's customary use of his professional title 'Honorary Consultant in Public Health Medicine' in letters to staff was viewed by many senior managers and clinicians as a considerable aid in the struggle to legitimate the reforms to professionals.

By the end of 1992, such were the perceived links that had been established between marketing and quality at Tyfu that one senior nurse, who complained of having to sell her profession's services to GPs, commented that 'while most staff are aware of marketing initiatives, these probably cannot be differentiated in their minds from quality . . . they are now indistinguishable'.

Function

A major empirical issue in determining the extent to which health-care professionals become involved in marketing roles within units has been the extent to which they perceive marketing activities as functionally *relevant* to their view of health-care provision. Certainly, doctors have always argued that they have practised in the interests of the individual patient (Thompson 1992) and are therefore, by definition, guided by a customer focus. Clinicians also have experience of 'managing'. Indeed, many consultants have managed their practices and many run the business aspects of their private practices. More recently, health-care professionals are being required to become involved in the management of the services they provide, through their involvement in areas such as the contracting process and in roles such as clinical directors and resource managers. In this sense, health professionals are following lawyers (Nelson 1988) and accountants (Greenwood *et al.* 1990) in becoming professional/managerial hybrids. This process began with the piloting of the Resource Management Initiative (RMI) in 1987 when clinicians were encouraged into resource allocation decision making.

However, professionals have proved reluctant fully to subordinate their practice values (MacIntyre 1990) to the marketeers' philosophy of meeting exchange parties' demands for a number of reasons. These include the perceived prioritization or targeting of some patients at the expense of others for financial reasons, and the perceived diminishing of their patient care ideals. Moreover, many doctors feel uncomfortable with the notion of competing with colleagues purely for income as opposed to clinical reputation. Keat (1991) explains how this process may lead to the 'exclusivity' of rewards and the discouragement of the sharing of ideas and new developments. Those UK health-care professionals who had their own private practices, were experienced in the more market-oriented systems such as the US system, or who felt that their specialities were well placed to benefit from the reforms were easier to convince of the relevance of marketing to the NHS. Of the enthusiasts, a number of clinical directors felt that their new budgeting responsibilities allowed them to increase the quality of the service that they provided. The most often quoted example encountered in this study occurred when clinicians spoke of improvements in the information at their disposal as a result of the reforms.

In both units, health-care professionals were encouraged to become involved in the collection and input of data which could be used for marketing-type activities. Where this was achieved, those involved generally believed that this extra work would result in an increase in service quality. For example, the installation of a new patient management system at the Marw radiology department was enthusiastically championed by the Superintendent Radiologist who believed it would reduce waiting times. The Consultant Radiographer, however, realized that it would also be able to give her the information she required to describe her service-mix in response to demands from management. Yet aside from these enthusiasts, very few instances were found of other health-care professionals becoming involved in the marketing function. Even at Tyfu, where a marketing manager was appointed, few had any idea what function the marketeer was performing or why. Conversely, the appointment of a GP liaison officer (a customer service manager) was generally well received as health-care professionals accepted that this post was needed to ensure that patients' views on quality were actioned. It is unsure whether most realized that it was GPs and not patients who were to be the focus of this person's responsibility.

The legitimacy of NHS marketing is also affected by the perceived origins and *ownership* of the change idea. The governmental origins of these reforms and the early control of marketing initiatives by finance departments negatively influenced the legitimacy of the ideas in the minds of occupational groups. Many nurses linked NHS marketing with the growth in power and numbers of finance departments, and to the perceived detriment of the nursing profession. An indication of Marw management's realization of the comparative legitimacy of quality over marketing was that while many existing marketing-type activities, such as those relating to contracting, emanated from the finance function, later expressions of marketing initiatives emerged from within the Directorate of Nursing and Quality's Quality Strategy Working Group (Marw 1991). Whilst this was justified publicly on the grounds of available space and personnel, management was keen to develop marketing techniques under the umbrella of quality. As the UGM put it:

> I appointed a quality coordinator . . . We created what we called a Unit Quality Council . . . linked with that has been a major push to get the views of our clients . . . It is through things like this and the King's Fund Audit that staff become aware that marketing is the vision we must promote.

Indeed, within the five main aims of this quality project was an embryonic marketing plan stressing:

> Purchasing Authorities and GP fundholders are clearly our consumers. We must identify existing and potential markets and competitors . . . examine our competitiveness . . . decide whether to adopt a strategy of service diversification or specialisation, target identified 'gaps' in the market, and market our products . . . A Unit profile must be the first step in working towards a more comprehensive marketing strategy

. . . particularly focusing on specialist services where there is the potential to win market shares in the contracting market.

(Marw 1991: 8)

This quality document articulated, perhaps more precisely than anywhere else, the emergent philosophy of the unit. Moreover, it is interesting that during early 1991, a period of supposed focus upon marketing as an issue, a quality manager was appointed instead of a dedicated marketing position, let alone a marketing department. Even in late 1992, this attempt to link the ownership of marketing to the quality department led one clinician to feel that quality 'is the biggest unit initiative and marketing must be linked to it'.

Overall, as both units show, the development of marketing in the NHS has to be understood by reference to the attempts to link marketing and quality. At the same time, the precise way in which clinical notions of quality have been used at unit level to legitimate marketing change has resulted in a marked reshaping of the intentions behind the original NHS reforms. The extent of management activity around marketing philosophy, process and functions has not led to any direct translation of strategic intention into operational form. On the contrary, the outcome has been conditioned by the processes of negotiation and accommodation involved. The very act of legitimating markets via quality has proved rich in unintended consequences.

CONCLUSION

Using a micro-political approach, this paper has shown that interpretations of change reflect the motives and concerns of pluralistic stakeholders. As a result, organizational change theory applied to the NHS must take serious account of the process of legitimization (Ham 1988: 24). It is evident that management and health-care professionals have interpreted the reforms in a variety of ways depending, to some degree, upon the subjective legitimacy they attach to the changes. This legitimacy is dependent upon a whole range of dynamic interests that disrupt any linear assumptions about the process of change. In the NHS, quality and the internal market are being used as a cross-disciplinary ideology for organizing professional work and binding actions together through an embryonic marketing philosophy. This form of standardization is similar to the standardization of clinicians' skills/knowledge during their education and training. This gives a dual set of levers for management to use in designing and coordinating hospital organization.

Standardization of ideology is 'tight' in the sense that it constitutes centralized control at the level of more professionals desiring external goods – but it is also 'loose' and highly decentralized because it relies on individuals interpreting legitimacy and operationalization at their localized level.

Using findings from structured case studies of professionals service organizations, the chapter reveals a number of subtle nuances at the heart of the NHS marketing change processes. Progress towards a market orientation is currently being undermined by a lack of attention being given to legitimating the reforms to the health-care professionals with their largely unchanged structural monopolies. Elsewhere, as part of a 'relationship marketing' approach, professionals are being persuaded that a market-orientation encompasses many of their professional practice standards and values (MacIntyre 1990). This chapter has shown how, following a trend established in the USA, some NHS managers are using the professionally acceptable vocabulary of quality as a means of legitimating some of the ideas and techniques traditionally associated with a market orientation. Some of these managers have introduced the 'internal market' (Gronroos 1990) concept to develop a customer–supplier paradigm, while simultaneously demonstrating a sensitivity to patient care by communicating the potential quality benefits of professionals becoming 'part-time marketeers'. In effect, these initiatives constitute an attempt to utilize quality and the internal market as a cross-disciplinary ideology for organizing professional work through the principles of the market.

The chapter also has something to contribute to the specific concerns expressed earlier in this volume. Kirkpatrick and Martinez (chapter 3) are right to stress the pervasive influence of the discourse of consumerism. Yet as the unit-level evidence in the previous sections showed, identifying the 'consumer' and 'customer' in the NHS is by no means straightforward. On a broader scale, the attempts to restructure the public sector have clearly been extensive in the past ten years and no-one doubts the advent of the 'new managerialism'. However, what this local study of hospital units shows, when set against the wider fabric of reforms in the NHS, is the extent of its fragility. In this sense, the evidence presented here is consistent with Reed's findings that quality initiatives have to pass through the micro-political filter within organizations. Hospitals are a strong example of the range of forces within public sector organizations which prevent any easy translation of political imperative into operational form.

This study has emphasized two key areas in this respect: professionals and marketing. In the first area it is abundantly clear that the reforms have provided new opportunities for professionals to shape unit structures and procedures, not least through their collective definitions of quality allied to their political strength. The second theme of markets is equally important. A detailed examination of the way the legitimacy of marketing has been socially constructed highlights how malleable market relations can be in the new public sector. Both managers and professionals have attempted to use the market to sustain their notions of quality. What stands out is the indeterminate nature of the internal market of the NHS, the transitory state of the current 'negotiated order' and the multiple contradictions within the discourse of quality. Their unravelling may take some time.

NOTE

For the sake of confidentiality all names are pseudonyms but all titles and role descriptions are accurate.

REFERENCES

Ackroyd, S., Hughes, J. and Soothill, K. (1989) 'Public services and their management', *Journal of Management Studies* 26(6): 603–19.

Ahmed, P. and Rafiq, M. (1992) 'Implanting competitive strategy: a contingency approach', *Journal of Marketing Management*: 49–67.

Alderfer, C. (1987) 'An intergroup perspective on group dynamics', in Lorsch (ed.), *Handbook of Organizational Behaviour*, Englewood Cliffs: Prentice-Hall.

Anthony, R., Dearden, J. and Govindarajan, V. (1992) *Management Control Systems*, Boston: Irwin.

Butler, J. and Vaile, M. (1984) *Health and Health Service: An Introduction to Health Care in Britain*, London: Routledge and Kegan Paul.

Calnan, M. and Gabe, J. (1991) 'Recent developments in general practice', in Gabe, J., Calnan M. and Bury, M. (eds), *The Sociology of the Health Service*, London: Routledge.

Christopher, M., Payne, A. and Ballantyne, D. (1992) *Relationship Marketing: Bringing Quality, Customer Service and Marketing Together*, Oxford: Butterworth-Heinemann.

Department of Health (1989) *Working for Patients*, Cmnd. 555, London: HMSO.

Dufour, Y. (1991) *The Implementation of General Practitioner Maternity Unit Closure Proposals in Hospitals*, PhD thesis, University of Warwick.

Ellis, R. (ed.) (1988) *Professional Competence and Quality Assurance in the Caring Professions*, London: Croom-Helm.

Fitzgerald, L. (1993) 'Clinicians into management: the agenda for change and training', paper presented at 'Professions and Management in Britain' Conference, University of Stirling.

Gardner, C. (1986) Dissertation proposal, George Washington University, Washington, DC, reported by Yorke, D. in Ford, D. (ed.) (1991) *Understanding Business Markets*, London: Academic Press.

Glover, I. and Kelly, M. (1992) 'From placebo to healing balm? The curious history of British management thought and of its application to the National Health Service', paper presented at the British Academy of Management Conference, University of Bradford.

Greenwood, R., Hinings, C. and Brown, J. (1990) 'P2 form strategic management: corporate practices in professional partnerships', *Academy of Management Journal* 3(4): 725–55.

Griffiths Report (1983) *NHS Management Inquiry: Letter to the Secretary of State and Recommendations for Action*, London: HMSO.

Gronroos, C. (1990) *Service Management and Marketing: Managing Moments of Truth in Service Competition*, Lexington: Free Press/Lexington Books.

Gummesson, E. (1991) 'Marketing-orientation revisited: the crucial role of the part-time marketeer', *European Journal of Marketing* 25(2): 60–75.

Harrison, S. (1990) 'UK provider markets in English health care: incentives and prospects', in Bengoa, R. and Hunter, D. (eds), *New Directions in Managing Health Care*, Leeds: The Nuffield Institute.

Harrison, S., Hunter, D., Marnoch, G. and Pollitt, C. (1992) *Just Managing: Power and Culture in the National Health Service*, London: Macmillan.

Heald, D. (1990) 'Charging in British government: evidence from the Public Expenditure Survey', *Financial Accountability and Management* 6(4): 229–64.

Hood, C. (1991) 'A public management for all seasons?', *Public Administration* 69(1): 3–20.

Houston, F. (1986) 'The marketing concept: what it is and what it is not', *Journal of Marketing* 50: 81–7.

Keat, R. (1981) *The Politics of Social Theory*, Oxford: Blackwell.

Keat, R. (1991) 'Consumer sovereignty and the integrity of practices', in Keat, R. and Abercrombie, N. (eds), *The Enterprise Culture*, London: Routledge.

Kitchener, M. (1992) 'Managing marketing change', *Journal of Industrial Affairs* 1(1): 29–31.

Kitchener, M. (1994) 'Investigating marketing change: a comparative-intensive approach', in Wass, V. and Wells, P. (eds), *Principles and Practice in Business and Management Research*, Aldershot: Dartmouth Press.

Kohli, A. and Jaworski, B. (1990) 'Market orientation: the construct, research propositions and managerial implications', *Journal of Marketing* 54: 1–18.

Le Grand, J. (1991) 'Quasi-markets and social policy', *The Economic Journal* 101: 1256–67.

MacIntyre, A. (1990) *After Virtue: A Study in Moral Theory*, London: Duckworth.

McKinlay, J. and Stoekle, J. (1988) 'Corporatisation and the social transformation of doctoring', *International Journal of Health Services* 18(2): 191–205.

McNulty, T., Whipp, R., Whittington, R. and Kitchener, M. (1993) 'Putting marketing into NHS hospitals: issues about implementation', *Journal of Public Money and Management* July: 51–7.

Major, J. (1989) 'Public service management: the revolution in progress', lecture, London: Audit Commission.

Marw Group of Hospitals (1990) *Business Plan 1990/91*, Marw: Marw Group of Hospitals.

Marw Group of Hospitals (1991) *Unit Quality Strategy*, Marw: Marw Group of Hospitals.

Meyer, A., Goes, J. and Brooks, G. (1991) 'Organisations in hyperturbulance: environmental jolts and industry revolutions', in Huber, G. and Glick, W. (eds), *Mastering Organisational Change: Enhancing Organisational Performance through Redesign*, New York: Oxford University Press.

Mintzberg, H. (1983) *Power In and Around Organisations*, Englewood Cliffs: Prentice-Hall.

Morgan, N. and Piercy, N. (1990) 'Barriers to marketing in professional service firms', *MEG Conference Proceedings*, Oxford: Oxford Polytechnic.

Narver, J. and Slater, S. (1990) 'The effect of a market orientation on business profitability', *Journal of Marketing* October: 21.

National Audit Office (1988) *Quality of Clinical Care in National Health Service Hospitals*, Paper 736, London: House of Commons.

National Consumer Council (1993) *Quality Standards in the NHS*, London: HMSO.

Nelson, R. (1988) *Partners with Power: The Social Transformation of the Large Law Firm*, Berkeley: University of California Press.

Owen, D. (1976) 'National Health Service: clinical freedom and professional freedom', *The Lancet* 8 May: 1006–9.

Pettigrew, A., Ferlie, E. and McKee, L. (1992) *Shaping Strategic Change*, London: Sage.

Piercy, N. (1991) *Market-led Strategic Change*, London: Thorsens/Harper Collins.

Plant, R. (1987) *Managing Change and Making it Stick*, London: Fontana/Collins.

Pollitt, C. (1990) *Managerialism and the Public Services: The Anglo-American Experience*, Oxford: Basil Blackwell.

Quinn, J. (1980) *Strategies for Change: Logical Incrementalism*, Homewood: Irwin.

Raelin, J. (1985) 'The basis for the professional's resistance to managerial control', *Human Resource Management* 24(2): 147–76.

Roach Anleu, S. (1990) 'The professionalization of social work? A case study of three settings', *Sociology* 26: 23–43.

Rooney, E. (1988) 'A proposed quality system specification for the National Health Service', *Quality Assurance* 14(1): 60–81.

Schatzman, L. and Strauss, A. (1973) *Field Research: Strategies for a Natural Sociology*, Englewood Cliffs: Prentice-Hall.

Schulz, R. and Detmer, D. (1977) 'How to get doctors involved in governance and management', in *Hospital Medical Staff: Selected Readings 1972–1976*, American Hospital Association.

Sheaff, R. (1991) *Marketing for Health Services*, Milton Keynes: Open University Press.

Shortell, S., Morrison, E. and Fiedman, B. (1990) *Strategic Choices for America's Hospitals*, San Fransisco: Jossey-Bass.

Stewart, J. and Walsh, K. (1992) 'Change in the management of public services', *Public Administration* 70(4): 519–32.

Strong, P. and Robinson, J. (1990) *The NHS Under New Management*, Milton Keynes: Open University Press.

Thompson, P. (1992) 'Public sector management in a period of radical change: 1979-92', *Public Money and Management* July–September: 33–41.

Todd, D. (1979) 'Mixing qualitative and quantitative methods: triangulation in action', *Administrative Science Quarterly* 24 December: 602–11.

Tyfu Hospital NHS Trust (1991) Management Team Briefings, January–October.

Walsh, K. (1991) 'Citizens and consumers: marketing and public sector management', *Journal of Marketing Management* Summer: 9–15.

Webster, F. (1988) 'Changing control strategies in industrial R&D', *Business Horizons* May–June: 29–39.

Welsh Office (1991) *Charter for Patients in Wales*, Cardiff: Welsh Office.

Whipp, R. and Pettigrew, A. (1991) *Managing Change for Competitive Success*, Oxford: Basil Blackwell.

Whittington, R. and Whipp, R. (1992) 'Professional ideology and marketing implementation', *European Journal of Marketing* 26(1): 52–63.

Winstanley, D., Sorabji, D., Dawson, S., Mole, V. and Sherval (1992) 'When the pieces don't fit: dilemmas in public sector restructuring', paper presented at BAM Conference, 'Management into the 21st Century'.

Wong, V., Saunders, J. and Doyle, P. (1991) 'The barriers to achieving stronger marketing orientation', in *British Companies: An Exploratory Study*, ESRC Ref WF 2025 0018, London: Economic and Social Research Council.

Yorke, D.A. (1990) 'Interactive perceptions of suppliers and corporate clients in the marketing of professional services: a comparison of accounting and legal services in the UK, Canada and Sweden', *Journal of Marketing Management* 5(3): 307–23.

Chapter 10

The emergence and use of quality in British Rail

Andrew Pendleton

INTRODUCTION

In the years immediately before privatization, 'quality' came to the forefront of management in British Rail (BR). Along with safety and the skills of the workforce, quality was proclaimed as one of the three areas on which the success of BR depended (British Railways Board 1993: 4). By the end of the 1980s, quality of service objectives had been added to the core financial objectives set by government and, in response to the Citizen's Charter initiative, BR issued a Passengers' Charter (British Railways Board 1992) setting out its performance targets and obligations to its passengers, now retitled customers. BR's charter was the first to provide for customer refunds when certain targets were not achieved. Moreover, the language of 'quality' had become an all-pervasive discourse used not only to market services to external customers, but internally to conceptualize and legitimize changes to organizational processes and patterns of human resource management. All major initiatives in these areas were justified in terms of improving service quality. Some of the most important incorporated the language of quality into their titles (e.g. *Quality Through Teamwork, Organising for Quality*). Yet although quality and human resource management innovations became increasingly conjoined from the late 1980s, the linkages between them were by no means as straightforward as implied by the Citizen's Charter.

Much of the appeal of 'quality' in recent management initiatives has been its multiplicity of meanings and applications (see Pfeffer and Coote 1991; Wilkinson and Willmott 1994; and ch. 1 in this volume), enabling its use as a catch-all concept to justify organizational change. Besides its traditional use to describe premium products and services, 'quality' has recently acquired a number of specific meanings in management discourse. One, associated especially with total quality management (TQM), refers to the degree to which a product or service specification is actually achieved and is encapsulated in such notions as 'zero defects' (Wilkinson 1993). A second is concerned with 'fitness for purpose', in other words, the extent to which a product or service meets a consumer need. A further meaning, especially associated with the public sector, is that of 'value for money' (see chapter 1 in this volume); the provision of goods or services at a price which optimizes consumer returns as recipients and/or funders. Underlying all of these in recent years has been the notion of of quality as organizational responsiveness to external market pressures, and the subjugation of producer to consumer interests. In this chapter we suggest that for a long time the dominant meaning of quality in BR has been that of the first type – that of maintaining adherence to production specifications. Recent initiatives, such as TQM programmes, extensive safety validation procedures, and the Passengers' Charter fall squarely in this tradition. Quality as 'fitness for purpose' and value for money have been less prominent, though not altogether absent. However, in recent years the discourse of the consumer has become highly prominent. Whilst this is consistent with the importance government has attached to exposing public sector organizations to market forces, the emergence of this language of quality has been, in part, a response to the shortcomings of government policies, both in terms of their effects on the provision of services and on internal patterns of management (Pollitt 1992).

The different meanings of 'quality', however, are potentially contradictory in their implications for organizational practices. This is shown particularly clearly in the area of human resource management. It has been observed by Wilkinson (1993) that tensions within total quality management, between 'hard' statistical process control approaches to quality control and 'softer' approaches aimed at encouraging employees to internalize the quality message, broadly correspond to the widely accepted distinction between 'hard' and 'soft' approaches to human resource management (Legge 1989), and also to Friedman's (1977) earlier contrast between 'direct control' and 'responsible autonomy'. Some versions of quality tend to be associated with an emphasis on the direct assertion of the management prerogative in the utilization of labour whilst others are more associated with training and employee involvement initiatives. The precise configuration of quality–HRM linkages in given organizations may be complex and contradictory, as well as heavily dependent on the prevailing labour management context.

In BR's case, the emphasis on achieving service targets has been associated with both kinds of human resource management approach, as has the recent discourse emphasizing responsiveness to consumer needs. Concern to improve employee performance by reducing formal and uniform regulation, as in the shift to performance-based payment systems, has co-existed with greater bureaucratization of some work roles. In some respects, therefore, quality has been associated with attempts to change the prevailing pattern of labour management whilst in others it can be seen as involving an intensification of traditional approaches.

THE TRADITIONAL CONCEPT OF 'QUALITY' IN BRITISH RAIL

The current emphasis on quality is an integral part of new approaches to public sector management which have become increasingly widespread from the late 1980s onwards (Walsh 1991; Stewart and Walsh 1992). In common with internal contracting and the creation of quasi markets, the encouragement of quality is aimed at improving organizational responsiveness to market forces and consumer needs. Although the philosophy and specific mechanisms of the Citizen's Charter are relatively novel, especially in relation to public services, in organizations like BR a concern with quality of service has a longer pedigree (Doern 1993). The aspects of service quality which were to form the cornerstone of BR's approach in the early 1990s were already in use when the Conservatives came to office in 1979. Indeed a Consumers' Charter was drafted by BR as early as 1980. At that time, the key dimensions of quality were reliability (i.e. the extent to which planned services actually ran), punctuality (the extent to which services kept to schedules), train cleanliness and safety (Monopolies and Mergers Commission 1980: 30). Reliability and punctuality were monitored internally by reference to performance targets. These performance targets, however, formed no part of formal governmental objectives for the railways, the only quality of service dimension to BR's statutory obligations being the requirement to use the Public Service Obligation grant (PSO) to maintain services at broadly the same level as in 1974. The approach to quality, therefore, was primarily concerned with achieving the service specification rather than defining the nature of the specification itself. In essence, the management of quality focused on devising a technically feasible timetable and on utilizing physical and human resources to ensure that this plan was successfully implemented each day. This conception of quality was consistent with the engineering and operations management values said to dominate BR at the time (Reid 1990). Quality was about the operational achievement of a technical specification. There was little explicit reference to the consumer in this discourse (which is not to say that consumer wants were ignored). For instance, in a statement on rail policy issued at the start of the 1980s, the only statistical information in the section on quality related to equipment failures (British Railways Board 1981).

This approach to railway management underpinned a pattern of labour management in which great importance was attached to predictability, consistency and uniformity (Pendleton 1994). To deliver the pattern of services scheduled in the timetable, managers had to be sure that suitably qualified staff would be available in the appropriate places at the appropriate times, often working without direct supervision. The 'conventional wisdom' in BR since nationalization has been that consensual approaches to labour management are necessary to secure these imperatives. Reliance on the management prerogative to govern labour deployment could have too many dysfunctional side-effects on the operation of the timetable. The emphasis on engineering and operations values was therefore interconnected with an extensive system of joint regulation. BR was characterized by an extensive 'web of rules' governing most aspects of labour management, including job grading, promotion, deployment, utilization and remuneration, for the most part determined jointly by management and unions. Alongside these, most aspects of train operation were governed by a comprehensive set of safety rules, detailing with some precision required staff actions across the anticipated range of operational situations. Both task content and industrial relations were therefore highly bureaucratized in BR.

Superficially, BR's approach to quality of service issues looked very different by the early 1990s but in reality there was considerable continuity with earlier practice. The main substantive development was that some of the operations-based quality of service targets had acquired a wider audience. Quality of service objectives were incorporated into BR's formal objectives in 1987 when the Secretary of State for Transport formally agreed the targets for punctuality, reliability, train loading, train cleanliness and booking office queuing times already in use by BR's Network SouthEast, and required that BR's achievements against targets be reported to the department each year (Monopolies and Mergers Commission 1987: 261–2). The government followed suit for BR's Provincial Sector in 1989. Then, in the wake of the Citizen's Charter, BR published a Passengers' Charter which set reliability and punctuality performance targets for each passenger profit centre, and undertook to publish details of actual performance at railway stations. A national target for booking office queuing was stipulated and BR gave various undertakings, though not expressed as targets, to avoid overcrowding, provide adequate information and to get passengers to their destinations (British Railways Board 1992). BR's charter was notable for being the first to provide for partial refunds where certain charter undertakings were not achieved (though the total compensation paid by BR to passengers has actually fallen compared with pre-charter days: *Financial Times* 13 March 1994).

In the early 1990s, quality was primarily operationalized in terms of achievement of a specification, just as it was fifteen years earlier. By contrast, quality as 'fitness for purpose' or value for money has been much less developed despite some rhetoric to the contrary. Most improvements to the quality of the service itself have been fairly marginal, though no doubt welcome, such as the introduction of Customer Welcome Teams to InterCity stations in 1992 and improvements to InterCity on-train buffets. The quality of rail services themselves – their frequency, their timings and their interconnections with other services – are viewed by government and BR as commercial issues for resolution by BR management, and unsuitable for the limited consumer dialogue embodied in the charter initiatives. Instead, it is assumed that BR's interpretation of consumer demand (in the light of its financial objectives) will lead to provision of appropriate services. Indeed, the logic of recent government rail policy is that the influence of other 'social' factors (e.g. the desirability of reducing pollution) should be steadily reduced in favour of the commercial considerations of BR's 'business needs'. These primarily financial considerations have justified a deterioration in service provision at various times in the 1980s and 1990s. The main obstacle to substantial improvements in the quality of service provision is that large increases in public subsidy would probably be required. This, of course, is entirely contrary to one of the main thrusts of government rail policy in the 1980s and 1990s – reductions in public financial support for the railways. The issue of quality as 'value for money' is coloured by similar considerations. Whilst on the one hand reductions in public subsidy can be justified on the grounds of securing value for money for the taxpayer, as they have in the case of public services, on the other they have led directly (in conjunction with profit targets) to real increases in the prices of BR services. From the customers' point of view, therefore, this aspect of service quality has probably worsened in recent years. For this reason little emphasis has been given by government and BR to this dimension in public discussions of quality.

Although the inference of our analysis is that there has been little fundamental change in the management of quality in BR, two developments are novel and worthy of note. One is the language of quality itself which has come to be all-pervasive, providing an overarching conceptualization of virtually all BR activities, both internally and externally. Passengers have been redefined as 'customers' and all staff coming into regular contact with them have been reclassified as 'retail' staff. Platform and train announcements now refer to '*your* service', '*your* buffet', which appears to breakdown the separation of consumption from production and to imply customer 'ownership' of the services provided by BR (Du Gay and Salaman 1992). These linguistic innovations even affect physical plant: traction and rolling stock depots are now known as 'traincare' depots. The second development is the use of quality as a legitimizing force for a range of innovations in labour management and internal management processes. In some respects, these innovations depart from the traditional emphasis on consistency, uniformity and equity, whilst in others, quality has increased bureaucratic standardization. In the remainder of the chapter we examine (a) the evolution of the configuration and discourse of 'quality' in BR over the last fifteen years or so, and (b) the nature of recent human resource management (HRM) initiatives associated with the concern for quality.

THE DEVELOPMENT OF 'QUALITY' IN THE 1980s AND EARLY 1990s

Whilst 'quality' only comes to the fore in management discourse from the late 1980s its origins have a longer pedigree. As might be anticipated, the reasons for its development lie largely in the political sphere; the emergence of quality has to be set in the context of an intensification of policies of 'commercialization' over the last fifteen years or so. However, BR's adoption of 'quality' is not simply a mirror-like reaction to the Conservative government's apparent conversion to consumer rights in the early 1990s, though some may wish to claim so for political purposes. The reality is far more complex. The concern with quality has emerged from a number of contradictory forces. Probably the strongest pressures for quality have come from agencies in the political domain but outside government itself. By contrast, government policies of commercialism for most of the period have been more focused on financial restructuring than product quality. The government's eventual

conversion to quality in the 1990s can be located in the political unpopularity of the consequences for service quality of its earlier policies
(Pollitt 1992). For electoral reasons the government needed to show its
concern for the state of public services, and the Major government
needed to distance itself from Thatcherism and to forge a distinctive
philosophy of its own. It is also possible to argue that the mechanisms
of the charter approach favoured by the government distance it from
failures of service provision and tend to redirect blame for service
deterioration from government to the organization itself (chapter 1 in
this volume).

The main thrust of government policy towards British Rail for most
of the 1980s was commercialization (Pendleton 1993). Although the
language of commercialization included copious references to markets
(and hence consumers, at least indirectly), its main practical component
was financial. The main objectives set for BR in 1983 (and renewed for
the rest of the decade) were essentially financial, incorporating reductions in financial support and the imposition of profit targets. From
1983, a series of stepped reductions in government grant (the PSO) were
imposed, with the result that by the end of the decade central government financial support for BR had been reduced by over 50 per cent in
real terms, and InterCity services removed from the subsidy regime.
Accompanying these were profit targets for those rail activities required
to act on a 'fully commercial footing' (freight, parcels and InterCity).
The government's rationale was simple: BR's costs were considerably
higher than they need be because financial protection weakened incentives for BR managers to pursue efficiency, and because the railway
trade unions had constructed a web of 'restrictive practices' governing
labour utilization, aided and abetted by a spineless management. A more
rigorous financial regime would encourage long overdue reforms of
working practices. Commercialization, therefore, also included an
industrial relations component. In fact, during the first half of the 1980s,
BR's core strategy centred on a programme of reform of working
practices, including flexible scheduling of traincrew, removal of the
train guard from some services and extensions to single staffing of
locomotives (Ferner 1988). For the most part the objective was to secure
economies by reducing headcount rather than to improve product quality
by changing labour utilization.

This particular definition of commercialization is highlighted by two
features of BR practice at the time. The first is BR's use of performance
indicators (PIs). By the end of the 1970s, BR (in advance of many other
nationalized industries) had responded to the Labour government's 1978

White Paper (Treasury 1978) by developing a comprehensive set of performance indicators. However, as Carter *et al.* note (1992: 147–9), BR's PIs (like those of other public sector organizations) were primarily concerned with finance and efficiency rather than quality of service (Pollitt 1986). In the 1982 Annual Report, for instance, only three of the twenty-one core PIs were concerned with quality of service, with most relating to labour and financial efficiency. A commentary on 'key performance indicators' talked only of efficiency and economy indicators (British Railways Board 1983). The second feature is the change of language that seemed to occur contemporaneously with commercialization. After the partial replacement of geographically based management structures with market-based business sectors in 1983, management policies increasingly came to be justified (internally and externally) by reference to 'the needs of the business'. This reification of the businesses was meant to signify a break from the engineering and production culture, and a conversion to the power of markets. However, the consumer was something of a lacuna in this ideology. The 'needs of the business' were overwhelmingly financial – unsurprising given the financial and political context – and centred on cost reductions. This mantra was therefore frequently recited to justify unpopular decisions with consumers, such as service reductions.

If government itself was largely interested in finance, efficiency and industrial relations, other bodies were more concerned with quality of service. In its investigation into BR's London and South-East services at the end of the 1970s, the Monopolies and Mergers Commission recommended that the quality of service standards already in partial use within BR be agreed and monitored in conjunction with the statutory consumer organization, the Transport Users' Consultative Committee (TUCC), and details of actual performance be published at railway stations (Monopolies and Mergers Commission 1980: 53). It further recommended that more precise operational targets be developed from core quality of service standards for management control purposes. Later reports by the Commission (in 1987 and 1989) also pursued this theme. Within Parliament, both the House of Commons Committee of Public Accounts (1986) and the House of Commons Transport Committee (1987) recommended that government develop and monitor quality of service objectives in conjunction with BR to ensure that the government's financial objectives did not harm service quality. The statutory consumers' body – the Transport Users' Consultative Committee – exploited these openings to press home its long-standing message that quality of service should be protected and advanced using performance targets and measures. In response to these political pressures, the government began to take on board the quality of service message and from 1987 some quality objectives were incorporated into BR's formal objectives. However, there is little evidence to suggest that the government had been converted to the cause of consumer rights. Rather, the primary concern seems to have been to neutralize political 'fall-out' from reductions in PSO finance, and the quality considerations introduced into BR's formal objectives were viewed primarily as constraints rather than substitutes for the core strategy of financial retrenchment.

However, the correlation between cuts in PSO and deterioration in quality of service did not go away. On the contrary, towards the end of the 1980s BR's operating performance deteriorated sharply, due to a combination of financial stringency, a sharp upturn in demand for rail travel and high levels of staff turnover (Pendleton 1993), especially in the politically sensitive South-East. In 1989, train cancellations in the South-East increased from 1.5 to 4 per cent, and the proportion of Network SouthEast and InterCity trains arriving 'on time' (i.e. within ten minutes of booked arrival time) fell sharply. Complaints to the TUCCs rose by 54 per cent from 5,228 in 1989–90 to 8,053 in 1990–1 (Central Transport Users' Consultative Committee 1991). At the same time, BR's hitherto creditable safety record was compromised by serious accidents at Clapham Junction, Purley and Newton. In two of these cases the root causes could be located in economy measures, even though human error was the immediate cause in all three cases (see, for instance, the Hidden Inquiry report into the Clapham Junction disaster 1991).

To summarize so far, the upshot of our analysis is that government strategy towards the railways in the 1980s, and the management response to it, centred on financial cutbacks and efficiency improvements. As the 1980s progressed, this led to a deterioration in service quality both in terms of BR's ability to deliver the service specification and the nature of the service specification itself. It is not stretching the point too far to suggest that the closing years of the 1980s can be characterized as a 'quality crisis'. It is in this context that the discourse of quality emerged centre stage in the management of the railways. 'Quality' provided the rationale and legitimation (and title in some cases) for reforms aimed at securing swift improvements to BR's operational performance. It also provided an 'upbeat' rallying call for a workforce demoralized by the effects of cutbacks, deterioration in services and abuse from the public, as well as the trauma of the series of fatal accidents. Appeals to quality also gave signals to politicians, consumers and the electorate that BR management was taking serious steps to rectify its faults, as well as taking market responsiveness seriously. By the time that the Major government discovered quality in the early 1990s, therefore, BR management had already been converted.

Developments in BR's case are therefore broadly consistent with Pollitt's analysis that the emergence of 'quality' in the public sector has been a reaction to the effects of the Thatcher governments' policies of retrenchment on service quality (Pollitt 1992: 180–7). As suggested above, an emphasis on quality provided a number of benefits to BR management in its efforts to deal with the dysfunctions of government strategy towards the railways. The approach to quality eventually adopted by the Major government in the form of the charter initiative did not transform BR's approach to quality; rather it reinforced the target-based approach in use internally within BR since the 1970s. This particular conception of quality provided a number of benefits to government. It left the important issues of the level and character of rail service provision more or less untouched. The charter ignored wider issues of transport and railway policy. Indeed, it can be argued that the focus on meeting targets could divert public attention from these issues, though hostile comments from rail travellers recorded in the media suggest rather mixed results in this respect (*Financial Times* 13 March 1994). A further possible benefit of the charter approach is that the charters issued by organizations like BR tend to focus culpability for failure to meet specified targets more squarely on the organization than government (Lewis 1993; chapter 1 in this volume). It can be argued, therefore, that the charter initiative did not fundamentally change the character of recent government policy towards organizations like BR (Doern 1993). Instead, it provided a mechanism for dealing with some of the political problems arising from the emphasis on financial retrenchment and commercialization. Many more fundamental aspects of rail policy remained unchanged. For instance, a big reduction in PSO grant in 1993 led to cuts in services and hence a reduction in the quality of the content of BR's services. Overall, the evidence from BR's case suggests that the development and character of 'quality' has been a function of the political interplay of various key groups of actors, in a context where the dominant policy has been one of retrenchment rather than the simple outcome of the spread of New Right notions of markets and consumer sovereignty.

QUALITY AND HUMAN RESOURCE MANAGEMENT

A hallmark of recent approaches to product quality, such as total quality management, has been an emphasis on the reform of internal organizational processes, though the linkages between quality management and HRM have generally been weakly developed and often contradictory (Wilkinson 1993; Wilkinson *et al.* 1992). Yet such linkages were asserted with some confidence in the Citizen's Charter. In that document performance related pay was clearly identified as a key HRM mechanism for securing improvements in service quality, and BR's adoption of this form of payment system for some of its manual staff was cited approvingly (HMSO 1991: 17). However, the reality is somewhat more complex. It is true that in BR a new approach to HRM and industrial relations issues emerged at approximately the same time as quality was moving to the centre of management discourse. Yet the origins of the two were distinct, though related, and although quality provided a rationale for HRM initiatives, it was not the most important factor in their development. The failure of this particular strategy, however, catapulted quality to the centre of HRM, and in the early 1990s, quality and HRM became increasingly synchronized.

Around the time that quality of service was assuming increasing importance in BR's relationships with central government, a new approach to HRM emerged which had a number of distinctive features compared with earlier practices. First, whereas BR's industrial relations strategy in the first half of the decade had been aimed primarily at reducing headcount and improving labour productivity, the new approach was much more concerned with increasing management control of labour selection, deployment and utilization. Those managers in the ascendant were concerned that the previous initiatives had not only been less successful in improving efficiency than had been hoped but that they had done little or nothing to weaken the 'web of rules' which governed labour usage (Martinez Lucio 1993). Indeed, some initiatives seemed to have made some aspects of labour management even more rule-bound (Pendleton 1991). The new approach was therefore concerned with weakening job regulation and enhancing the management prerogative. Inevitably, in the BR context this implied a reduction in the trade unions' involvement in labour management. The second feature of the new approach, therefore, was that unions were given a smaller role in the application of new policies and practices. Third, in contrast to even the recent past, union agreement to the introduction of HRM changes was not viewed as essential and, indeed, some innovations such as performance related pay were introduced over the heads of the unions. In the light of these characteristics 'hard human resource management' seems an appropriate characterization of the new approach which emerged around 1987/8 (Pendleton 1993). Some reference was made to quality of service in the rationales for these new policies – a reduction in joint regulation would give BR a freer hand to respond to customer needs – but the primary logic was to transform industrial relations to meet the dictates of the government's strategy of financial cutbacks.

The origins of the new approach can, like the emergence of quality, be located in movements in the 'political contingency', that is the complex of forces emanating from government and other agencies in the political domain which provide the context and, on occasions, the primary influence on organizational decision making (Batstone *et al.* 1984). A number of factors can be identified such as changes to the composition of BR's board by government to include a greater proportion of private sector business leaders; dismay in government agencies such as the Monopolies and Mergers Commission and those BR managers in the ascendant at the results and timescale of earlier industrial relations reforms; 'gung-ho' industrial relations confidence post miners' strike, etc. (Pendleton 1993). Given that a primary objective of 'hard human resource management' was to replace joint regulation of various aspects of labour management with unilateral management control, conflict with the railway trade unions was almost inevitable. It came over BR's plans to reform industrial relations institutions. During spring 1989, there were a number of one-day strikes against BR's plans which, by common consent, BR 'lost' very badly.

This industrial relations disaster for BR coincided with and intensified the 'quality crisis' described earlier. By mid-1989, BR was faced with the twin imperatives of rebuilding relationships both with its customers and its employees, whilst at the same time maintaining much of the substantive content of the HRM initiatives then in progress to achieve the dictates of government's financial strategy. The solution adopted was to replace the confrontational approach to industrial relations with the more traditional reliance on consensus (Pendleton 1993). At the same time, 'quality' moved to the fore as the rationale for changes to labour management. Now that consensus was valued again, a legitimating force was needed to justify radical and often unpopular changes. The discourse of 'quality' served a number of purposes here. First, its upbeat tone could provide a rallying call for a demoralized workforce. Second, appeals to product quality could disarm the opposition of those employees and their representatives who had traditionally used the concept of public service as a defence against strategies of retrenchment. Third, an emphasis on customer needs could secure greater management control over employee performance without management appearing to wrest control from employees directly (Fuller and Smith 1991). In highlighting the functions of quality in these respects, however, we do not wish to suggest that quality provided the linchpin of a conspiratorial 'master plan' amongst top management. However, the advantages of quality in these respects were perceived by management, though not necessarily in the same terms presented here (Welsby 1991), and for this reason the early years of the 1990s were characterized by an ever-closer alignment of quality and human resource management. Yet though the discourse of quality became much more central to the rationale for HRM changes in the early 1990s, the substantive content of these initiatives differed little from the earlier phase of 'hard HRM'. Furthermore, the linkages between quality and HRM were often contradictory in character. To explore these contentions we now outline the main innovations in HRM from the late 1980s.

The first set of changes were those associated with pay and performance. In the late 1980s and early 1990s there were a number of attempts to link pay to performance, which increasingly focused on 'quality of service', as might be expected given the emphasis of the Citizen's Charter on performance pay. In 1988, BR imposed personal contracts and performance related pay on all of its management grades. Collective bargaining over managerial pay ceased, except over the establishment of minimum points in each salary band and henceforth each manager's pay was to be determined by an annual appraisal with his or her superior. The appraisal process was based on meeting objectives, of which at least one was a quality of service objective. Although in the early years of the scheme the variations in pay awards were quite large, more recently the range has become compressed, mainly because of financial difficulties and the Major government's public sector incomes policy limiting pay increases to 1.5 per cent of pay bill costs. Both developments seem to have had a demotivating effect; annoyance at the discrepancies found in early pay awards has been followed by dismay that performance has not been adequately reflected in more recent awards (Pendleton 1992). Concern about the fairness of performance pay may not have been allayed by the introduction of a new scheme by government in which the chairman of BR can earn a bonus of up to £25,000 if Passengers' Charter targets are achieved (*Independent* 9 March 1992). Performance payments have also been extended to some blue-collar staff and with an explicit link to quality. A new grading system for signals and telecommunications technicians (cited approvingly in the Citizen's Charter) was introduced in 1990 with provision for promotion to higher grades being explicitly related to achievement of quality targets. Finally, before the privatization initiative killed off initiatives of this type, InterCity was pressing for senior conductors on InterCity trains to be put on to a performance related pay scheme in which the key criterion was to be the quality of service delivered to the customer.

A hallmark of performance related pay schemes is that they usually diminish the role of unions and increase individual management judgement in pay setting. A similar development can be seen in the approach to employee selection and promotion. The governing principle for determining promotion and job movements amongst blue-collar and many white-collar jobs for many years had been seniority of service. In the late 1980s, BR made increasing use of aptitude tests and other guides to future performance in the selection of employees. In particular, staff selected from BR's existing pool of train guards to become senior conductors on InterCity trains were selected on merit rather than seniority using a battery of tests to predict how they would deal with the public. Similarly, those guards wanting to become train drivers in the wake of the Traincrew Agreement were required to take a number of selection tests. Achieving quality became a central component of the rationale for these innovations – it was argued by BR management that the seniority system resulted in unsuitable employees securing promotion. This appeal to quality placed the rail unions in something of a conundrum. The principle of seniority had long been central to their approach to labour management. Equally, improvements in the quality of rail services had been an important campaigning objective, especially in the 1980s when unions were concerned to counter the retrenchment policies brought about by the government's financial strategy. The rail unions, therefore, focused their bargaining efforts on the generation of rules to ensure that selection criteria would be administered fairly rather than opposing the dilution of seniority per se.

Alongside these measures were a variety of employee involvement initiatives with some aimed at securing greater management control of employee performance in the short term, and others more concerned at winning 'hearts and minds' in the medium term. The discourse of 'quality' has come to be especially strong in initiatives of this type. Originally, many of the initiatives under this heading were implemented by specific regions of BR. The Western Region, for example, embarked on a programme of studies of organizational culture in the mid-1980s with the objective of identifying ways of changing the prevailing culture (Bate 1990). Slightly later, the Southern Region embarked on a programme aimed at encouraging more 'positive' attitudes amongst employees to BR in the hope that in time this would lead to performance improvements (Guest *et al.* 1993). Some parts of BR also flirted with the then fashionable team briefing. Many of the earlier initiatives were somewhat tentative, in part because top managers were uncertain of their benefits and in part because any industrial relations benefits could well be outweighed by their costs. One of the rail unions, for instance, threatened to take legal action to prevent an employee attitude survey taking place on the grounds that the existing industrial relations machinery was the proper mechanism for transmission of this kind of information.

However, the 'quality crisis' towards the end of the 1980s changed all this. A number of programmes were instigated with the objective of changing attitudes, developing teamwork and improving quality. The discourse of quality was central to these. In 1989, a Quality Through People programme of training was set in motion for 25,000 managers and supervisors, aimed at heightening awareness of the barriers to quality and how these could be overcome by an emphasis on putting the customer first. This programme was followed by Quality at Work, a programme of training in quality for the rest of BR's workforce. Much of this was aimed at developing competencies and was linked to the formation of a Rail Industry Training Council and the award of NVQs. At the same time, BR functions from maintenance depots to booking offices were encouraged to develop their procedures for improving and maintaining quality, with a view to acquiring BS5750 accreditation. Related initiatives have included an annual quality fair, where groups of staff put on exhibits of quality innovations, and an annual quality conference to review the progress of quality initiatives (British Railways Board 1993).

A final aspect of the use of quality is in its legitimation of a comprehensive overhaul of BR management structure in 1991–2. Known as Organising for Quality (or 'O for Q' to its detractors), this simplified the matrix structure of business sectors and production regions created in the early 1980s. That structure had been developed to give greater prominence to 'business' considerations in management decision making than had been the case with the previous production/engineering-based structure (Pendleton 1994). Sectors were given 'bottom-line' financial responsibility whilst the regions were charged with the production of the service specified by the sectors. The architects of this structure had hoped that this matrix would be a more flexible and market-oriented structure than its predecessor. In practice, however, it was riven with conflicts between sectors and regions with the primary means of conflict resolution being the generation of additional rules to govern the sector–region relationship. The bureaucratic features of BR were therefore intensified rather than diluted by the sector structure (Bate 1990). A further problem was that the customer was one step removed from the parts of BR responsible for service specification (Welsby 1991). Organising for Quality in 1991–2 was meant to overcome these problems. The matrix structure was replaced with a simplified structure in which the business sectors took over production responsibilities. 'Proximity to the customer', 'responsiveness to market forces' and 'improvements to service quality' were the key legitimating concepts used to justify this change of structure. The language of quality found further expression in the division of BR profit centres into operations and retail functions, with all staff coming into regular direct contact with the customer classed as 'retail staff'. As might be anticipated, this substantial over-haul of the management structure caused a fair amount of discontent amongst managers, weary of repeated reorganizations since the early 1980s to meet financial cutbacks. In this context the language of quality played a vital role. As well as providing a more uplifting justification for upheaval than financial stringency, it undermined one of the key bar-gaining positions developed by the rail unions in the 1980s to respond to policies of contraction.

Overall, then, there has been a close synchronization of quality and HRM initiatives in the first half of the 1990s. The language of quality has come to be the main rationale for HRM change, and HRM changes are seen to be necessary to achieve quality objectives. However, these linkages are by no means simple or consistent. As the foregoing has indicated, quality has been linked with both 'soft' HRM initiatives – those concerned with 'winning hearts and minds' – and harder policies aimed at increasing direct control of employee performance. On balance, as in other parts of the public sector, the harder policies predominated. This is not altogether surprising given the dominant conception of quality as the achievement of the service specification. Meeting these kinds of target in an organization like BR, where a high degree of coordination of tasks is necessary to provide services, almost inevitably requires a heavy reliance on standardized rules. The solution to many of the shortcomings experienced by BR during the 'quality crisis' of the late 1980s has been the generation of additional rules. There is now much greater formal specification of tasks and their inter-relationships than there was in the 1980s, especially in those functions where safety is

very important. By contrast, the new discourse of customer responsiveness can be seen to imply a measure of debureaucratization of work
tasks so that staff can react flexibly to consumer demands. In practice,
however, financial stringency and the need to coordinate tasks and
functions has meant that rules have had to be developed to indicate when
staff can be flexible in their response to customers. For instance, alongside the expansion of the customer assistance role of train guards in
recent years there has been a generation of rules to guide the provision
of this assistance, e.g. when to offer free phone calls if trains are delayed.
Finally, although some aspects of joint regulation have been weakened,
new rules have had to be created to guide managerial activities. Although
a reduction in trade union influence on labour utilization has no doubt
been an aspiration here, in practice the rail unions have been able to
exploit the perceived necessity for rules to secure new forms of regulation, as has occurred in bargaining over the content and application of
suitability criteria for employee selection and promotion.

CONCLUSION

In BR's case, the current vogue for quality has both elements of novelty
and continuity, and it would be wrong to view the development of
quality as the simple unfolding of a New Right strategy to enhance the
responsiveness of public corporations to their customers. The dominant
conception of quality on the railways in the early 1990s has been the
achievement of the timetable specification. In other words, making sure
the trains run on time. This view of quality, however, has a long pedigree
and predates the Citizen's Charter by a considerable period of time. The
development of this notion of quality during the 1980s was primarily a
reaction to the effects of government policies of retrenchment and
commercialization. Only later did government itself adopt it as a way of
distancing itself from the political difficulties stemming from other
government policies. Quality as 'fitness for purpose' and quality as
'value for money' were much less developed in relation to BR than other
public services because one could awaken issues of transport policy
which the government preferred not to face, whilst the other was likely
to invite hostility from those paying higher rail fares as a result of
government financial strategy. The particular configuration of quality in
BR, therefore, can be seen as a function of the contradictions of government policy towards BR from the 1980s onwards.

The language of quality, which became increasingly prominent after
BR's 'quality crisis' in the late 1980s, has been not only a central feature

of the BR–government relationship but of BR's relationship with its employees. From the late 1980s, 'quality' has been increasingly used to legitimate a range of labour management initiatives and BR's quality and HRM strategies have become increasingly conjoined. Quality fulfilled a number of needs in this respect. First, it provided a rationale for change to a workforce deeply suspicious of management initiatives. The emphasis on quality was one that was difficult for opponents of change to counter because they had traditionally used the notion of service quality themselves, albeit with a different language, to oppose management policies of retrenchment and work reorganization. Second, the language of quality has something of an upbeat tone, useful for reinvigorating a workforce demoralized from a decade of government spending cuts and uncertain of the prospects for a privatized railway. Third, quality could encourage employees to improve their work performance. Whilst it would be extremely difficult in current circumstances to increase employee commitment to BR, as the study by Guest *et al.* (1993) indicates, improvements in task performance might be secured if the focus is the user of rail services. In a sense, quality provides a link between the public service ethos of old and the new philosophy of markets and commercialization. However, there is little evidence that the new philosophy of consumer responsiveness has led to a debureaucratization of labour management. Whilst some aspects of joint regulation have been weakened in the name of quality, new forms of unilateral and joint regulation have emerged in response to the quality imperative. It may well be, therefore, that the vogue for quality has drawn on and even intensified traditional characteristics of public sector organizations like BR rather than transformed them.

REFERENCES

Bate, P. (1990) 'Using the culture concept in an organization development setting', *Journal of Applied Behavioural Science* 26(1): 83–106.

Batstone, E., Ferner, A. and Terry, M. (1984) *Consent and Efficiency: Labour Relations and Management Strategy in the State Enterprise*, Oxford: Basil Blackwell.

British Railways Board (1981) *Rail Policy*, London: British Railways Board.

British Railways Board (1983) *Annual Report and Accounts 1982*, London: British Railways Board.

British Railways Board (1992) *Passenger's Charter*, London: British Railways Board.

British Railways Board (1993) *Annual Report and Accounts 1992–1993*, London: British Railways Board.

Carter, N. (1991) 'Performance indicators: "backseat driving" or "hands-off control"?', *Policy and Politics* 17(2): 131–8.

Carter, N., Klein, R. and Day, P. (1992) *How Organizations Measure Success*, London: Routledge.

Central Transport Users' Consultative Committee (1991) *Annual Report for 1990–1991*, London: Central Transport Users' Consultative Committee.

Doern, B. (1993) 'The UK Citizens' Charter: origins and implementation in three agencies', *Policy and Politics* 21(1): 17–30.

Du Gay, P. and Salaman, G. (1992) 'The cult(ure) of the customer', *Journal of Management Studies* 29(5): 615–34.

Ferner, A. (1988) *Governments, Managers and Industrial Relations: Public Enterprises and their Political Environments*, Oxford: Blackwell.

Friedmann, A. (1977) *Industry and Labour*, London: Macmillan.

Fuller, L. and Smith, V. (1991) 'Consumers' reports: management by customers in a changing economy', *Work, Employment and Society* 5(1): 1–16.

Guest, D., Peccei, R. and Thomas, A. (1993) 'The impact of employee involvement on organisational commitment and "them and us" attitudes', *Industrial Relations Journal* 24(3): 191–200.

HMSO (1991) *The Citizen's Charter: Raising the Standard*, Cmnd. 1599, London: HMSO.

House of Commons Committee of Public Accounts (1986) *36th Report from the Committee of Public Accounts: The Effectiveness of Government Financial Controls over the Nationalized Industries: Departments of Energy, Transport and Trade and Industry*, Cmnd. 343, London: HMSO.

House of Commons Transport Committee (1987) *Third Report from the Transport Committee: Financing of Rail Services*, London: HMSO.

Legge, K. (1989) 'Human resource management: a critical analysis', in Storey, J. (ed.), *New Perspectives on Human Resource Management*, Oxford: Basil Blackwell.

Lewis, N. (1993) 'The Citizens' Charter and next steps: a new way of governing? *Political Quarterly* 64(3): 317–26.

Martinez Lucio, M. (1993) 'The Post Office', in Pendleton, A. and Winterton, J. (eds), *Public Enterprise in Transition: Industrial Relations in State and Privatized Corporations*, London: Routledge.

Monopolies and Mergers Commission (1980) *British Railways Board: London and the SouthEast*, London: HMSO.

Monopolies and Mergers Commission (1987) *British Railways Board: Network SouthEast*, Cmnd. 204, London: HMSO.

Monopolies and Mergers Commission (1989) *British Railways Board: Provincial*, Cmnd. 584, London: HMSO.

Pendleton, A. (1991) 'The barriers to flexibility: flexible rostering on the railways', *Work, Employment and Society* 5(2): 241–57.

Pendleton, A. (1993) 'Railways', in Pendleton, A. and Winterton, J. (eds), *Public Enterprise in Transition: Industrial Relations in State and Privatized Corporations*, London: Routledge.

Pendleton, A. (1994) 'Structural reorganization and labour management in public enterprise: a study of British Rail', *Journal of Management Studies* 31(1): 33–53.

Pfeffer, N. and Coote, A. (1991) *Is Quality Good For You? A Critical Review of Quality Assurance in Welfare Services*, London: Institute of Public Policy Research.

Pollitt, C. (1986) 'Performance measurement in the public services: some political implications', *Parliamentary Affairs* 39(3): 315–29.

Pollitt, C. (1992) *Managerialism and the Public Services: The Anglo-American Experience*, Oxford: Basil Blackwell.

Reid, R. (1990) *Preparing British Rail for the 1990s*, London: British Railways Board.

Stewart, J. and Walsh, K. (1992) 'Change in the management of public services' *Public Administration* 70(4): 499–518.

Treasury (1978) *The Nationalized Industries*, Cmnd. 7131, London: HMSO.

Walsh, K. (1991) 'Quality and public services', *Public Administration* 69(4): 503–14.

Welsby, J. (1991) 'Organised for quality', *Transport* September/October: 138–9.

Wilkinson, A. (1993) 'Managing human resources for quality', in Dale, B. (ed.), *Managing Quality*, London: Prentice-Hall.

Wilkinson, A., Marchington, M., Ackers, P. and Goodman, J. (1992) 'Total quality management and employee involvement', *Human Resource Management Journal* 2(4): 1–20.

Wilkinson, A. and Willmott, H. (1994) 'Introduction', in Wilkinson, A. and Willmott, H. (eds), *Making Quality Critical*, London: Routledge.

Chapter 11

Quality and 'new industrial relations'

The case of Royal Mail

Miguel Martinez Lucio

INTRODUCTION

The Post Office, and in particular Royal Mail, is one of the earliest forms of modern state intervention in Britain. Its symbolic and economic value within the state is fairly substantial; its successful position when compared to the postal services of virtually all other countries makes it a relatively unique public institution.

The adoption of a quality-oriented strategy within Royal Mail in the late 1980s occurred in response to the limited, and indeed contradictory, aspects of decentralization and commercialism. Following the 1988 industrial dispute, there was an organizational need – as far as higher levels of management were concerned – to introduce a cultural dimension to the process of organizational change. The assumption was that this would allow for external considerations, such as market realities and customer expectations, to be wedded to the priorities and behaviour of Royal Mail employees. Such an ideological dimension would undermine the potential for internal resistance, as well as transform the extent of internal organizational autonomy in employee relations which had been able to resist the impact of 'decentralization' and 'commercialism' by maintaining a very strong formal and informal trade union role at the workplace level.

By actively representing new interests and subjects within the sphere of work itself (e.g. the 'internal customer'), Royal Mail would be complementing the wider institutional aspects of change that had been a characteristic of the first ten years of Conservative government policy. More specifically, this emphasis on quality crystallized with the proposed introduction of teamworking and the reorganization of the labour process around separate units of 'internal customers' structured along the lines of internal competitive relations.

Management's reference to an increasingly hostile market and the obsessive customer in order to bring about restructuring, along with the specific introduction of new quality-driven working practices, will be examined. In addition, some of the problems involved with such a project will be discussed. For example, management's referencing to performance measurement, levels of service quality and the desires of the public have been countered by trade union and political strategies and responses that emphasize public support for *public* services. At the level of the workplace, differences and disputes on matters related to teamworking and new employment practices have evolved in part due to the belief that previous practices were, indeed, both flexible and operationally successful. The very discourse of quality may therefore appear to legitimate restructuring (Du Gay and Salaman 1992), and reorganize relations between the workplace and the market (Reed chapter 2). In so doing, however, it *potentially*, and even unintentionally, transforms the politics and management of labour in ways that were initially unexpected.

The objectives of this chapter are, first, to explain how the adoption of a prevalent discourse of quality management within Royal Mail has developed out of a need to provide an ideological dimension to the project of commercialization and decentralization. Second, the chapter aims to explain the subtle relation between such ideological projects – with their reference to performance, markets and, in particular, customers – and a desire to alter the relative autonomy of organizational and employment practices. Finally, the chapter will show how this project has encountered difficulties due to the way in which counter references to both quality and the customer have been used by various organizational stakeholders. It also demonstrates how such a project of change leads to a potential 'politicization' of workplace behaviour. The chapter draws on case study research carried out at various levels of Royal Mail throughout England and Wales. The period of research spanned two years up to late 1993, covering the development and implementation of quality-oriented programmes of change and new management practices more generally. It has been based on semi-structured interviews with managers and trade unionists, the observation of specific critical incidents, and the collection of a vast range of secondary data.

ORGANIZATIONAL BACKGROUND AND MYTHOLOGY

The Post Office consists primarily of three key divisions: letters (Royal Mail), parcels (Parcelforce) and retail (Counter Services). Such is the scale of operations that its counter services are considered to be the largest retail business in the country. In 1991–2, the Post Office, of which Royal Mail is the largest part, had a turnover of just over £5 billion and delivered 16 billion items of mail per year. The Post Office employed, in 1991–2, 197,000 staff, of which 166,000 worked in Royal Mail. It had been in profit throughout the entire period of the Conservative government since 1979 and had actually contributed £74 million to government funds during the financial year 1991–2, bringing the total to £750 million for the previous ten years (Post Office 1992). In addition, what has also been a peculiar characteristic of this organization, when compared to other organizations in the public and private sectors, has been its unquestionable 'success' in financial and service delivery terms. This is especially the case when it is compared to the post offices of other countries. This argument could be validated with reference to the extremely high levels of end-to-end letter delivery in 1992–3 which exceeded 90 per cent for first-class post received on the following day.

Part of the mystique of this organization is not only its sheer size and coverage, but its historical feature of having been a central pivot, alongside the police, railways and the army, in the creation of the modern nation-state. This is the case in many other countries where postal (and telegraphic) services were one of the bedrocks of the modern state. At one point, when the Post Office included telephony, it was a ministerial department on a par with education and defence. The existence of the Post Office has also been of great symbolic importance. The presence of the rural sub-post office as an outpost of the central state, keeping communities in touch with each other and providing the public with a range of official documentation, has proved to be an important feature of Post Office services.

Furthermore, the uniformed postman or postwoman delivering mail early in the morning in various weather conditions, along with the very real terror of the canine species, has contributed to a positive image of this employee in the public eye. This image has been steadily enhanced over the last century through a range of publicity and marketing campaigns developed by the Post Office itself. It has been added to by the fact that the sorting of mail during antisocial hours and, on occasions, on fast-moving special trains inspired various provincial poets and filmmakers. These mythical features of Royal Mail's workforce are relevant to understanding the problems within the current government's attempts to reorganize the Post Office, and Royal Mail in particular. One should not ignore this fact as such cultural characteristics can, in a context of political and organizational change, be used as ideological resources by those in opposition to it (Hemingway 1982). They can be viewed as elements in the ideological dimension of the organization that may be rearticulated by organizational stakeholders at different times in order to contest the legitimacy of change (Laclau 1977).

Finally, in terms of its industrial relations and personnel tradition after the Second World War and prior to the 1980s, the Post Office has never experienced significant levels of industrial conflict. For some, the 1971 strike on pay, and the 1977 dispute surrounding the delivery of post to the anti-union firm Grunwicks, did not seriously unsettle what was a relatively peaceful industrial relations tradition (Clinton 1984). If anything, Post Office industrial relations as a whole seemed to be constituted since the First World War by some very interesting features that, according to one observer, were similar to the enterprise unionism currently apparent in the Japanese model of industrial relations, e.g the centrality of seniority, the degree of employee loyalty, and the nature of the 'partnership' principles that exist in the relationship between unions and management (Grint 1993). This appeared to be in keeping with the consensual practices of Whitleyism that underpinned a range of public services in the immediate pre- and postwar periods (Sheldrake 1988). In terms of the organization's main unions, these are dominated by the Union of Communication Workers (UCW) which represents the vast bulk of the workforce. More skilled and technically oriented employees are represented by the National Communications Union (the predominant union in British Telecom) which merged with the UCW in 1995 to form the Communications Workers' Union (CWU), whilst the National Union of Civil and Public Servants and the Communication Managers Association represent distinct grades of managers and supervisors. To date, the 'consensual' characteristics appear to dominate the organization's industrial relations. These unions continue to negotiate within a traditional and relatively formalized system of collective bargaining at the national level of different operations and through a range of formal procedures at local levels of the organization, although, as this chapter will illustrate, changes have steadily been made.

Overall, the Post Office has exhibited, and continues to exhibit, a range of particular ideological and organizational features that tend to set it apart from most other public services. These features provide a specific cultural and organizational context within which the project of *commercialization* (see Introduction) has had to be implemented (Batstone *et al.* 1984). It is a context that consists of cultural characteristics which are not closed, but which are open to diverse interventions and political rearticulation by a range of organizational stakeholders.

THE IMPERATIVES FOR CHANGE AND THE INTENSIFICATION OF CHANGE

The background to change in relation to the Post Office is complex. It cannot solely be reduced to the ideological orientation of the post-1979 Conservative governments and their obsession with privatization, even if this did contextualize the organizational change within the Post Office, and Royal Mail in particular, in certain ways. There were in fact very specific obstacles to privatization that were related to the 'monarchic' identity and image of the organization, its relative popularity amongst citizens, its limited profitability (making its organizational commodification within share markets awkward), and its highly regulated and universal pricing system (Martinez Lucio 1993).

Regardless of these obstacles to privatization, there were a range of imperatives for change (Martinez Lucio and Noon 1995). The commercialization of the organization was emphasized in the form of piecemeal (and contradictory) workplace reforms (e.g. Improved Working Methods), cost containment exercises, and an emphasis on financial criteria developed in response to new market threats within postal services both in Britain and abroad (Dearing 1986). New parcel carriers and specialist business postal services were emerging in the international and national transportation of mail. The divisionalization and reorganization of the Post Office was initiated in 1986 in response to these market changes. As a result, its corporate structure was reorganized around several business units (letters, parcels and counter services). The letters business, in the form of Royal Mail, remained the core operational service.

Royal Mail's Business Development Plan of 1992 took the project of decentralization even further. This plan reorganized Royal Mail along two lines. First, nine regional divisions were created which were to coordinate critically specific operations. Within this structure, a set of different functional divisions was established which split the core letter functions into three separate units: distribution, processing/sorting and delivery. These, in turn, would be coordinated at the regional level. What one therefore witnesses in Royal Mail is a drastic reorganization in the form of a functional and regional decentralization. In turn, the structure of Royal Mail's local industrial relations system, beyond formal collective bargaining, was reorganized (as were the unions) in relation to these new structures. New branch and workplace union structures were elaborated that were to parallel the new divisional and functional structures of the organization as a whole. Whilst the transition towards such structures was not straightforward, due to a broad internal debate within the UCW and the threat at one stage by Royal Mail of a withdrawal of union facilities, the guarantees made regarding the continuing role of national collective bargaining structures in Royal Mail ensured an element of union compliance.

There were two logics underpinning this project. The first at that time was one of functionalizing Royal Mail in order to allow for a type of privatization that would later involve the possibility of selling off or decentralizing specific parts of Royal Mail's operations. The processing function with its automated sorting offices could be part of a network that did more than just official Royal Mail work. Similarly, the distribution section could be used for more than just the transporting of mail traffic and the delivery section could be franchised at the local level with, as was suggested in certain locations, postmen and postwomen possibly 'buying their walk' and setting up businesses. The second logic was one of creating nine regional divisions in order to remove substantial decision-making power from the previously more numerous local districts. Operations would acquire a more strategic and coordinated approach from higher, regional levels of the organization. Information and objectives could be more easily transmitted from above through these new structures. More systematic control within the organization and at work would, it was hoped, emerge from such new structures. This systematic control would be based on a more precise measurement of outcomes and processes, financial controls, new points of management coordination for establishing objectives, and basic strategic leadership.

Second, paralleling these developments in the commercialization and reorganization of the Post Office was the re-emergence of the technological imperative for change (Martinez Lucio and Noon 1995). A new wave of automation was being systematically introduced within Royal Mail. The nature of this automation, it was felt, would allow for significant labour savings; yet the introduction of automation along with its successful operation would require a high level of employee commitment and participation along with a reprofiling of skills (Scott 1993). Hence, within certain management circles, the 1985 *Safeguarding the Future of the Mail Business* agreement with the unions, regarding issues such as the introduction of new technology, was steadily being perceived as being too restrictive given the nature of the guarantees in the document.

Third, there were further imperatives for change that emerged as a consequence of the inherent limitations that were deemed to exist within the traditional industrial relations system itself. Attempts to extend the logic of decentralization to industrial relations activity in the form of pay supplements for the South-East in 1988, which was registering high staff turnover rates in the London area in particular, led to a major dispute in 1988 which then spread throughout the country as a consequence of management's use of casual labour to clear the backlog of mail. This was a significant dispute given its scale as well as the level of worker solidarity. But it was also an indication, as far as many managers were concerned, of the increasing cultural and political gap that existed between the workforce and the management. It was believed that the intensification of change would be confronted by an organizational and industrial relations tradition that could lead to industrial conflict. This conflict had in fact been steadily rising during the 1980s (Martinez Lucio 1993).

Coupled with a renewed political interest in privatization in the late 1980s, these diverse imperatives for change and perceived organizational constraints led to a major and strategic re-evaluation of organizational strategy which involved a range of external consultants. The basic features of this shift in higher management thinking was the belief that direct communication *and* a new industrial relations strategy would have to parallel traditional links with the unions. Such alternative contacts with the workforce would facilitate the relaying of commercial and market considerations which had hitherto been marginal in traditional industrial relations forums. This strategic development would also support and internally market the changes in organizational structure, and the implementation and operation of new technology. The subject of the 'customer' was therefore steadily emerging as a point of reference within such developments, allowing management demands for change to be legitimated by drawing on this alternative stakeholder. This allowed for a 'triangular' relationship within industrial relations to be justified (i.e. relations between management, unions *and* employees). This was one of the basic ideas that created an interest amongst higher tiers of management in the whole practice of total quality management and the discourse of the 'customer'.

THE ORIGINS AND IMPLEMENTATION OF CUSTOMER FIRST

In line with so many other organizations in the country, Royal Mail developed its own variant of total quality management (TQM) under the title of Customer First. Royal Mail's employment of Rank Xerox's former head of TQM complied with the government's desire to draw from what they considered to be proven private sector experience. There was a range of features to this renewed interest in communication, but this chapter will focus on the formal strategy of Customer First and the way in which this concept of the customer emerged within the various changes proposed in the organization of work.

In 1988, a management structure was constructed with the aim of developing and implementing Customer First. Organized nationally, this structure was coordinated along regional and functional lines through Quality Service Managers (QSMs). In addition, a series of national conferences was periodically held to allow for a certain degree of coordination. As well as holding a range of sessions on customer identification (relating to both internal and external customers), these individuals had to support the Quality Improvement Projects (QIPs) that were set up in various parts of the country. These were, for example, an advanced form of suggestion schemes, with committees that consisted of management, the unions and individual worker representatives in delivery and sorting offices. These committees discussed and oversaw the implementation of agreed suggestions.

Emerging from the personnel division of Royal Mail, the Employee Communications Managers (ECMs) paralleled the QSMs and QIPs as a vehicle for direct communication. The ECMs were used in situations where drastic and problematic changes to working conditions had to be explained to the workforce. The objectives were explicit in its own communiques on Customer First; Royal Mail had to 'transform itself from a bureaucratic, complacent, self-confessed Leviathan into a responsive, customer driven, market focused business' (Van den Elst 1993: 13).

What, therefore, emerged from the strategic reorientation in the late 1980s was an emphasis on a more systematic and direct engagement and communication with employees which had as its referent and point of legitimation the 'customer'. Change was very explicitly presented to employees of Royal Mail in terms of the demands and desires of the 'customer'. Specific meanings of customer demands were developed: 'speed of service', 'time guarantees', 'regularity', 'security', efficient delivery and 'employee identification'. Quality was primarily defined in terms of time and efficiency, with less reference to the public nature of the service and the actual coverage of the traditional range of services offered. This very specific and centrally driven feature of the project related to quality was clear from the organizational structure of the project itself. Such was the hierarchical nature of this management structure, which was based on the cascading principle of training for 'quality and customer awareness', that QSMs were not always up to date on developments and pilot schemes in other parts of the country, which is ironic given the contemporary interest in 'flatter' organizational structures and the restructuring of Royal Mail's organization.

THE DISCOURSE OF THE CUSTOMER AND THE INDUSTRIAL RELATIONS TRADITION

These very specific understandings of quality and the customer were mobilized within three distinct spheres of employee activity. The description of these will serve as the basis for this part of the chapter.

First, in broader terms, the discourse of quality appeared to act as a source of legitimation for the divisionalization and functionalization outlined above, providing it with a market-based rationale. The relaying of both the uncertainties and the new demands emerging within the market were considered to be a fundamental prerequisite for legitimating any changes to organizational strategies and structures that were seen as being incapable of dealing with these new exigencies. The external environment had to be redefined and represented within the organization, and redefined in order to emphasize the necessity for change. During the interviews, some quality-related managers actually expressed their concern with their medium- to long-term role as a consequence of this process. They also raised the question as to whether they were merely being used as a marketing mechanism for the Business Development Plan.

It would, nevertheless, be unwise to reduce such changes in the external environment to purely political and ideological considerations as if these existed in an economic vacuum. New demands for a speedier service were actually emerging from business customers, who were in some cases using more expensive alternatives such as Business Post in London to such an extent that, by 1992, Royal Mail was being seriously undermined within the London market for business mail. Developments in the form of the fax machine and electronic mail contributed further to this pressure for change (although items of mail dealt with by Royal Mail have been increasing since the early 1980s). Indeed, the National Mail Users Organisation, which consisted of key business customers, intervened and made Royal Mail transform the way it was measuring mail delivery performance rates. This collective consumer constituency brought to bear on Royal Mail the 'pressure' of the market (especially as business customers constituted approximately 87 per cent of Royal Mail revenue in 1993). At the same time, the European Union's proposals for deregulating postal services, allowing for greater competition in the delivery of mail, were further promoting the desire for reorganization and an opening up to competition throughout the twelve member states.

Second, there was a reinterpretation and utilization of these market-level developments and this was apparent in the way the external customer was constructed and represented within Royal Mail's organization and workplace. For example, it was argued that the new divisional and functional structures required that employees locate themselves within a specific area of employment and at a specified time (settled attendance). In addition, the emerging interest in teamworking as a consequence of technological developments in the sorting of mail further added to this management demand for what were called fixed duties and settled attendancies. One of the problems with these demands is that they contradicted the internal labour market traditions of Royal Mail's workforce. These traditions were based on extensive internal employee mobility across different functions and tasks (Martinez Lucio and Noon 1995). In attempting to push through these changes, especially in the area of postal deliveries, the image of the external customer was conjured up by management. For example, management argued in a vast range of meetings throughout the country that the customer wanted to identify, trust and be familiar with their postman or postwoman. This was used to justify the fixing of duties and the settling of attendances within postal deliveries which would in turn allow, it was argued, for the possibility of the introduction of teamworking and/or the establishment of a postal delivery franchise system that involved employees or other interested parties. Hence the reference made to postal deliverers of the possibility of 'buying your walk'.

Third, not only was the customer solely *represented* within the confines of the workplace in the form of the external customer but he/she was *constructed* within it in the form of the 'internal customer' – that peculiar characteristic within the discourse of total quality management. In the cascade training sessions, employees were asked to think of their fellow employees as their 'customers', i.e. reviewing their work and dealing with their colleagues just as they would external customers. Regardless of the diverse and even competing definitions of teamworking within Royal Mail management, its (attempted) establishment was (to be) based on the the construction of teams as separate customers passing mail ('products') on to each other.

The significance of such developments is not clearly visible from their implementation and their formal rhetorical content. Nevertheless, such new management practices are seen by many academic observers to have a significant effect on the role of worker representatives and industrial relations regulations as trade unions become bypassed, employees involved directly in the organization of work, and employee roles and behaviour reconditioned by the discourse of the 'customer' (Guest 1989: Garrahan and Stewart 1992: Martinez Lucio and Weston 1992; Storey 1992). In the case of Royal Mail, there are three related developments and characteristics that illustrate the way the discourse of quality is organizationally used.

First, the constant reference to the uncertainties of the market can contribute to the uncoupling of traditional organizational relationships within Royal Mail. The 'presence' of the 'market' and the 'customer' destabilized the traditional relationships between management and unions. It contributed to the erosion of the relative autonomy of workplace institutions vis-à-vis the external commercial environment (chapter 2 in this volume). This means that the form and content of workplace regulation related to a discourse of the social and an understanding of worker rights which evolved as counterpoints to the arbitrary qualities of market mechanisms. This autonomy was historically constructed within (a) the context of social democratic public policies, (b) the construction of the Keynesian welfare state, and (c) the autonomy within the state of those processes that regulated both public sector professionals and employees generally, and which emphasized political stability. Within this political context, worker representation was constitutionally and socially fixed on the basis of a differentiation of interests and roles between organized labour and management (Clegg 1951).

Second, the managerial use of the customer in order to uncouple such relationships and roles developed on the basis of a steadily increasing measurement of activity in mail traffic and productivity. Without these developments in performance measurement the task of relating employee activity to outcomes in the market (both external and internal) would be difficult to achieve. Isolating and insulating considerations within the employment relationship such as staff allocation, temporal considerations in the form of rotas and grading structures tends to become more difficult within such a new context of transparency (chapter 4 in this volume).

Third, such developments as those outlined above contribute, it is believed, to an undermining of traditional 'worker solidarity' as competitive relations are established between workers. These competitive relations are developed both within and between teams, relating to the levels of their activity as well as to the allocation of various shifts and duties, for example. The undermining of traditional forms of labour deployment and even matters related to working conditions, for example, would not always involve the union or be based on traditional allocative mechanisms such as seniority principles, instead it would be achieved – as far as management was concerned – by workers themselves acting autonomously of traditional rules and regulations once teamworking was established and in collaboration with management. Hence, the necessity of direct communication and the new triangular relation with its greater emphasis on workplace controls: 'team ideology succeeds where quality circles in the past failed. This is largely because the latter failed to extend ideologies into the very identities of workers themselves' (Garrahan and Stewart 1992: 111).

The sum total of these developments is that the discourse of quality was a central component of Royal Mail's organizational changes. With regards to the institutional structures of the workplace, these were being re-established within the discourse of the enterprise with reference to the market and its constituent, the customer, along the lines suggested by Sabel (1990) and referred to by Du Gay and Salaman (1992): 'Through the discourse of the enterprise, the relations between "production" and "consumption", between "inside" and "outside" of the corporation, and crucially between work and non-work based identities, are progressively blurred' (Du Gay and Salaman 1992: 624). But these are developments that consisted of very specific (and almost rigid) representations of the 'customer' and meanings of quality within the organization; representations that were precisely tied into changes in working practices in the case of Royal Mail, such as the establishment of new 'fixed' employment activity and the attempted and piecemeal introduction of teamworking.

THE 'CULT OF THE CUSTOMER' AND ITS UNINTENDED USES: POSSIBLE FUTURE DEVELOPMENTS

Developments along the lines of those outlined above have given rise to a range of pessimistic interpretations regarding the fate of 'traditional' organizational relations within the employment sphere of the public sector. Yet my research within Royal Mail parallels a set of arguments which state that such transitions in the world of work are not straightforward and unproblematic (Kelly 1988). There are difficulties in constituting new organizational relations in the form of ideal-typical managerialist conceptions of quality-driven organizations (Keenoy 1991; Blyton and Turnbull 1992; Storey 1992; Martinez Lucio and Simpson 1992).

In the case of Royal Mail, we can identify a range of contradictions that emerged within the sites of employee activity discussed above and that were related to, and in part conditioned by, the discourse of quality. Each of them indicates how the politics of quality is not closed and acting as some instrument to be readily utilized within any specific project of organizational change. The constituent elements of quality – market relations, the customer, the cult of surveillance-driven involvement – are subject to reinterpretation, altering traditional relationships in ways that were initially unexpected due to the strategic calculations of actors (e.g. trade union responses) and alternative cultural contexts (the organizational culture outlined earlier). History and agency cannot be suspended when deliberating on the effects of management strategy.

Originally, at the broader level, the discourse of quality was in some cases being associated by a range of union activists with the objectives of further restructuring and potential redundancies, let alone the prospect of privatization. Political motivations were in various cases seen by trade unionists and employees to be behind the managerial interest in quality. Subsequently, the extremely high levels of demoralization registered by an internal survey organized by Royal Mail, with over 70 per cent of staff registering that they were 'unhappy at work' in 1993 (*Financial Times* 8 June 1993), may be attributed to the prospect of privatization, the constant government vacillations on this matter and the very real prospect of redundancies. But it is also possible that the constant reference to market uncertainties and changes in competition within the discourse of quality may have contributed unintentionally to this demoralization. The 'changing' market was represented to Royal Mail employees within the Customer First programme as an external and independent entity which had to be reacted to and accounted for at work, but which could not be controlled or regulated at the micro- or macro-level, or by the public or even the private sector.

Second, the use of the 'external' customer and the partial erosion of organizational boundaries had, in certain circumstances, the effect of transforming the subject of the customer into a point of contention. Management's drawing in of the customer in order to legitimate change and as a way of focusing employees on the exigencies of the market contributed unintentionally to a series of counter references during key moments of conflict. In Melton Mowbray in 1992, a five-week strike by postmen and postwomen regarding fixed duties saw union representatives question management as to how it was that customers required to know and familiarize themselves with the deliverer of their letters. In the case of Cardiff, a strike in the processing/sorting area over settled attendances/shifts in the summer of 1993 saw the union refer to the potential deterioration of the 'quality' of working life for those workers with 'eternal' late shifts, for example. The union also referred to customer satisfaction with the service as organized historically. The local trade union activists referred to opinion polls that registered that the public considered it the most efficient public service. The customer and the public were explicitly drawn into the industrial relations debate on change, putting local management in a difficult position vis-à-vis local public opinion and the media, even if it was clear that local management had consulted heavily with the workforce over such changes for nearly two years. Alternative interpretations of the market were possible which made the tasks of Customer First increasingly difficult as such counter-references were mobilized by activists within the workplace.

In effect, the supposed erosion of any boundaries between workplace and the market has no necessary outcomes. If anything, this erosion may further contribute to the steady, albeit uneven, 'politicization' of public sector industrial relations which had been emerging due to the incomes policies of the 1970s (Winchester 1983) and the response to the resource restrictions since the 1980s. References to a wider set of interests, in this case those of the 'customer', further undermined the traditional character of public sector industrial relations making its development and desired 'pacification' more problematic.

Third, this potential politicization occurred within the 'confines' of the workplace itself. In part, this was facilitated by the fact that the reference to quality was not compensated by any real and coherent changes in the reward system of employees. In one sorting office, teams were to be rewarded with 'tea breaks and Christmas pints' (internal circular) raising memories of the farcical Christmas bonus of 1991 (a packet of cabbage seeds) which drew the attention of the front page of the *Sun* newspaper and which temporarily undermined credibility in the new wave of management ideas. Furthermore, line managers have commented on the contradiction between references to quality and 'arbitrary budget allocations'. Unions have not been slow to highlight these problematic developments. A range of local union responses emerged that went beyond simply rejecting change, such as the UCW conference rejection of teamworking, taking quality true to its word. For example, suggestions from employees were thoroughly followed through by union representatives in some QIPs programmes – especially the expensive ones (Darlington 1994). Throughout the country, the UCW branches began to exchange information on the implementation of quality and its contradictions. The national leadership was in turn steadily developing a range of interesting strategies regarding such issues (even if it appeared to be slightly divided). This type of union strategy and response, along with others, continued to test management resources and their approach to the concept. This exposed a fundamental weakness in management strategy: the inability to allocate substantial resources to employee relations change due to the continuing pressure for financial results emerging from both the Department of Trade and Industry and the Treasury, and not necessarily due to the traditional industrial relations system.

The relevance of this is that an instrumental and political rationale behind the practice of quality management was being inferred by the workforce and its representatives (even in instances when local management did not see the bypassing of unions as a central issue). Union representatives were steadily beginning to respond seriously to team-working and direct communication along the lines seen in industries such as the automobile industry by emphasizing and enhancing their own lines of communication and representation (Martinez Lucio and Weston 1992). But of particular relevance is that the different uses of the customer and new forms of employee involvement along competitive lines were being rearticulated within the politics of work, as were the outcomes of service measurements. This rearticulation was facilitated by the specific historical and cultural context of the organization, outlined earlier in the chapter, with relation to its popularity and highly transparent service delivery.

Conflicts subsequently emerged which included, directly or indirectly, the issues of public interest, customer satisfaction and the broader politics of privatization regardless of Royal Mail management's attempt to restructure the workplace and its institutions, with the aim of moving them away from traditional Whitleyist 'insularity'. The outcomes of such developments may depend on future strategic calculations on behalf of the union leadership and local rank and file, amongst others, who have not been slow to rearticulate customer interests in their anti-privatization campaigns. Indeed, it may also depend on how management depoliticize such strategies and unintended outcomes. Either way, the advent of the market and its representation within the employment structures of Royal Mail have activated and not necessarily marginalized the traditional institutions they were intent on reforming.

ACKNOWLEDGEMENTS

This chapter is dedicated to the memory of Joyce Brown and her support of the project. The author assumes sole responsibility for the research and arguments in this chapter.

REFERENCES

Batstone, E., Ferner, A. and Terry, M. (1984) *Consent and Efficiency: Labour Relations and Management Strategy in State Enterprise*, Oxford: Blackwell.

Blyton, P. and Turnbull, P. (1992) *Reassessing Human Resource Management*, London: Sage.

Clegg, H. (1951) *Industrial Democracy and Nationalization*, Oxford: Basil Blackwell.

Clinton, A. (1984) *Post Office Workers*, London: George Allen.

Darlington, R. (1994) 'The challenge to workplace unionism in the Royal Mail', *Employee Relations* 15(3): 13–25.

Dearing, R. (1986) *The Commercial Public Sector: A Changing Face*, London: The Post Office.

Du Gay, P. and Salaman, G. (1992) 'The cult(ure) of the customer', *Journal of Management Studies* 29(5): 615–33.

Garrahan, P. and Stewart, P. (1992) *The Nissan Enigma*, London: Mansell.

Grint, K. (1993) 'Japanization? Some early lessons from the British Post Office', *Industrial Relations Journal* 24(1): 14–27.

Guest, D. (1989) 'Human Resource Management: its implications for industrial relations and trade unions', in Storey, J. (ed.), *New Perspectives on Human Resource Management*, London: Routledge.

Hemingway, J. (1982) *Conflict and Democracy*, Oxford: Oxford University Press.

Keenoy, T. (1991) 'The roots of metaphor in the old and new industrial relations', *British Journal of Industrial Relations* 29(2): 313–28.

Kelly, J. (1988) *Trade Unions and Socialist Politics*, London: Verso.

Laclau, E. (1977) *Politics and Ideology in Marxist Theory*, London: Verso.

Martinez Lucio, M. (1993) 'The Post Office', in Pendleton, A. and Winterton, J. (eds), *Public Enterprise in Transition: Industrial Relations in State and Privatized Corporations*, London: Routledge.

Martinez Lucio, M. and Noon, M. (forthcoming 1995) 'Organisational change and the tensions of decentralisation: the case of Royal Mail', *Human Resource Management Journal*.

Martinez Lucio, M. and Simpson, D. (1992) 'Discontinuity and change in industrial relations: the struggles over its social dimension and the rise of human resource management', *International Journal of Human Resource Management* 3(2): 173–90.

Martinez Lucio, M. and Weston, S. (1992) 'Human resource management and trade union responses: bringing the politics of the workplace back into the debate', in Blyton, P. and Turnbull, P. (eds), *Reassessing Human Resource Management*, London: Sage.

The Post Office *Report and Annual Accounts*, London: The Post Office.

Sabel, C. (1990) 'Skills without a place: the organisation of the corporation and the experience of work', paper presented to the British Sociological Association Annual Conference, University of Surrey, Guildford.

Scott, D. (1993) 'Managing change', *Automation*, Swindon: Royal Mail.

Sewell, G. and Wilkinson, B. (1992) 'Someone to watch over me: surveillance, discipline and the just-in-time labour process', *Sociology* 26(2): 271–90.

Sheldrake, J. (1988) *The Origins of Public Sector Industrial Relations*, Aldershot: Avebury.

Storey, J. (1992) *Developments in Human Resource Management*, Oxford: Basil Blackwell.

Van den Elst, K. (1993) 'Customer First, five years on', *Enterprise* Autumn: 13–16.

Winchester, D. (1983) 'Industrial relations in the public sector', in Bain, G. (ed.), *Industrial Relations in Britain*, Oxford: Basil Blackwell.

Chapter 12

Market-driven reforms in education
Performance, quality and industrial relations in schools

*Jackie Sinclair, Roger Seifert
and Mike Ironside*

INTRODUCTION

This chapter is based on the findings of Economic and Social Research Council-funded research* carried out at Keele University between 1991 and 1993. The study concerns the impact of the market-driven education reforms upon employment and industrial relations in state sector schools. In common with other parts of the public sector such as the NHS (Lloyd and Seifert 1992), the government has introduced structural changes to the school system, designed to introduce a form of market-based competition at the expense of elected local authorities' traditional role. The most recent changes were instigated by the Education Reform Act of 1988 which introduced local management of schools (LMS) and a national curriculum. The reforms were accompanied by arguments about 'quality', 'choice' and 'value for money' – for example, the White Paper *Choice and Diversity* (Department for Education 1992) – whereby parents were considered as consumers in a market.

Our findings highlight some contradictions between the rhetoric of 'excellence' and the reality of school managers struggling with budgetary constraints. Many reforms rely on the cooperation of teachers, yet there has been an adverse impact not only on their workload and terms and conditions but on their professional autonomy. We argue that the school system is potentially destabilized by the uncertainties generated by the reforms. Insecurity, discrimination and exploitation are inherent in the system, and it is not clear how managers will come to terms with the inevitable school-based conflicts that will arise.

This chapter elucidates some of the policy contradictions which go some way to explaining the lack of enthusiasm for many of the reforms. The fuelling of discontent was, unsurprisingly, a major consequence of the reforms.

IMPLICATIONS OF EDUCATION REFORMS

A central purpose of the reforms is to reduce state spending on school education. Under pressure of recession the government's objective is to reduce expenditure without appearing to lower standards. Teachers' salaries amount to just over £11 billion in total (School Teachers' Review Body 1993: 61) and make up about 80 per cent of the average school's budget, which means that cutting the cost of schooling necessarily involves cutting the cost of the teacher workforce. Under these circumstances quality becomes a key concern, as standards of education continue to be a matter of both public debate and political calculation. The objective of maintaining standards of quality while reducing costs in a labour-intensive service raises the central industrial relations issues of pay and performance (Ironside and Seifert 1994). In addition to government control over total expenditure on schools, through the power to place limits on Local Education Authority (LEA) budgets, the government has taken control of some aspects of education standards and classroom activity through the establishment of the national curriculum and the standard testing arrangements for pupils. The contradictions and unpopularity of government policy in this area have been amply illustrated by the industrial action begun during 1993 in the form of a teachers' union boycott of pupil testing, supported by governors' and parents' organizations. This demonstrates that the state cannot simply impose new 'systems' unproblematically. As Walsh (1987) points out, divisions exist between branches of the state also, such as ministers, LEA officials and politicians at national and local level. Our findings lend weight to this and highlight the endurance of relations between the LEAs, school managers and local trade unions. Nevertheless, there is potential for massive centralization of power which, coupled with the provisions for schools to opt for grant-maintained status, undermines the LEAs, even though less than 1,000 schools had taken up this option by 1994. The LMS system weakens LEAs further by transferring control over school budgets and staffing issues to school governing bodies. Under LMS, the LEA is required to distribute most of the aggregate budget to schools in accordance with a government-approved formula, a market-type mechanism which allocates funds mainly on the basis of numbers of pupils attending a school. This has the effect of generating competition between schools, which can only maintain budgets by attracting greater pupil numbers. The reforms place various employment powers, including pay, staffing and performance, in the hands of school governors and managers, although the LEA remains the employer in law (Smyth 1993).

League tables of examination results, truancy rates and other performance indicators add a further dimension of market competition among schools. Schools are under pressure to provide evidence of high standards of quality to the parents of both existing and potential pupils. The combination of budgetary and competitive changes places an imperative on management to extract higher levels of teacher performance at lower cost. This can be achieved in a number of ways: by altering the skill mix so as to substitute more expensive staff with cheaper staff; by reducing the number of teaching staff while maintaining pupil throughput, thus increasing workload; and by keeping staff numbers and pay static while increasing throughput. School managers are required to maintain quality while increasing both the volume and the intensity of the teachers' workload, and this involves the mobilization of human resource management (HRM) techniques.

RESEARCH METHODS

During our research we explored these issues in detail through fieldwork in three LEAs in the Midlands. These were a Labour-controlled county council containing both a large industrial conurbation and isolated rural areas; a Conservative-controlled shire county with large population centres and smaller villages; and an industrialized metropolitan district, with control changing during the course of the study from Labour to a Conservative/Liberal Democrat coalition. The research programme included a documentary study, interviews with union and LEA officers, including observation of joint consultative committee meetings, and case studies of individual schools. A questionnaire survey was also conducted among all head teachers and school-based union representatives (various aspects of our findings are written up in Sinclair *et al.* 1993a and 1993b and in Ironside *et al.* 1993).

The case study research at seventeen schools involved face-to-face interviews with over 150 teaching staff and follow-up interviews with head teachers and union representatives.

In this chapter we begin by setting out the main features of the school sector workforce, trade union organization and collective bargaining arrangements. We then discuss the context of the reform process, identifying some of the quality issues, including the notion of performance measurement for schools, and the implications of market controls replacing democratic accountability. We then outline findings from our research, looking first at some of the general effects of declining budgets on schools, before taking up three major themes in order to illustrate the contradictions between the rhetoric of the 'freedom' of LMS and the reality of declining standards under the impact of market-oriented reforms in schools. The three themes on which we focus are:

1 The use by governing bodies of flexible pay supplements, and views on performance related pay in particular.
2 The impact of the reforms on teacher workload and the consequences for staff and pupils.
3 The responses of school managers, LEA officers and unions to the reforms.

Throughout, we consider the implications for industrial relations as a result of reforms and the resultant shift in managerial authority introduced by LMS.

SCHOOL SECTOR WORKFORCE, UNION ORGANIZATION AND COLLECTIVE BARGAINING

The education service has a workforce of 969,000 full-time equivalent employees. Of these over 440,000 are teachers employed in 26,500 schools in England and Wales. Over half are graduates, and the gender composition of the teaching workforce is three fifths women, while men just outnumber women in secondary schools (Department for Education statistics). Teachers from ethnic minorities are estimated as 2 per cent of the teacher workforce, concentrated on the lowest scales and in support services such as language training (Commission for Racial Equality 1988: 65).

The statistics for the total workforce in education indicate a significant number of staff outside the teaching profession, and at school level these include a range of manual and non-manual staff whose jobs have been affected not only by the wider reforms and budgetary constraints, but by the provisions of compulsory competitive tendering. We elaborate on these specific groups elsewhere (Sinclair et al. 1994).

State schools have always been highly unionized with density around 80 per cent (Coates 1972; Ironside and Seifert 1994). On the teachers' side there are six main unions, with the National Union of Teachers (NUT) the largest and the Association of Teachers and Lecturers in third place; only the NUT and the National Association of Schoolmasters and Union of Women Teachers (NASUWT) are TUC affiliated. The last decade has seen a substantial redistribution between them which has often followed the contours of industrial action at national level.

Membership figures for the three largest classroom teacher unions are set out in the following table, illustrating patterns in recent years.

Table 2: Teacher trade union membership

	1986	1988	1990	1992
NUT	229,601	216,614	218,194	213,656
NASUWT	166,583	159,256	166,331	190,637
AMMA (ATL)	123,601	131,500	138,571	152,795

Source: Certification Officer's reports

The remaining smaller unions, the Professional Association of Teachers (PAT), the National Association of Head Teachers (NAHT) and the Secondary Heads Association (SHA) claim 41,000, 38,000 and 8,000 members respectively (Certification Officer).

These figures should be treated with caution as they include students and retired members. Nevertheless, they do indicate high levels of union density among this significant occupational group.

School sector industrial relations and collective bargaining institutions took the form of multi-employer, multi-union bargaining characteristic of Whitleyism. The forum for settling teachers' pay was known as the Burnham Committee (Saran 1985), in operation from 1919 to 1987. Abolished by the Secretary of State following a period of industrial action, it was replaced by the Interim Advisory Committee, the forerunner of the School Teachers' Review Body (STRB). In addition to restructuring of the national pay system, this policy, at a stroke, reduced the influence of trade unions and LEAs at national level.

Whilst pay review has been substituted for national bargaining, and pay scales, conditions and codified duties are laid down by statute, the teachers' unions are still recognized by LEAs, and facilities agreements remain at this level. Furthermore, the unions can obtain bargaining rights at workplace level over a range of school-based issues. To this extent, therefore, the status of unions in educational establishments remains intact or, arguably, has been extended. The response of the workforce and its collective organizations, is therefore crucial in the context of the simultaneous centralization and decentralization of managerial powers heralded by LMS.

QUALITY, COMPETITION AND PERFORMANCE MEASUREMENT IN THE EDUCATION SERVICE

Government policy makers have assumed that commercial criteria borrowed from the profit-seeking private sector would be a solution for perceived inefficiencies in the public services. Industrialists and Conservative politicians have challenged both the benefits of comprehensive education and the dominance of the teaching profession and LEAs in the education sub-government, accusing them of failing business needs and therefore the country (Simon 1991: 526–7). In recent years, policy documents have been peppered with the terminology of 'quality' and 'excellence' associated with total quality management (TQM). As an accompaniment, the government has insisted on the adoption of a hotchpotch of strategies and practices familiar to private sector HRM approaches. These include the introduction of teacher appraisal, annualized hours contracts, flexible payments and performance related pay. In addition to school competing with school, the performance of teachers is the subject of evaluation and competition.

The ideologically loaded management concepts of quality and efficiency have been mobilized to weaken the influence of teachers and their organizations on educational standards. Instead of being participants, through centralized negotiation and LEA-level consultation, in the management of the school system, the aim is that teacher unions are to be excluded from all areas of decision making. The head teacher's role is transformed from that of first among professional equals to one of chief executive, and one of the primary tasks of this manager is the enforcement of quality management procedures.

Teachers, their organizations, pupils, parents, employers and the state have all been concerned with pupils' abilities since the First World War, as explicit policy concerns. The shift in emphasis from professionally defined concern with *standards* to management-defined concern with *quality* stems from the Labour government's Great Debate in the late 1970s. This political initiative was taken up and developed by successive Conservative administrations throughout the 1980s, formally expressed by the White Paper *Teaching Quality* which incorporated views expressed by Sir Keith Joseph on the desirability of linking teacher performance with pay (Department of Education and Science 1983). The thrust of Conservative policy since has continued to focus on teacher performance, in particular blaming the nation's economic and moral decline upon teachers and their collective organizations. Ideological attacks upon teachers and local authorities have been used to justify a uniform national curriculum applicable in every state school and the undermining of local democratic controls (Simon 1991).

DEMOCRATIC VERSUS MARKET CONTROLS?

Prior to LMS, LEAs were major partners in the education system with significant powers over planning, finance, organization and staffing. The shift of power away from LEAs began in the early 1980s with severe cuts in all budgets, rate-capping and the creation of new rights and responsibilities for governors.

The following, taken from the White Paper *Choice and Diversity*, sums up the government's aspirations for the education sector in the 1990s: 'Five great themes run through the story of educational change in England and Wales since 1979: quality, diversity, increasing parental choice, greater autonomy for schools and greater accountability' (DFE 1992: 2). Schools, it was claimed, should have the freedom to manage their own affairs, to vary terms and conditions of employment, and to break away from national and LEA controls: 'All schools now have the freedom under local management of schools to take decisions reflecting their own priorities and circumstances in a way that was not possible a few years ago under the bureaucratic rule of local government' (DFE 1992: 4).

LMS represented a fundamental shift ideologically, and in terms of funding arrangements, from educational and staffing needs to a more competitive basis and an acceptance of the inevitability of 'winners' and 'losers'. Parental choice of schools has partially replaced LEA planning, and is dependent on reliable published information in line with the Citizen's Charter. This information is provided in the form of league tables of GCSEs and originally was to include results of pupil testing of national curriculum subjects. Further information is to be provided through the now deregulated schools inspection service, whose role is to publicize strengths and weaknesses of the state-maintained sector at four-yearly intervals. Failure by governors to retain or increase their school's share of the 'market' will therefore have severe consequences. The logic of this system is the creation of a multi-tiered education system, consisting of successful GMS or grammar schools, City Technology Colleges and the independent sector. Remaining LMS schools would, under this policy, provide low-quality, low-cost education for the majority of children.

Proponents of the reforms have applied the terminology of the marketplace as if the new relationships that are being established in the school sector are equivalent to market relationships in the private sector. Several commentators have been critical of the attempt to replicate market competition and to commodify the public services. Kaser (1988) argues that commercialization introduced by new management systems into the public sector is far from simply a commitment to cutting waste, but is saturated with ideology. Keep (1990) has pointed out fundamental flaws in attempting to draw parallels between education and business. Analogies between market forces and, say, retail do not apply as the 'product' has little to do with consumer preferences, stemming largely from political decisions made by the Secretary of State. Furthermore, the notion of a 'customer' would normally imply someone paying for a service. Yet in the school system who is the customer? The pupil is the direct user of the service, yet does not pay. The parents may pay through taxation, yet are not direct users of the service. The customer, in the sense of paying for the service, is the taxpayer, yet there is no direct mechanism for the majority of taxpayers to intervene in the market and influence levels of quality and provision.

The research we have conducted in schools attempts to disentangle these issues and our findings reinforce these various critiques, highlighting how the vocabulary of the market is used to confuse rather than clarify. It is at the level of the school that many of the reforms are to be implemented or even resisted. This is within the context of considerable financial constraints for schools and a weak labour market for teachers whereby recruitment and turnover problems are alleviated.

THE IMPACT OF DECLINING SCHOOL BUDGETS

Even where schools were classified as 'winners' under the LMS formula, a major issue in most schools was the lack of funds. In the overwhelming majority of case study schools, funding was the biggest concern of most heads, staff and governors, their main fear being the effect on pupils and general educational provision. Many head teachers found the idea of marketing and fund-raising for their school offensive, others saw it as the only way to survive and embarked on courting the local press in an effort to raise the school's profile within the community. Staff in some schools had refused to undertake fund-raising activities unless they were considered entirely voluntary.

In the largest schools, a form of quasi 'internal market' has developed in which departments or faculties have been turned into 'cost centres' and in which the heads can make bids for departmental funding. In some cases, this created gender divisions; one head teacher noted that women, for example, in languages departments had not been as assertive in making demands compared with male colleagues working in design and technology.

What explains this apparent underfunding? Reports by the Organization for Economic Cooperation and Development (OECD) and the London School of Economics showed an actual fall in Britain's real per capita spending on education throughout most of the 1980s (*Guardian* 13 January 1992: 11). In any case, under LMS the complexities of the rigid formula for funding schools has produced an uneven financial pattern among comparable schools.

A main factor of the formula funding is the treatment of teachers' salaries; the 1994 settlement of a 2.9 per cent increase was to be implemented without additional Treasury funding, and any savings must be made out of school budgets. Yet schools receive only the 'average' teacher's salary rather than the actual cost. Thus, schools with a higher proportion of older, more experienced staff at the top of the incremental scale, protected salaries or women returners cost more than the average and these groups are an additional expense to the school. The Department for Education (DFE) now appears to have decided their fate: 'the problems of schools inheriting high salary costs should have been addressed by a combination of transitional arrangements, subsequent staff turnover, and the existing options open to LEAs to mitigate higher than usual salary costs' (DFE 1993). A high profile of 'expensive' teachers was a common explanation for the budgetary problems in many case study schools. A variety of other reasons were advanced, however, most of which were not under the control of school managers regardless of pupil numbers, such as the physical condition of the school.

There were disagreements from time to time with the LEAs over responsibility for payment of sickness benefit, for certain repairs, collection of dinner money, or even items such as window-cleaning. The services which remained within the LEA, such as sports and support services, also had been cut back and the effects were felt within schools, sometimes leading to potentially dangerous situations:

> One of my colleagues asked me to take a class of children into town last week, in my car. I told her I was not insured but she said, "well it's not far". I agreed to take them as we cannot get transport from the local authority and so we have to take these kinds of risks.

In addition to deteriorating quality of educational provision and restructuring of non-teaching jobs, the funding problems have directly affected overall levels of teaching staff, since the most significant savings can be made on teachers' salaries. The job losses and redundancies which have continued over the last two or three years have intensified the labour of remaining staff. New management strategies resembling those of HRM are necessitated which include the utilization of new flexible methods of payment explored below.

PERFORMANCE RELATED PAY

Since Burnham's abolition, the trend has been away from national bargaining and towards the setting of a minimum rate through the review body with more local control of pay through flexibility to allow for variations in local labour markets or individual performance. The attraction of this mechanism is that it allows the DFE and the Treasury to control budgets and enforce public sector pay limits, while allowing the unions a public voice in pay determination. From 1990, individual incentive payments were made available for the specific criteria of extra responsibility, for special needs teaching, for recruitment and retention difficulties, or for outstanding performance. These incentive payments have now been incorporated into one pay spine along which teachers can progress. Acceleration is allowed for 'excellence' and each teacher's 'point score' is reviewed annually, suggesting a potential shift towards individual bargaining. In addition heads and deputies were allowed additional accelerated spinal point increases after 1991, to reflect their new managerial duties and as a 'reward' for implementing LMS.

The main focus of recent debate has been over the method of linking pay supplements to the performance of the school and/or the individual staff member within it, in accordance with the Citizen's Charter initiative (STRB 1993: 34) The government's suggested performance measures for payments have included school 'league tables', examination results, truancy rates, school leaver destinations and teacher appraisal.

Performance related pay (PRP) is visualized as a means to free school managers from LEA bureaucrats and overpowerful trade unions. Proponents have provided scant evidence for their claims but such thinking, illustrated by the following quotation, continues to inform government policy for the public sector:

> It might not be inappropriate, if somewhat grandiose, to suggest that the collapse of the bureaucratic centralist East European economies is a testimony to the mistaken assumptions which underline the NAS/UWT model. It is precisely this very different culture of performance, possibly based on Japanese-style total quality management . . . which we have to create in schools.
>
> (Tomlinson 1992: 4)

The imperfections of performance related pay systems and fallibility of relevant criteria are well documented, however (Stenning and Stenning 1984; Johnson 1984). The six teacher unions have also opposed or have reservations about PRP on the grounds of the lack of suitable performance indicators, potential divisiveness and equity of treatment, and they are particularly adamant that payment should not be linked to appraisal, which should be for staff development only.

The review body also is aware of the shortcomings of performance indicators for schools, bearing in mind such features as the relationship between socio-economic background of pupils and school performance in terms of examination results (STRB 1992: 13). It has therefore expressed a preference for a PRP scheme which 'rewards schools that can demonstrate year-on-year improvements in performance' (STRB 1992: 15). The government has however rejected this approach and insists on merit pay for individual teachers, perhaps linked to appraisal, but without additional funding 'because of the desirability of rewarding good teachers in poor schools but not poor teachers in good schools' (STRB 1993: 34).

Yet the government's policy of limiting the paybill and introducing flexibility has not so far produced the results it may have hoped for. Since 1990, schools have had available the criterion 'outstanding classroom performance' for awarding incentive allowances to individual teachers, and our study presented an opportunity to investigate the attitudes of school managers and staff towards this form of reward (Sinclair and Seifert 1993). Our findings reveal a low take-up of flexible payments except for specific duties and responsibilities. This is in common with the observations of the School Teachers' Review Body which found only 1 per cent of incentive payments were awarded for classroom performance (STRB 1993: 17). The review body cited financial constraints, but also noted the 'cultural resistance' to differentiation between individual teachers' pay where they have equivalent responsibilities (STRB 1992: 22).

School managers in our own study were under similar financial constraints. In primary schools, the government requires at least 55 per cent of teaching staff to receive some form of incentive allowance. This rule has not been fulfilled in a number of schools whose head teachers said the school could not afford it. There appeared to be tacit agreement, when the issue was discussed at JCCs, that pressure to fulfil the requirement would not be applied by LEA or union officers to schools whose budgets were critically low. But there was considerable opposition to the *principle* of PRP and most head teachers held strong views that allowances should be distributed fairly, which meant applying the criterion of extra duties to any award. Most school union representatives agreed with the policy of avoiding payments for 'excellence' although a small number of individual teachers felt they personally would benefit; an NUT representative at a secondary school said his members were in favour of PRP, 'as we felt we would do well out of it, and people say "yes, let's have it . . . that will teach all those dossers who go home at 3.15".'

At selective/grammar schools with 'high academic standards' it might be expected that head teachers might have an interest in using pay awards for excellence. Of the schools in the sample this was not the case; two head teachers explained that with high achievement reflected in their GCSE and A level results *all* teaching staff believed themselves to be outstanding performers. The chair of governors at one school, a businessman experienced in negotiations with trade unions, said PRP was 'great in principle, but in every case, you cannot say that it is an individual's effort . . . it's collective activity and most teachers are in a team'. He was aware of the dangers of leapfrogging action if the basic scale was varied.

Another head of a selective/grammar school thought PRP was a 'can of worms', but he described a constant stream of teachers at his door asking for incentives. He said, 'Yes, the begging bowl is out at the moment. Three or four requests have gone to the governors. If I tell you about all the informal approaches I've had, we'll be here all night.' There were similar expectations, however, in some inner-city schools, where staff felt they had a hard job in motivating classes with larger numbers of pupils suffering from economic deprivation and lack of motivation.

It was because of these pressures and fears of divisiveness that many heads felt the need to ward off problems by adopting formal pay policies for the school. The LEAs urged caution when making awards, warning of potential equal pay claims or leapfrogging. Most heads in the case study sample were keen to stick with the LEA model but some wanted to allow for discretionary payments in the event of future recruitment problems.

There was a slightly less cautious approach on the subject of heads' and deputies' pay. Nationally, approximately 30 per cent of heads and deputies have been awarded an average of three to four additional spinal points since the provision was introduced (STRB 1993: 28). Of significance is that, in general, school governors made the awards for head teachers in line with their LEA's recommendations. In the Conservative shire county, the unions negotiated with the LEA that one pay policy was considered for all teachers simultaneously to prevent head teachers being singled out for favourable treatment. Only one head and deputy among the eight case study schools in that county had received increases, in comparison with the other two LEAs where over half of head teachers received significant increases. A small number refused to accept such increases when offered them by governors, however, explaining the moral dilemma of announcing cutbacks while receiving a benefit themselves. In one school a head had attempted to have his salary *reduced* due to the school's dire financial position. On other occasions the money was used to make general staff-room improvements.

Overall, the concept of payments related to individual performance is problematic in schools. There is awareness of the potential for divisiveness, undermining teamwork and collegiality, and discrimination. All head teachers, as well as classroom teachers, can claim they have extra workload and duties, however, so the isolation of 'outstanding performance' as a criterion need not necessarily be stated when making an incentive payment. In addition, frustration was continually expressed over funding in almost all case study schools. It was not only a school's ability to make decisions over flexible pay or 'extras', but the quality of school life in general that severely affected staff and pupils. Particularly affected was the ability to retain a full complement of teaching staff, with detrimental consequences for those who remained.

TEACHER WORKLOAD

The questionnaire survey found redundancies, redeployments or early retirements in a quarter of all schools and in four-fifths of secondary schools during 1991–2. This labour shedding affected 250 teachers in 145 of the schools responding. These job losses resulted from the financial position of schools under the new system, although a transition period allowed some to have a breathing space, avoiding compulsory redundancies by natural wastage and early retirements. In schools which did have a financial gain under the formula, the knowledge of redundancies and problems in neighbouring schools enabled school managers to exploit new managerial powers, claiming impending financial crisis even where none existed. One of the two GMS schools had a surplus of £180,000 prior to going grant maintained. The head admitted that he nevertheless 'engineered a budget crisis' to prevent complacency and 'to make them aware we were overstaffed'.

Measures for reducing staff costs required other strategies including the employment of younger teachers or probationers, utilization of short-term contracts and reducing part-time teachers' hours. The job losses and other mechanisms had a considerable impact on labour intensification in terms of effort and workload. This contradicted the codification of teachers' hours as laid down in the Teachers Pay and Conditions Act 1987. Following the industrial action of 1985/6 over pay, teachers had an annual hours contract imposed on them, specifying their availability of 195 days or 1265 hours per annum when their working time must be available for allocation by the school manager. Our findings revealed that most teachers found the hours requirement to be totally unrealistic. Typical of comments by interviewees were:

> The 1265 hours . . . we just pay lipservice to it. The school plan mapped this out, but with meetings stemming from the new curriculum, task groups, etc. so more meetings are required. You record the hours at first but it tends to fall flat. It's a vicious circle, but you don't want to let the kids down. It's a reflection of the conscientiousness of teachers, working longer hours to maintain standards.
>
> (Head of faculty, suburban comprehensive)

This codification, however, has raised awareness among teachers of the limits of their obligations. Where attempts had been made to extend the length of the working day by extra hours or 'twilight teaching' this was resisted by staff at two comprehensives. Extra timetabled hours of work or fund-raising events at weekends – activities outside 'directed time' – teachers insisted should remain on a voluntary basis.

The extra duties expected in the form of more timetabled hours, cover for absence and larger class sizes had inevitable consequences on sickness and absence levels. Some heads were taking steps to reduce the levels of casual absenteeism through the mechanism of non-renewal of insurance schemes which had enabled them to recover the cost of supply staff. Pressures on absenteeism were felt in other ways; a primary school NASUWT representative said, 'a year ago, it was implied that when it came to losing staff, those with an absence record would be looked at'. Other strategies included devolving responsibility for cover down to line management at faculty or department level where staff only covered for colleagues within their own departments. This induced guilt and dramatically reduced absentee levels. Cutbacks in support staff for domestic science, language or special needs also added to workload. In primary schools, it was often the head teacher who took over support roles and some heads said they felt obliged to 'let the staff have a break' by standing in for them while they did curricular preparation. There was increasing reliance on parental volunteers or students to help with practical activities or reading and most teachers were grateful for the appearance of another adult in class.

The combination of budgetary pressures, job losses and ever-changing content of the national curriculum occasionally produced shortages of available subject teachers. In this event, the head would try to utilize existing staff and, in a number of secondary schools, teachers were asked to take subjects they were not qualified for or had not taught in many years. Functional flexibility, referred to as 'skill diversification' (Apple 1988: 106), was evident in around half of the secondary schools in the study. For example, a science teacher was not qualified to teach French and German, but he was asked to teach them as he happened to speak those languages.

In most of the case study schools, examples were given of larger class sizes. At national level, the proportion of primary school classes with over thirty pupils has risen from 18.2 per cent in 1989 to 21.6 per cent in 1993 (STRB 1994: 71). There were complaints at interview of oversized classes and in the event of teacher absence in primary schools it was common to combine two classes of over thirty. In secondary schools there was particular concern over large classes in practical subjects such as science, where there were potentially dangerous situations.

The consequences for school staff of cutbacks are evident from our research. This is in spite of government claims and the rhetoric of quality in policy documents. The new environment, workload and fears for job security sometimes put particular pressures on staff, in addition to workload demands. High levels of stress were reported in every case study school, including nervous breakdowns. On occasion, individual teachers face disciplinary, professional incompetence or parental complaints, mostly resolved without recourse to formal procedures. There was a notable increase in formal disciplinary cases in one LEA, predominantly on the grounds of striking children. Yet the host of changes has introduced enormous problems for staff, as discussed above. With head teachers' new responsibilities for their schools' market share and league table position, there is pressure on them to ensure high standards in teachers' conduct, delivery of the curriculum and general competence.

Nevertheless, announcements of cutbacks, changes in staffing or terms and conditions were not always received passively. Clearly, some forms of resistance to the pressures are being voiced, both on an individual basis and collectively. A series of one-day strikes was organized by the NASUWT in one county, and in many areas unions and the local community lobbied and petitioned against education cuts and job losses. It is the various initiatives employed locally and at workplace level, and the dialogue which is gradually being established over these issues, which the next section addresses.

MANAGEMENT AND UNION RESPONSES

The changes described provide ingredients for localized conflicts, now the direct responsibility of head teachers in conjunction with governing bodies. Seifert predicted that LMS 'will generate a range of complex and possibly intractable problems over pay and conditions of service' (Seifert 1991: 43). How these issues are grappled with, and what procedures and institutional frameworks would be set up, formed part of our enquiry.

Although our research is concerned with the changing context of industrial relations with the emphasis on decentralization, we have been mindful of the centralization of management powers upwards to the Secretary of State, and events at national level. The boycott of pupil testing undertaken by the three classroom unions has brought about the collapse of one of the government's main education policies for enabling competition between schools: league tables based on test results. The government was also forced to agree to 'slim down' the national curriculum and methods of pupil assessment in line with the Dearing recommendations. However, with the abolition of the Burnham Committee, no official forum exists at national level for the resolution of such conflicts. The locus of industrial relations activity has been disturbed and now takes place on three levels – nationally, at LEAs and at schools.

The emerging pattern is determined by a whole range of factors often relating to historic relations between unions and school managers, but our study has revealed a significant role for the LEAs in personnel related issues. All three LEAs studied have produced manuals and guidelines advising on personnel practice and employment law. These have been drawn up in consultation with five or six of the teacher trade unions and head teachers' associations. It is at the area level that the facilities agreements remain, although budgets have been reduced or frozen despite increasing demands upon local union officers.

This retention of the LEA–union influence reflects the success of the national unions' policies which discouraged the fragmentation of a well-established local system of industrial relations and pushed for its retention. Despite their status as mainly advisory, all non-GMS schools in the case study research had 'opted in' to their LEA's arrangements.

That the guidelines had been drawn up in consultation with the major unions, including head teachers' associations, was seen as a 'selling point' by school managers.

It is the *monitoring* of local agreements and guidelines at school level by the representatives which was under-developed in the main, however. At one end of the spectrum, school managers marginalized unions and decision making was unilateral, while at the other extreme, but in only one or two larger comprehensives, was the emergence of relatively formal school-level bargaining units. More usual was an *ad hoc* approach. Meetings between school managers and unions were generally unco-ordinated but gradually some form of consultation was emerging in schools. Many heads regarded their style of management as 'open' and felt that any teacher with concerns 'could knock on my door anytime'. Staff echoed this response. Most teachers are accustomed to the practice of the 'whole school' meeting, or layers of meetings at faculty or department level, which are a normal part of the calendar for discussing school business. The tendency in many schools is for localized industrial relations issues to be tagged on to these forums. Issues such as alterations to the school day often cascaded down from heads and deputies to faculty heads, development groups, or small groups of departmental staff, in the form of team briefings.

Many teaching staff, including union representatives, expressed satisfaction with this system; many failed to recognize the managerial tone of team briefings or that separate forums should be held for issues relating to terms and conditions of employment. On the other hand, some staff expressed open dismay that they had such issues landed on them with no prior notice, and some did realize the management tone of such meetings:

> She can turn on people if they disagree with her, although officially there is freedom to speak openly, so you have to do it gently or deviously.
>
> (Deputy head, primary school)

> Consultation is mainly with the management team, but usually things have been decided and we are told rather than consulted.
>
> (NASUWT rep., same school)

Even serious issues like redundancy were often discussed at this level; staff were in some instances given a 'choice' of redundancies or larger classes and less non-contact time, even voting on the issue at this level.

In spite of the *ad hoc* approach, our survey shows that school representatives now see the issues of job security, workload and appraisal as warranting discussion in the workplace. Our questionnaire and case study findings confirm that the teacher trade unions are deeply embedded in the workplaces (Ironside *et al.* 1993). Virtually all schools have at least one teacher union representative performing the minimal function of distributing union literature, but in many, and in most secondary schools, the level of activity is much higher than this. School representatives attend union training courses, have networks of contacts with other activists and full-time officials, and have contacts with both their members and their managers to an extent that is comparable with the establishments covered by the WIRS surveys.

We have identified high levels of cooperation between workplace-based representatives from the three unions but there are clear differences between them. On most indicators of activity, the Association of Teachers and Lecturers (ATL) representatives are less active than the others, reflecting this union's organizational and political focus on professionalism and on the pay review process. If control over pay and conditions becomes further consolidated at the level of the workplace then ATL's influence may decline.

NASUWT representatives are generally more active than NUT representatives in the secondary sector. In the primary sector the picture is mixed, with the NUT representatives more active according to some indicators and NASUWT representatives more active according to others. NASUWT's issue-driven orientation towards the defence of the skilled practitioner provides a clear organizing principle for activity in secondary schools. However, the NUT's broader political perspective and its wider base in both the primary and secondary sectors may prove more suitable for the development of an inter-school steward committee type of organization within its more highly developed regional structures.

CONCLUSION

Our study has revealed some of the emergent trends since the introduction of decentralized management and other education reforms from the late 1980s. The attempted fragmentation of the education service under LMS was accompanied by measures to introduce competition among schools and to fund them according to their success in attracting pupils. At the same time, financial arrangements have led to persistent claims of underfunding by the schools participating in our study and these have been found detrimental to the quality of school life in general. The objective of a cheaper and more tiered education service has brought the issue of quality to the fore, raising the question of how standards can be maintained at the same time as costs are reduced. To this end, HRM techniques are targeted at gaining the commitment of employees to the aims of the organization. The new climate necessitates new mechanisms for controlling costs and teacher autonomy through a range of practices emphasizing more casualized conditions of employment, flexibility, and controls on performance through appraisal related not only to pay but to promotion and redundancy.

The changes were bound to have profound implications for industrial relations in schools, and there is a great potential for dissatisfaction among teachers over these issues. Nevertheless, our findings show that market mechanisms and HRM techniques cannot simply be transplanted into the system as though they are neutral instruments. Several factors are important here. First, school teachers and heads are highly unionized – we found 99 per cent union membership among the head teachers surveyed, and teacher militancy over local and national issues has featured historically as well as in recent periods (Seifert 1987). This provides a basis for organizing some form of resistance to attacks on spending, quality of education and managerial offensives. Second, the LEA remains the employer in law and still has some authority; the highly formalized system developed in the 1960s and 1970s has generally been retained in amended form to reflect school managers' new powers. Furthermore, bargaining or consultation between LEA officers and union representatives ensured relative stability in schools for several decades and its resilience is evident in spite of central government attempts at fragmentation. Finally, it is by no means clear exactly what would replace the formal system of LEA-based industrial relations.

It is this last point that raises the most interesting and important questions. The planned further extension of budget delegation will place LEA-provided services under increasing strain. The continuing role for LEA officers in establishing procedural frameworks through negotiations with teacher union officers may be removed, and school-based managers stand to lose the support of these negotiators at a time when they are required to make increasingly difficult and unfamiliar decisions about issues such as redundancy and performance related pay. Where there is disagreement, how will conflict be resolved in the absence of the LEA's advice or disputes procedures? There is little experience among school managers and union representatives, especially in primary schools, of negotiating settlements to disputes. Governing bodies in many schools will be unable to find solutions to deep-rooted conflicts, which could blight relationships for years.

The government has not convinced many of those involved of the benefits of a school system free from either local democratic controls or union influence. If the government does abolish LEAs, either through restructuring local government or by squeezing their resources until their function becomes the mere distribution of school budgets, then school managers will be entering a very uncertain future.

NOTES

*   The support of the Economic and Social Research Council for this study is gratefully acknowledged: Award Reference No. R–000–23–2733.

REFERENCES

Apple, M. (1988) 'Work, class and teaching', in Ozga, J. (ed.), *Schoolwork: Approaches to the Labour Process of Teaching*, Milton Keynes: Open University Press.

Central Statistical Office (1993) *Economic Trends* 471 (January).

Coates, R. (1972) *Teacher Unions and Interest Group Politics*, Cambridge: Cambridge University Press.

Commission for Racial Equality (1988) *Ethnic Minority School Teachers: A Survey in Eight Local Education Authorities*, London: CRE.

Department of Education and Science (1983) *Teaching Quality*, Cmnd. 8836, London: HMSO.

Department of Education and Science (1988) *Education Reform Act: Local Management of Schools*, Circular 7/88, London: Department of Education and Science.

Department of Education and Science (1989) *Local Management of Schools and Further and Higher Education Colleges: Order Under Section 222 of the Education Reform Act 1988*, Circular 13/89, London: Department of Education and Science.

Department for Education (1992) *Choice and Diversity: A New Framework for Schools*, London: Department for Education.

Department for Education (1993) *Consultation Paper on LMS*, London: Department for Education.

Harris, N. (1990) *The Law Relating to Schools*, London: Fourmat.

Interim Advisory Committee (1990) *Third Report of the Interim Advisory Committee on School Teachers' Pay and Conditions*, Cmnd. 973, London: HMSO.

Ironside, M., Seifert, R. and Sinclair, J. (1993) 'Change in the teacher unions', paper for the University of Wales College of Cardiff Employment Research Unit Conference.

Ironside, M. and Seifert, R. (1994) *Industrial Relations in Schools*, London: Routledge.

Johnson, S. (1984) 'Merit pay for teachers: a poor prescription for reform', *Harvard Educational Review* 54(2): 175–85.

Kaser, G. (1988) 'Value for money in the public services', *Capital and Class* 36: 31–57.

Keep, E. (1990) 'Do borrowed clothes fit? Some question marks concerning the importation of private sector management practices and market models into secondary education', paper presented to the Annual Conference of the British Education Research Association.

Lloyd, C. and Seifert, R. (1992) 'Industrial relations in the NHS: a study of four hospital units', in *The Challenge of Change: The Theory and Practice of Organizational Transformations*, proceedings of the Employment Research Unit Annual Conference, Cardiff Business School.

Saran, R. (1985) 'The politics behind Burnham: a study of teachers' salary negotiations', *Sheffield Papers in Education Management* No. 45, Sheffield: Sheffield Polytechnic.

School Teachers' Review Body (1992) *First Report*, Cmnd. 1806, London: HMSO.

School Teachers' Review Body (1993) *Second Report*, Cmnd. 2151, London: HMSO.

School Teachers' Review Body (1994) *Third Report*, Cmnd. 2446, London: HMSO.

Seifert, R. (1987) *Teacher Militancy: A History of Teacher Strikes 1896–1987*, Brighton: Falmer Press.

Seifert, R. (1989) 'Industrial relations in the school sector', in Mailly, B., Dimmock, S. and Sethi, A. (eds), *Industrial Relations in the Public Services*, London: Routledge.

Seifert, R. (1990) 'Prognosis for local bargaining in health and education', *Personnel Management* June.

Seifert, R. (1991) 'The conflict potential', *Managing Schools Today* 1(1): 41–3.

Seifert, R. and Ironside, M. (1993) 'Industrial relations in state schools', Thames Business Paper No. 19, presented at Symposium on Public Sector Employee Relations in the 1990s, September 1991, University of Greenwich Business School, London.

Simon, B. (1991) *Education and the Social Order 1940–1990*, Lewes: Falmer Press.

Sinclair, J. and Seifert, R. (1993) 'Money for value', *Managing Schools Today* 2(9).

Sinclair, J., Ironside, M. and Seifert, R. (1993a) 'Classroom struggle? Market oriented education reforms and their impact on teachers' professional autonomy, labour intensification and resistance', paper to International Labour Process Conference.

Sinclair, J., Seifert, R. and Ironside, M. (1993b) 'The road to market: management and trade union initiatives in the transition to school level bargaining under LMS', paper given to the British Universities Industrial Relations Annual Conference.

Sinclair, J., Seifert, R. and Ironside, M. (1994) 'The restructuring of non-teaching jobs in schools: the two pronged attack of CCT and LMS', paper given to University of Wales College of Cardiff Employment Research Unit Conference.

Smyth, J. (1993) *A Socially Critical View of the Self-Managing School*, London: Falmer Press.

Stenning, W. and Stenning, R. (1984) 'The assessment of teachers' perform-
    ance', *School Management and Organisations Abstracts*.
Tomlinson, H. (ed.) (1992) *Performance Related Pay in Education*, London:
    Routledge.
Walsh, P. (1987) 'The failure of meso-corporatism: the politics of education in
    the United Kingdom', paper presented to Annual Conference of the
    Australasian Political Studies Association, University of Auckland.

Conclusion
The politics of quality and the emergence of new issues and tensions within the public sector

Miguel Martinez Lucio and Ian Kirkpatrick

Our interest in this book has been to investigate the political uses of 'quality' as part of the government's incremental strategy of reforming the public sector. The objective of this concluding chapter is to summarize the different contributions to the book and consider a range of new problems and tensions which have arisen out of attempts to implement quality. Finally, we outline briefly some of the alternative ideas and debates which are emerging in the public sector around the whole issue of quality and consumer empowerment.

'CHANGE' AND THE USES OF QUALITY

Through the contributions to this volume, two broad aspects of the political use of quality have been identified. First, quality has been associated with greater managerial *control* over the activities of professional and other 'street-level' staffs. An emphasis on measuring quality as 'value for money', using a host of performance indicators, was an integral part of this process. Second, and more generally, a rhetoric of 'quality improvement' was used to *legitimate* internal organizational changes in management structures, working practices and in employee terms and conditions. Many of the contributors have shown how this rhetoric often involved making numerous references to the interests of external consumers as a way of justifying internal organizational changes.

In the first instance, the issue of quality as a vehicle for increasing managerial control over professional work processes was illustrated in the chapter by Davies and Kirkpatrick. In particular, the development of performance indicators was seen to be steadily eroding the traditional role of professional librarians, giving rise to more rigid forms of bureaucratic control. Such controls were exerted in a context of declining real-term resources and attempts to increase 'value for money' in higher education more generally. In chapter 6, Ian Shaw also talked about how quality projects might become associated with increasing managerial control over professionals. Looking at social services, Shaw described how the introduction of quality measures had contributed to a strengthening of management which, due to its own professional background in the social services, was actually able to exert a considerable degree of control. In both higher education and social services, the use of performance indicators has led to a greater transparency of professional work which, in turn, is facilitating closer managerial control.

Quality was not only associated with managerial controls but was, as mentioned, used as a legitimation device for a wider range of changes. This point was illustrated in the chapters by Pendleton and Martinez Lucio on British Rail and Royal Mail respectively. They described how 'quality improvement' projects such as TQM were being utilized to underpin wider changes in industrial relations and attempts to introduce human resource management. New 'flexible' working practices such as teamworking were being established; such practices were explicitly and implicitly circumventing unions and their traditional priorities. The chapter by Sinclair *et al.* also revealed how managerial attempts to introduce performance related pay in secondary education were supported by the rhetoric of quality improvement. In all three cases the 'interests' of the external consumer had been invoked in order to justify internal organizational changes in working practices and in employee terms and conditions.

Beyond the area of labour management, Kitchener and Whipp argued that quality was used as a vehicle for establishing and reorienting marketing relations and professional identities within the health service. In order to persuade certain professional groups to support new 'marketing' objectives, NHS managers have made constant references to the future benefits of such changes in terms of quality improvement. Also looking at the health service, Potter and Morgan argued that local conflict has arisen in some trust hospitals because of competing approaches to quality improvement. Whereas TQM, which emphasizes radical cultural change, might be supported by hospital managers, powerful clinicians' groups prefer quality assurance and its more limited concern with conforming to standards (most of which are established professionally).

Whilst concerned with the way quality has been 'used', top–down, to enforce greater managerial controls and legitimate change in working practices, most of the contributions to this book also point out how attempts to use quality in this way have been mediated and negotiated at the micro level through the political interplay of organizational actors. Contributors have insisted on emphasizing the cultural, organizational and micro-political contexts within which such quality-related policies and strategies have developed. Their approaches have varied, as have their methodologies, but there has been a common and broad concern with questions of agency, reflexivity and rearticulation, i.e. the ability of groups of individuals to reflect upon and characterize situations, providing distinct elements of their working and organizational environments with different meanings and interpretations. As Mike Reed reminds us, one needs to be cautious of reifying 'quality' and suggesting that its use will inevitably lead to greater controls and unproblematic organizational transitions.

QUALITY AND THE EMERGENCE OF NEW ISSUES AND PROBLEMS IN THE PUBLIC SECTOR

In this section our aim is to describe how a range of contradictions and tensions has emerged within the British government's project of reforming the public sector. We show how these contradictions and tensions have problematized the government's espoused objective of improving the quality of public services. Three issues are of particular importance for our discussion. First, major contradictions have arisen between the theory and practice of improving quality through greater user exit and choice. Not only in reality have there been important structural constraints on choice, but there are also certain philosophical problems associated with the whole idea of using exit mechanisms in the public service context. Second, there has been a noticeable gap between the rhetoric and reality of various management-led initiatives designed to increase user voice. Many of these initiatives have been of a 'cosmetic' nature, limited to formal policy statements, with little or no real effort to democratize and open producer interests to new external considerations. Finally, contradictions between the different approaches to quality and deeper objectives of economy and retrenchment have been identified. A narrow emphasis on 'value for money' and conformance, for example, has not sat well with the more ambitious talk about extending the involvement of users in the design, delivery and assessment of public services (a point reflected in many of this book's contributions).

These types of difficulty lead us to question any assertions that in practice (a) user involvement or choice has increased and (b) 'quality' itself (however defined) has improved. As will become clear, the failure of many quality initiatives has helped foster the development of counter-references to quality improvement which are potentially politicizing relationships within public organizations and broadening the scope for innovation beyond the narrow confines of governmental and managerial agendas of financial retrenchment and control.

The limits of choice

Many of the contributions draw attention to the fact that, despite government reforms aimed at extending and imposing quality through consumer exit, the choices of individual users of public services remain limited. This is a result both of the limits of structural reform and, we argue, of the particularly 'individualistic' nature of the discourses of consumerism which have been adopted. In terms of structure, most of the so-called 'markets' which have been created in health and local government are not ones which involve the direct participation of consumers, but are rather 'bureaucratically managed' and mediated by the choices of professional experts (Appelby *et al.* 1990; Cochrane 1991) (see also Harris chapter 7, Kitchener and Whipp chapter 9, and Thompson chapter 3). Key decisions are made by oligopolistic institutional purchasers with very little (or no) 'choice' left for the individual user. In this way, there exist important structural constraints which have so far restricted user 'choice' in public services and have almost certainly not led to real improvements in 'quality'. Furthermore, rather than allow greater choice for all consumers, Conservative government reforms have actually led to the creation of a two-tier welfare system (Wilding 1992). That is, a state of affairs in which those who possess the money and knowledge to gain access to high quality (mainly private) services will do so, while those who are less fortunate will be tarnished increasingly with the brush of 'dependency' and have access only to the 'basic no frills state system' (Stoker 1989).

Further limitations on user choice derive from the more obvious financial constraints facing most public sector organizations. As Wistow and Barnes suggest, 'limitations on public resources rather than private means dictate that not all wants can be met' (Wistow and Barnes 1993: 297). This fact has also led some to question the whole relevance of the exit mechanism in the public sector context. As Stewart and Walsh argue, for example: 'In the public domain, public purposes have to be realized, which may not conform to the wishes of individual members of the public. Public purpose can set limits to responsiveness to the customer' (Stewart and Walsh 1992). Not only, then, are there serious structural constraints placed on user choice but there are serious flaws within the theory itself when applied to the public sector context.

The limits of voice

If user choice has been limited in practice, then so has consumer voice. Here, too, there was a gap between rhetoric and reality, not to mention serious problems of actually trying to extend the role of users in the management and decision-making processes of the public sector.

In Britain, successive Conservative governments adopted a rhetoric of empowering the 'sovereign consumer' and altering the balance of power between producer and consumer interests. Only by forcing producers to adopt a want regarding standpoint whereby they serve only the consumers' interests, it was argued, could the greater voice of 'sovereign consumers' be heard and quality itself improved (Keat and Abercrombie 1991). The mechanism for bringing about such change was seen to be a new public management, more effective in controlling professional power, responding to external developments and generally acting in the 'consumer's interest'.

In practice, what the rhetoric of extending voice often meant was not increased consumer participation and involvement in public services, but the empowerment of a management claiming to act in the consumer's interest. Talk of making public services more responsive and bringing them 'closer to the customer' actually meant limited decentralization and attempts to gain greater control over professional work processes. In many cases, however, even this objective was largely unsuccessful. In the NHS, for example, despite managerial efforts to introduce quality assurance systems, clinical freedom has remained strong. According to Pollitt, 'the dominant model seems to be that of professional development without the awkwardness of wider public accountability, still less actual user participation in the design or operation of the Quality Assurance system' (Pollitt 1990: 448).

In many areas, the continuing dominance of professional experts has led to continued asymmetries of information between them and managers who wish to exert greater control. There have, of course, been good technical reasons why this has been so (many complex professional work processes remain indeterminate and difficult to measure or standardize). Generally, the failure to increase the transparency of professional work across the board has placed limits on the extent to which managers can exert control, and has also undermined claims that public services are becoming more 'responsive' to consumer interests.

Another way of understanding this development is that such information asymmetries may, in some cases, be used by the government and various managers deliberately to restrict any real participative public role in the process of state restructuring; that is, by forging strategic alliances with certain professional groups whenever their resistance has been relatively effective. The co-opting of key professional groups into managerialist developments was, in the case of health, greatly facilitated by the use of quality-related management techniques (Kitchener and Whipp chapter 9). Within such developments, it hardly needs to be said that consumers may be effectively marginalized. Such marginalization, however, was acceptable to the government because it allowed it to pursue wider objectives of financial control and retrenchment with the limited support and involvement of certain key professional groups.

By and large, efforts to extend user voice in public services have so far been limited, cosmetic and of 'the superficial window dressing variety' (Harrison *et al.* 1992). Despite a rhetoric of getting 'closer to the customer', few attempts have been made actually to involve users in either the setting of priorities or the design of services (Wrinkler 1987; Pollitt 1988; Wistow and Barnes 1993). The emphasis instead was on empowering managers using a rhetoric of the sovereign consumer. As the various contributions to this book demonstrate, such a rhetoric has been used to mask other, less ambitious initiatives geared towards achieving greater control over professional work processes through limited decentralization and performance measurement. The consumer's 'interests' were more often invoked in a passive manner in order to add legitimacy to such developments.

This brings us to the third set of problems relating to the way different approaches to quality have come into conflict with each other and with deeper objectives of cost containment and economy. Such dissonance emerged due to the complex and uneven development of the government's reform project more generally (see chapter 1). There was, in particular, a problem of rival messages of consumerism and 'value for money' being used as a smoke-screen to mask the effects of intensifying pressures on resources. This occurred in the case of performance indicators which have used the language of consumerism, but focused almost exclusively on measuring inputs and processes rather than outputs or impact factors which might take into account users' views and rights (see Davies and Kirkpatrick). The chapter by Fitzgeorge-Butler and Williams also reveals how plans to introduce TQM in housing associations have so far led only to increased bureaucracy and efforts to cut costs (see also Pendleton chapter 3 and Martinez Lucio chapter 11 on this aspect). Such contradictions have generated widespread 'demoralization' and cynicism amongst public sector employees, and even managers (Poole *et al.* 1994), who are often told to increase quality while, at the same time, being expected to cut costs and work in environments that are financially scrutinized in a centralized manner. In the NHS, for example, Pollitt discovered 'widespread scepticism among staff concerning "consumerist" initiatives because, it was believed, general managers were obliged to give priority to cost saving' (Pollitt 1990: 444). The irony of this is that greater user and employee scepticism and demoralization can, in turn, undermine efforts to improve 'quality'.

To sum up this section, we argue that efforts to bring about 'quality improvement' in the British public sector have been riddled with internal tensions problematizing their use both at the micro and macro level. These tensions and contradictions are realized and accentuated in efforts to 'improve' quality through the restructuring of public sector organizations. They are also inherent within the discourses themselves due to the way they have been constructed politically. These problems arise, in part from a wider set of contradictions and tensions which lie at the heart of the successive Conservative governments' reform project more generally (see chapter 1). That project itself continues to be neither internally consistent nor linear. It involves a mixture of input and output orientations which have developed unevenly and have in some cases come into conflict with each other. Such incremental features are in part an outcome of the diverse and competing external factors that gave rise to the project of reform in the first place.

THE NEW LOGICS OF QUALITY AND PROBLEMS OF CONTAINMENT

It is not just the case that the development and uses of quality-related initiatives will give rise to a range of new contradictions and sites of struggle. A range of actors in the form of consumer bodies, groups of professionals and trade unions, amongst others, may actually develop systematic counter-references to quality with diverse understandings of quality indicators and public empowerment. These will interpret and define the meaning of performance measurement, accountability, citizenship, collective consumption and new participatory processes in a variety of ways that could be difficult to contain as far as any government or, certainly, group of managers is concerned.

The objective of developing a 'public service orientation' that is *for* and not directed *to* the public is one which many insist is not necessarily related to New Right definitions of consumerism (Stewart and Clarke 1987), and which does not involve any denial of employee and professional rights. At the level of the local state, there have been various attempts since the late 1970s to involve the public in novel and alternative ways, such as through increased decentralization of organizational structures and decision making.

The whole question of voice has been re-emerging as the focus of attention for many participants and academics, especially in the areas of local government, housing and health. In the case of local government, Burns *et al.* (1994) described a range of alternative developments and experiences in the establishment of new voice mechanisms that have not been centrally imposed or manufactured. In the first instance, representative democracy has in various (albeit a limited number of) local councils either been improved through providing greater facilities to citizens in the electoral process, or even extended by establishing area committees and more direct forms of communication between the public and local government (Burns *et al.* 1994: 35). Second, representative structures have been infused with participatory democratic features with the direct co-option of community representatives on to council committees. In certain circumstances, such participative processes have been extended through the direct funding of non-statutory groups and social movements (*ibid.*). Examples of these developments exist in various parts of the country and they suggest a range of alternative understandings of 'consumer' involvement and a widening understanding of 'customer roles'.

Such developments cannot solely be reduced to the area of local government. For some years now, the government has been attempting to legitimate the development of purchaser–provider relations within health by reference to the role of customer relations. Increasingly, the government has been forced into trying to convince certain groups of the non-rhetorical status of such claims. Hence, since the early 1980s, there have been attempts to develop local participatory structures through community health councils, neighbourhood health advisory forums and others, which may involve both individual citizens and local interest groups (Felvus 1994). In this book (chapter 3) Andy Thompson also talks at length about the emergence of alternative professional roles in health services. He suggests not making professional experts totally subservient to user and managerial demands (as is the case in New Right understandings of consumerism), but rather encouraging professional experts to exercise 'responsible autonomy' and allow users to play a more active role in the negotiation of service outcomes. The credibility and sincerity of many of these developments may have been questioned, but they nevertheless represent an ongoing need to cope with the plethora of interest and possible voice mechanisms that constitute the area of health at the local level.

Furthermore, a range of diverse and alternative understandings of quality, consumption rights and voice mechanisms are being directly propagated by a range of interest groups and social movements themselves. These have emerged for a variety of reasons and are in many cases beginning to locate themselves in the expectations and demands of individuals which have developed in response to some of the public policy rhetoric discussed in this book. In the case of Britain, the presence of social and consumer movements has actually increased, regardless of the lack of broad, macro-level participation structures at the level of the central state. Transportation, health, education and various other sectors consist of increasingly organized interest groups which represent citizens' views on a whole range of consumption issues. As for trade unions, their supposed 'decline' has been paralleled by a broad, albeit embryonic, interest in micro-political alliances and networks that, in certain instances, are capable of traversing both production and consumption concerns (Hyman 1995). What is of interest is that such broad political developments and networks are contributing to a range of counter-discourses regarding the politics of quality and consumption. Furthermore, these are increasingly and explicitly addressing many of the contradictions within the 'dominant projects' raised above.

It is for this reason that the contradictions referred to above will not contribute to any 'termination' or 'abandonment' of the issues of quality and public empowerment. The issues of accountability and broad consumption politics are as significant as ever. In part this is due to the continuing social and economic changes discussed above. Moreover, structural changes – the state's fiscal crisis, changing patterns of welfare consumption, and the dilemma of 'Fordist' public administration – which gave rise to quality-related projects and state reform projects in the first place (see chapter 1) have remained significant environmental factors. They have continued to contribute to the financial constraints, increasing public expectations and demands, and transitional bureaucratic arrangements, all of which have modified the development and restructuring of the politics of quality itself. Hence there is a need to emphasize the incremental character of such developments at the policy level, even if they have emerged from what many would consider to be a fundamental political break from previous post-war administrative practices in the state.

Finally, the issues of accountability and broad consumption politics will also remain significant to the management of public services due to the government's ongoing use of 'quality' relations in order to exert controls within a 'post-bureaucratic', 'decentralized' context of contract relations (Hoggett 1991), as well as the contradictions and tensions this is subsequently giving rise to and which were outlined above. Such strategies are very complex as a form of organizational control, testing the political, material and intellectual resolve of any government. In the context of increasing political uncertainty the outcomes cannot be clearly stated.

The question, therefore, appears to be increasingly one of *how* the politics of quality will develop and condition the management and objectives of the public sector; especially as there is at present no stable material or ideological basis for a coherently hegemonic and dominant project of quality. It is this which will contribute to a new, albeit fragmented, politics of public organization for the rest of the decade at least, and to a need for a more analytical and critical approach to the study of administration in public services that is more sober in its attitude to the dictats of management gurus.

REFERENCES

Appelby, J., Robbinson, R., Ranade, W., Little, V. and Salter, J. (1990) 'The use of markets in the health service: the NHS reforms and managed competition', *Public Money and Management* Winter: 27–33.

Boreham, P. (1983) 'Indetermination: professional knowledge, organization and control', *Sociological Review* 31: 293–718.

Burns, D., Hambleton, R. and Hoggett, P. (1994) *The Politics of Decentralization*, London: Macmillan.

Cochrane, A. (1991) 'The changing state of local government: restructuring for the 1990s', *Public Administration* 69: 281–302.

Felvus (1994) *Consumer Participation in the Public Sector*, MBA dissertation, Cardiff: Cardiff Business School.

Hambleton, R. and Hoggett, P. (1993) 'Rethinking consumerism in public services', *Consumer Policy Review* 3(2): 103–11.

Harrison, S., Hunter, D., Marnoch, G. and Pollitt, C. (1992) *Just Managing: Power and Culture in the National Health Service*, London: Macmillan.

Hoggett, P. (1991) 'A new managerialism in the public sector?', *Policy and Politics* 19(4): 243–56.

Hyman, R. (1995) 'Changing trade union identities and strategies', in Ferner, A. and Hyman, R. (eds), *New Frontiers in European Industrial Relations*, Oxford: Blackwell.

Keat, R. and Abercrombie, N. (eds) (1991) *Enterprise Culture*, London: Routledge.

Pfeffer, N, and Coote, A. (1991) *Is Quality Good for You? A Critical Review of Quality Assurance in Welfare Services*, Social Policy Paper 5, London: Institute for Public Policy Research.

Pollitt, C. (1988) 'Bringing consumers into performance measurement: concepts, consequences and constraints', *Policy and Politics* 16(2): 77–87.

Pollit, C. (1990) 'Doing business in the temple? Managers and quality assurance in the public services', *Public Administration* 68: 435–52.

Poole, M., Mansfield, R., Turner, B. and Martinez Lucio, M. (1994) 'Contrasts between public and private sector managers in Britain and the effects of the "Thatcher Years"', paper presented at the Cardiff Business School's annual Employment Research Conference on 'The contract state: the future of public management'.

Stewart, J. and Clarke, M. (1987) 'The public service orientation: issues and dilemmas', *Public Administration* 65(2): 161–77.

Stewart, J. and Walsh, K. (1992) 'Change in the management of public services', *Public Administration* 70: 499–518.

Walsh, K. (1991) 'Quality and public services', *Public Administration* 69: 503–14.

Wilding, P. (1992) 'The British welfare state: Thatcherism's enduring legacy', *Policy and Politics* 20(2): 201–11.

Winkler, F. (1987) 'Consumerism in health care: beyond the supermarket model', *Policy and Politics* 15(1): 1–8.

Wistow, G. and Barnes, M. (1993) 'User involvement in community care: origins, purposes and applications', *Public Administration* 71: 279–99.

Index

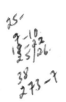